HALF A CENTURY OF JAPANESE THEATER
IV
1980s Part 2

HALF A CENTURY OF JAPANESE THEATER

IV

1980s Part2

Edited by
Japan Playwrights Association

KINOKUNIYA

Arts Plan 21

THE SAIS⊕N FOUNDATION

Translation and publication of this book has been supported by a grant from the Agency for Cultural Affairs.

Publication of this book has been supported by a grant from the Saison Foundation.

Publication of this book has been supported by a grant from the Japan Foundation.

First published 2002
Published by Kinokuniya Company Ltd.,
13-11, Higashi 3-chome, Shibuya-ku, Tokyo 150-8513, Japan.
ISBN 4-314-10148-2
Printed in Japan

CONTENTS

Editors' Notes

1. Japanese names in the plays are given in their original order, last name followed by first name.

ACKNOWLEDGMENTS

We would like to express our gratitude to the Agency for Cultural Affairs, the Japan Foundation, and the Saison Foundation for their assistance, without which the publication of this book would not have been possible.

We are also indebted to many individuals and organizations that extended their assistance to us. Playwrights, troupes, and photographers kindly provided information and photographs, otherwise unattainable, for this volume. We would like to express particular thanks to: Dr. Takahashi Yasunari, Vice President of the International Shakespeare Society; Dr. J. R. Brandon, Professor at the University of Hawai'i, Manoa; Ms. Matsuoka Kazuko, translator; Mr. Kuroda Shinjirō, the general manager of the Publishing Department of Kinokuniya Company Ltd.; Mr. Fukui Kensaku, legal advisor concerning the rights of translators and playwrights; and Kawabata Ryōko. Of great assistance in the formatting of the manuscripts was Kondō Satoko.

In closing, we would like to note that the opinions of the playwrights and critics are their own and do not necessarily reflect those of the translators, editors, and publishers.

Japan Playwrights Association Editorial Committee
(in alphabetical order)
Betsuyaku Minoru
Mari Boyd
Matsuda Hiroko
Ōta Shōgo
Senda Akihiko
Robert Witmer

FOREWORD

Betsuyaku Minoru
PRESIDENT OF THE JAPAN PLAYWRIGHTS ASSOCIATION

Recently, theater as a means of communication is being reassessed. It goes without saying that theater is a noticeably restricted method of communicating information. Due to the seating capacity of any one auditorium, a performance can only reach a limited number of people in a day; and as a performance cannot be simply copied and distributed, its message cannot be disseminated quickly on a wide scale. In today's society, it is like pitting a bicycle against a deluxe express bus on the highway.

The reasons theater is being reassessed are that: 1) due to these restrictions, theater has retained the ability to convey information in a sensuous and visceral way from actor to audience; and 2) theater has been largely unaffected by the global consumerism that has taken us by storm.

It is said that what can be copied, distributed and communicated to a million people is simply information for mass consumption, but what is conveyed among people in a group of a 1000 or less can be experienced as culture. Indeed a large theater is not essential, as the smaller the space the more intense the experience, and when there is a remarkable performance, word of mouth will often suffice to lure many more viewers to the theater. Cultural dissemination can spread in waves through the populace.

What distinguishes theater from many other communication systems is its anti-mass media activity and anti-consumerist economy. As one of the few remaining collective transmission systems of culture, which have not been exploited by a media-dominated society, theater retains an antiquated yet elegant mode of expression.

I hope you will keep this in mind as you read the five plays in this volume.

RADICALISM IN THE THEATER OF THE 1980s

Nishidō Kōjin
TRANSLATED BY MARI BOYD

1. The Significance of the "Third"

Modern Japanese theater reached a major transition in the 1980s. The politicized period of the 1960s through the 1970s came to an end, and a totally different decade began. The fundamental structures of economics and society changed and with them culture and the arts. Theater changed spontaneously from within as well as in inevitable reaction to the changes in the larger society.

The keyword of this period then is the "third." The appellation, the third generation of little theater,[1] was often employed by the public as new theatrical troupes like The Third Erotica[2] (f. 1980) and The Third Stage[3] (f. 1981) emerged. On a global scale, the growth of the Third World was striking. In this way, a new order became apparent. What then is the significance of the "third"?

Let us first consider the third generation of the little theater movement. This movement began in the latter half of the 1960s and constituted a revolt against *shingeki*, or New Theater, and its the realistic orientation. Young theater artists like Kara Jūrō (b. 1940) and Terayama Shūji (1935-73) organized avant-garde theater troupes independent of established *shingeki* troupes. These founders made up the first generation of little theater practitioners and their theater was alternatively referred to as the *angura* (underground) little theater. The artists of the next decade were known as the second little theater generation, and those who became active around 1980 came to be known as the third generation. This is not merely a chronological rendering, but an indication that, over the years, the *angura* little theater fostered legitimate successors.

However, the third was different from the second generation that continued the experiments of the first in that they did not consider themselves successors of previous generations. Instead by actively creating new working conditions and setting themselves apart from the former generations, they attempted to relate differently to them. In this way, the theater revolution of the 1960s can be viewed as the creation of a new theatrical paradigm, and not just a temporary phenomenon.

Another way of interpreting "the third" is to see it as the third turning point in modern Japanese theater history. If the 1920s constitute the first phase in modern theater, which broke away from the traditional theater arts of *nō* and *kabuki*, and the *angura* from the mid-1960s comprises the second phase, the 1980s can be seen as a new beginning.

The purpose of this essay is to outline the social events of the 1980s, to sketch the theater of those times, and, taking world events into consideration, to position Japanese theater in a global context.

2. Culture and Rupture

Discussion of the theater of the 1980s requires some knowledge of the 1970s. If the 1980s was a turning point, there must have been a rupture preceding it. The 1979 Manifesto of the theatrical troupe Black Tent 68/71[4] (f. 1968) (commonly known as the Black Tent) is an indication of such a severance. Opening with the statement, "There is no theater here," the Manifesto criticized from within the *angura* theater movement, which had shrunk to a minor phenomenon, and declared a parting of the ways with it. That a theater company which had been a major force in *angura* should have put forth such a manifesto was an anomaly. Yet this declaration aptly summed up and criticized the theater situation of the times.

First it recognized that there had been a theater movement that had reflected the events in the larger world. This was of course the *angura* theater revolution of the 1960s and 1970s, which had paralleled the theater movement in Europe and the US and gained a global currency. The theories on physical movement and theater buildings and the creative work of small troupes constituted a movement of theatrical expression that criticized the mainstream *shingeki* from its foundations and broke the boundaries of modern theater. Furthermore, this revolutionary theater movement had corresponded to the worldwide student movements and changing tide in politics and thought. This *angura* was an alternative theater that had provided a countercultural force against the dominant social order.

However, after the 1980s, with theater lacking a visible cultural enemy, and Japanese society becoming increasingly "soft" and managerial, the cultural conflict diminished to a minor phenomenon within the larger society. In these circumstances, theater was also forced to transform. Compared with the theater of the preceding decades, few 1980s theater practitioners professed politics in their work. And as young audiences filled the auditorium, political apathy grew and the orientation toward entertainment strengthened. Serious art became a subcultural matter.

Some critics who evaluated this change negatively labeled the 1980s a period of vacuity, in other words, a dearth of political and social concern. Others viewed the rapid spawning of young artists favorably, interpreting the abandonment of *angura* as a sign of maturity and preparation for a different kind of theater. But they did not indicate the presence of any vision. Two points can be inferred from the summation by the Black Tent: 1) *angura* had ended and the end was characterized by internal collapse, and 2) the Manifesto was written at a transitional period in which a new paradigm was not yet perceived.

This was the situation on the eve of 1980. The most important task at hand is to find a way to explain logically the continuities and discontinuities of theater arts through time.

3. Theater and a Media-dominated Society

The relations between media and theater are essential to understanding the changes in theater. Media-dominated society, a keyword that aptly describes this period, refers to a new development in capitalism, in which the focus is on the consumption of information rather than material goods. Critic Konakawa Tetsuo named this new stage, media capitalism. An enormous amount of information had become easily available and world trends could be observed without leaving Japan. The world had grown smaller.

Changes were clearly manifest in criticism and the academic world. A major change was the advent of new academism that appeared after the decline of the universities and leftist movements that had comprised the intellectual milieu of the postwar period. In this new wave, the influence of western culture and learning, especially of French post-structuralism and deconstruction, was powerful and operative in breaking up conventional thought structures. Together with the changes in lifestyle and values, the new academism also brought about playfulness in thought and brand labeling of philosophy. Postwar ideology, such as postwar democracy, lost ground and the beginning of a new era seemed to be at hand. The old order collapsed. However the result was an emptiness in ideology and culture. Theater was not unrelated to these shifting events. Movements like *shingeki* and *angura* lost efficacy and lapsed into vacuity.

What then filled the emptiness of theater? Eventually, the word that comes to mind is entertainment. Besides meaning to treat with hospitality or to give pleasure, this term has the nuance of intellectual pleasure. But applied to the 1980s situation in Japan, it came to mean the pleasure of consumption on the subcultural level.

The cultural phenomenon of the 1960s was termed "counterculture," but as it faded, it was superseded by the term "subculture" with its narrower application. The proliferation of troupes in the 1980s is related to the formation of subculture. People in their twenties rapidly made many theater companies and performed for equally young audiences. Theater that was neither clearly amateur nor professional burgeoned and cliquish communities formed.

The media supported this trend with a phenomenal expansion in the publication of magazines, but the concomitant increase in sales of magazines did not induce an improvement in quality of theater. If anything, the excessiveness seemed like a *cul-de-sac*.

4. The Emergence of a New Generation

The appearance of a new generation of theater practitioners was much awaited. By the end of the 1970s, the first generaton of *angura* artists had become part of the establishment and had reached a high level of artistic performance. How was the following generation performing? Director-auteur Tuska Kōhei (b. 1948), who whirled through the latter half of the 1970s with his fast-paced performances, attained heights of popularity, but soon showed symptoms of exhaustion. In 1981, he astonished everyone when he announced an artistic moratorium. He was not alone. Many of his contemporaries were forced to change directions or shift gears at this time. Punning on the name of Yamazaki Tetsu's theater company, Transposition 21[5] (f. 1980), this period was called the season of transposition or transition. For example, Ryūzanji Shō's theatrical troupe, called Theater Group[6] (f. 1970), entered its second phase and became The Second Theater Group in 1981,[7] while Yamazaki's Deaf Gallery[8] (1970-79), Ikuta Yorozu's Makamaka Company (1970-81), and Sakurai Daizō's Performing Horse Hall[9] (1972-82) were all forced to disband. In this way, theater entered a blank period, and the theater world looked for new young artists.

Theater journalists searched for post-Tsuka Kōhei artists and found Noda Hideki (b. 1955) and his student theater troupe, the Dream Wanderers (1976-92), at the University of Tokyo. His stage performances were clearly different from *angura*. Lively, healthy actors pranced and jumped across stage. However, in their dialogue and dramaturgy, his troupe continued the methodology of the earlier generations.

Inspired by him, amateur student theater groups continued to arise: Kisaragi Koharu (1956-2000) and her theater troupe Kiki (f. 1976) at Tokyo Women's University; Ōhashi Hiroshi and his New Waseda Theater,[10] now Da·M, at Waseda University; Kōkami Shōji's Third Stage at Waseda University; and Kawamura Takeshi's Third Erotica at Meiji University. This generation of artists, born in the second half of the 1950s, had not been exposed to political strife and had been able to enjoy the growing postwar prosperity wholeheartedly. Consequently their view on life had little to do with darkness or *ressentiment*. It was tantamount to a dissociation from previous generations.

What was expected of them? Was it not to survey and comprehend the theater of previous generations? Reviewing theater from its beginnings, they were to create anew, not leave theater to the whims of changing times. That endeavor comprises the second revolution of theater. If *angura* was, after *shingeki*, the concluding chapter in the making of modern Japanese theater and because of that, *angura* was the theater of transition, then the second revolution was to create a new paradigm. This set the stage for the beginning of a contemporary theater.

At this historical turning point in theater, the artist who spearheaded the revolution was Kitamura Sō (b. 1952) with his play *Ode to Joy* (1979). At that time Kitamura was the head of the Total Produce Organizers★Company[11] based in Nagoya. His first Tokyo performance at the Rocking Horse Theater[12] in Asakusa was an eye-catching event—comedy with a subtly different quality to that of Tsuka Kōhei had emerged.

Kitamura's major characteristic is his light touch. The setting of *Ode to Joy* is a city in ruins after a nuclear war. A husband-and-wife team of artists, who are eking out a living, encounter a man called Yasuo, who seems to be an incarnation of God. The dialogue is such that it is difficult to ascertain whether the speakers are serious or not. The fancifulness of their speech creates a tension between the images conjured up and the actuality of the situation. For example, they talk about atomic bombs and missiles as if they were colorful fireworks.

> KYŌKO: Look, it flashed again. This time, over there. Gesaku-don. Do you think it's another missile?

Furthermore, in the final scene the couple pulls a cart filled with household goods and fade into the darkness with "Una Sèrie di Tokyo,"[13] playing in the background. The juxtaposition of darkness and song is deeply moving.

In terms of lightness, Fukuda Yoshiyuki's *The Heroic Exploits of the Sanada Clan*[14] (1962), performed on the eve of the inception of *angura*, was a pioneering work. Fukuda used frequently the term "lightness as methodology," but Kitamura's is a nonchalant, easygoing kind of lightness.

Thus in 1979, on the one hand the Black Tent presented a manifesto summing up the *angura*; on the other, Kitamura emerged. The former signals an ending and the latter a beginning. In this way, the new and old forces passed each other as the 1980s began.

5. *Many Beginnings*

The commonality among the playwrights treated in this volume is that, committed to little theater as opposed to *shingeki*, they all represent new beginnings.

Kawamura Takeshi (b. 1959) and his Third Erotica shocked the theater world with a performance style expressive of the sensibility of the 1980s. His stage overflowed with violence and aggression. Noting these very aspects, critics have frequently called attention to his similarity with earlier generations and have viewed him as being a kindred spirit of Kara Jūrō. However, Kawamura's appearance was, in fact, an indication of the beginning of the post-Kara period. For example, let us compare his major work *Nippon Wars* (1984) and Kara's *A Virgin's Mask*[15] (1969). *A Virgin's Mask* is about the struggle of the great Takarazuka star of the 1960s, Kasuga Yachiyo, to regain her body, which was "stolen" by her fans. Recovering her physicality is her frantic attempt to shore up her identity and is akin to a scream of pain. In contrast, the protagonist in *Nippon Wars* is an android whose memory belongs to someone else. As memory is what anchors identity, the android's sense of self is always already nonexistent. As there is no subjectivity to protect, there is no basis on which to ground one's existence. Putting aside the question of where to draw the line between the 1960s and the 1980s, it is clear that the starting point of these two kinds of artists is diametrically opposed when it comes to the theme of personal identity.

In addition to having great talent as a storyteller, Kawamura developed a self-referential performance style that questioned stories themselves. For example, *The Shinjuku Version of the Tale of the Eight Dogs*[16] (1985-91), of which four of the projected five volumes have been written, portrays thrilling episodes of embattled people in urban settings. His characters boldly embark on daring adventures in the labyrinthine streets of a lust-driven city. Borrowing material from the dramatic works of the Edo period (1603-1868), Kawamura wrote a dynamic story. From the latter half of the 1990s, Kawamura turned to the theme of history and its documentation in plays such as *Tokyo Trauma* (1995) and *Hamlet Clone* (2000). Kawamura attempted to separate himself from *angura* by attacking their theater.

A new trend in the 1980s that attracted much attention was the emergence of women playwrights. Although there had been women playwrights earlier, the women in this period were also directors and often leaders of their own theater companies. Kisaragi Koharu and her group Kiki, Watanabe Eriko (b. 1955) and her company Three Circles[17] (1980-1997), and Kino Hana (b. 1948) and the all-female theater company Blue Bird[18] (f. 1974) enjoyed great media coverage. They responded to the general sense of a new era for women. Kishida Rio (b. 1950) was also one of this new breed of women.

Kishida joined Terayama Shūji's Peanuts Gallery in 1974, and became his right-hand collaborator in creative writing. She was also editor of the theoretical periodical *Underground Theater*[19] and, until 1983, she was Terayama's closest collaborator. Besides her work at the Peanuts Gallery, she formed her own theater troupe, Kishida Company[20] (f. 1981), and produced her own plays. These were extremely aesthetic works with polished language, quite unlike the highly experimental works at the Peanuts Gallery. The masterpiece of her theatrical art is *Thread Hell*[21] (1984). Written after Terayama's death, it is in a sense her voyage out of his influence.

The life of women is always portrayed in Kishida's works. Women are depicted as the playthings of the times, the victims of those in power and authority. The criticism of a male-dominated community is central to her theater, which attacks sexual exploitation. In her revision of history from a female perspective are the seeds of feminism. But for that social issue to become apparent in the larger society, more than a decade had to pass until the latter half of the 1990s, when the criticism of male-centered society eventually gained the momentum to turn society on its head. In the 1990s, Kishida became more experimental again and extended her activities beyond Japan, as will be explained later.

Together with the theme of women, the issue of resident foreigners arose in the 1980s. The problem of minorities appeared frequently and the theatrical troupe, Shinjuku Ryōzanpaku, founded in 1986, was a pioneer in this area. This troupe was formed by the junior members of Kara's Red Tent company and the Black Tent, and as the core members were resident Koreans and Chinese, the predicament of minorities was always an issue that added dimension to their productions.

Chong Wishing (b. 1957), playwright of Shinjuku Ryōzanpaku, originally aspired to become a scenario writer. He entered the actors training school of the Black Tent, became a highly competent actor, and then turned to writing plays. As Shinjuku Ryōzanpaku is a traveling tent troupe that tours around the country, Chong's plays are written with tent performance in mind. Attracting critical attention with *A Thousand Years of Solitude* (1989), he came into his own with *A Legend of Mermaids*[22] (1990). Based on the life in his home town, this work is in fact Chong's version of Maxim Gorky's *The Lower Depths* and depicts people living in barracks by the sea. There are six brothers always in emotional turmoil, the parents who try to save the family from total destruction, and the kind and cruel people around them—such characters provide variation on the resident foreigner theme.

The maximum utilization of tent space and spectacle based on fire and water go hand in hand with the socially concerned objectives of Shinjuku Ryōzanpaku. This troupe carried on the *angura* tradition, created in the 1960s by the Red Tent and Black Tent, of traveling throughout the country and performing in a tent pitched in a vacant lot. This kind of activity, however, requires considerably more labor than performing in a small theater building. It cannot be done without mobilizing a large number of troupe members and gaining local cooperation.

The little theater movement became a "boom" during the latter half of the 1980s due to the bubble economy, but in the 1990s with the prolonged economic recession it lost momentum. Theater units with a nucleus of two or three persons became the prevalent form. If *angura* was the ugly duckling of the high economic growth period, theatrical activities are obviously not unrelated to the economic order of the day. In that sense, Shinjuku Ryōzanpaku could be called the last of the *angura* troupes.

Chong left the company in 1996 and is now an independent playwright and scenario writer.

6. Collaborations, Overseas Productions, and Asia

As explained above, the 1980s theater can be presented as a coherent narrative. It is about how riding the economic prosperity of the country, youth culture arose; how light, speedy plays became popular; and how a sense of celebration overtook the theaters, as if people were partying night after night in discos. However there is a sequel. When the economy nose-dived in the 1990s, the celebratory atmosphere quickly evaporated and drama that depicted life seriously replaced it.

It goes without saying that the 1980s theater cannot be summed up in such a simplistic manner. What is shared by the five playwrights in this volume is that their work in the 1990s was different in standpoint from what they did in the 1980s. Thus it would be inappropriate to end this discussion of their theater with that decade. To ascertain the overall significance of these playwrights, attention must be given to their activities in the 1990s. Thus detailed discussion of individual accomplishments will be relegated to the introductions provided for each playwright, and the scope of this essay will be enlarged to address a number of issues that arose in the 1990s.

The 1990s was a decade of historical transition on a global scale, beginning with the collapse of the Berlin Wall in 1989, the dismantling of the Soviet Union, the collapse of socialism in eastern Europe, the Gulf War, and the civil war in Yugoslavia. On the domestic front, the death of the Shōwa emperor in 1989 and the Great Hanshin Earthquake and the Aum incident in 1995 were followed relentlessly by brutal criminal acts, such as juvenile crime, child abuse, and random killings.

In its treatment of society, was theater able to do justice to the rapidly changing conditions? The 1990s was a time when the efficacy of theater was questioned fundamentally. Compared to the happiness syndrome (Kara's term) of the 1980s, the past ten years have been deeply engaged with reality. In cultural and economic terminology it is the "lost decade"[23]; and artists have had much trouble in expressing its quality.

But simply criticizing the status quo is insufficient as the social system will cover up its inadequacies. Thus it is necessary to work within the social reality, and at the same time find a philosophy and method to engineer a change in the social mechanism on a fundamental level. Naming this form of criticism "radicalism," I will delineate the ways in which the playwrights exercised it.

One is collaboration. Theater turned towards crossing borders and cultural exchange rather than demanding independence or purity of genre. This trend had already begun in the 1980s and became established in the 1990s. In addition, overseas productions increased in leaps and bounds. Productions abroad by relatively new theater companies began in the second half of the 1980s, but financed by Japanese public and corporate funding, they were showcasing Japan's economic success. These overseas productions were after all unrelated to culture. Instead of a genuine interest in Japanese theater, foreign audiences were curious of the phenomenon of "Japan Today."

In the 1990s, contemporary theater companies were invited to famous arts festivals abroad. To cite some examples, Shinjuku Ryōzanpaku and The Third Erotica were invited to the world famous Theater der Welt in Essen, Germany. The festival program director visited Japan and viewed many stage performances before deciding on the two troupes. In this way, it was contemporary theater which lives and breathes the spirit of the times that was chosen to encounter the world, not *nō*, *kabuki* or *angura*.

Collaboration and overseas productions are not separate matters. They are the two sides of the same issue. When the *raison d'etre* or conventions of theater implode, exchange with other performing arts becomes desirable. The rapid development of collaborations with foreign theater artists was a characteristic of the 1990s. Singaporean artistic director Ong Keng Sen's ambition was to create a collaborative work on an Asian scale, and it was Kishida Rio that joined his project as playwright. Noda worked with Thai actors to produce *The Red Demon Akaoni*[24] (1996). These collaborations went beyond the level of international exchange to that of hybridity.

The topic of Asia quickly became a focal point. Contemporary Asian theater, such as that of Korea, came to Japan with increasing frequency, taking international exchange between comparable age groups to new heights. From showing foreign audiences a play written and performed by Japanese, Japanese artists moved on to creating a new play with their foreign counterparts. For example, Kishida collaborated with Lee Yung-tek, a major Korean artistic director, in the first Japan-Korean collaborative production, *Sewoli-Chota*.[25]

Compared to the closed and domestic tendencies of the 1980s, the internationalization of theater in the 1990s was a major development. Little theater troupes were oriented towards the outer world and with multilingual and multinational encounters becoming real possibilities, Japanese theater in general opened its doors to the world.

7. Towards Radicalism

Noda Hideki, the pioneer of the youthful theater of the 1980s and a synonym for entertainment-oriented little theater, disbanded his Dream Wanderers at the peak of its popularity and went to London for a year of study. On his return to Japan, he founded a theater unit called Noda Map. Discarding the troupe system in favor of a workshop method, he gathered actors anew for each production. Besides the main productions, he started small shows with a handful of players in a limited space. There he tried various experiments and called them "off-the-Map."[26] *The Red Demon Akaoni* was one of them.

A tragi-comedy about a man who finds himself in a strange community and treated as a monster, the play was conceived as a four-actor-multiple-role virtuoso piece. In the premier production in 1996, three Japanese actors played many different roles and one British actor, the part of the red demon.

In 1997, this work was produced as a Japan-Thai collaboration. Thai actors performed the Japanese play with Noda performing the red demon. Although the text was the same, the meaning of the performance was transformed. The red demon Noda played was a threat to the Thai community and signified the Japanese as aggressor. In the context of an Asian collaboration, a post-colonial perspective arose, which had not been apparent in the original production in Japan. In little theater it was customary for the theatrical troupe to have de facto exclusive rights to performing the resident playwright's plays. Noda broke this convention and the work gained depths of meaning.

The collaboration between Kishida Rio and Ong Keng Sen was more volatile. In the Japan Foundation production of *Lear* (1994), actors from six Asian countries performed together while maintaining their own performance style and native tongue. Thus in this play, *nō* actors and Beijing opera actors shared the stage. Through the mazy exchange of multiple languages, Ong materialized his world view that the "world is after all a disharmonious and dissatisfying place." To assume disharmony is to recognize mutual difference and to present difference as difference on stage. Asia is overflowing with diversity. Often lifestyles, religions, customs, and stages of industrialization vary from area to area. In order to express the diversity of Asia, Kishida and Ong chose this collaborative method.

Their subsequent project *Desdemona* (1999) was more experimental. Taking the wife's perspective in Shakespeare's *Othello*, their play portrays Desdemona as representative of Asian women. She will not submit to her indecisive husband. By placing Shakespeare's original in an Asian context, the collaborators rewrote western colonialism.

Kawamura Takeshi, who was often invited to produce his plays at international theater festivals in the 1990s, was also invited as a visiting artistic director to New York University. There he directed the college students in a production of Mishima Yukio's *Modern Nō Plays*, Mishima's ambitious attempt to give the essence of traditional theater a modern expression while honoring the style of *nō*. What is notable is that for Kawamura, directing performances overseas was no longer an unusual event, but an activity on par with his daily work. Japan and the world had become connected by such a permeability.

Kitamura Sō produced *Ode to Joy* at the Seoul Theater Festival in 1999. In the same year, Chong Wishing's *City of Images*[27] was performed by a Korean troupe. Such international exchange has grown rapidly in the past few years. Cutting-edge groups like dumb type, (f. 1984), and Deconstruction Company,[28] (f. 1979), are part of the avant-garde theater market of the world. Expanding imagination and networking can no longer be kept within domestic bounds.

If the term "radicalism" can be applied to these developments as well as to violence of expression, then theater is being reconsidered and restructured at a fundamental level. As globalization intensifies and nations draw more closely together in their needs and concerns, theater too must of course repeatedly transcend boundaries, cross-fertilize, and hybridize. This radicalism did not begin suddenly in the 1990s, but had its beginnings in the 1980s. The striking characteristic of theater today, so often taken for granted, is that this consciousness now produces results on the level of praxis. This survey of plays and playwrights from the end of the 1970s to the mid-1990s indicates clearly that, at the very foundations of modern Japanese theater, a new paradigm was emerging.

Notes

1. For further information, refer to Section 2, "The Little Theater Movement and New Plays" in the General Introduction of *Half a Century of Japanese Theater*, Vol. 3.
2. Daisan Erochika.
3. Daisan Butai.
4. Kokushoku Tento 68/71. Founded by former troupe members of the Freedom Theater and June Theater, playwrights Satoh Makoto, Yamamoto Kiyokazu, and Katō Tadashi were central in the socio-politically concerned theater activities of this group.
5. Ten'i 21.
6. Engeki-dan.
7. Dainiji Engeki-dan. The name of the troupe was again changed to Ryūzanji Company in 1985.
8. Tsunbo Sajiki.
9. Kyokuba-kan.
10. Waseda Shin Gekijō.
11. TPO★shidan.
12. Mokuba-kan.

13. A song by the Peanuts, twin sisters popular in the 1980s.
14. Sanada fūun-roku.
15. Shōjo kamen.
16. Shinjuku hakken-den.
17. Sanjū-maru.
18. Aoi Tori.
19. Chika Engeki.
20. Kishida Jimusho.
21. Ito jigoku.
22. Ningyo densetsu.
23. Ushinawareta jūnen.
24. Akaoni.
25. Happy days.
26. Bangai kōen.
27. Eizō toshi.
28. Kaitai-sha.

Ode to Joy

Kitamura Sō

TRANSLATED BY MITACHI RIHO

*

Introduction

Kobori Jun
TRANSLATED BY MARI BOYD

This translation is based on the 1989 Jiritsu Shobō publication of
Ode to Joy: Eiyaku Hogiuta.

Kitamura Sō
(Courtesy Kashiwamoto Katsunari, Studio Kit's.)

Kyōko looks up at the missiles in the far sky and says, "Look, it flashed again. Just like fireworks." From left: Kyōko, Yasuo, and Gesaku. Fusō Cultural Hall, Aichi Prefecture 1995. (Courtesy Kashiwamoto Katsunari, Studio Kit's.)

The three finish a rare meal of rice. Kyōko says, "Eating fast, shitting fast—both great skills to be proud of. Thanks for the good meal." Gesaku responds, "Uh-huh, don't you be moving around right after a meal." From left: Gesaku, Yasuo, and Kyōko. Fusō Cultural Hall, Aichi Prefecture 1995. (Courtesy Kashiwamoto Katsunari, Studio Kit's.)

After parting with Yasuo, Kyōko says, "It was a phantom. He was a PHANTOM." Center: Kyōko. Fusō Cultural Hall, Aichi Prefecture 1995. (Courtesy Kashiwamoto Katsunari, Studio Kit's.)

Driven out of Parutai town, the three are hurt and take a rest. Gesaku narrates the parable of the four faithful animals. From left: Yasuo, Gesaku, and Kyōko. Fusō Cultural Hall, Aichi Prefecture 1995. (Courtesy Kashiwamoto Katsunari, Studio Kit's.)

The couple head for Mohenjo-Daro. Kyōko asks, "D'you think it's snowing in Jerusalem? [. . .] D'you think it's snowing in Mohenjo-Daro?" All Gesaku can say is, "Dunno." From left: Kyōko and Gesaku. Fusō Cultural Hall, Aichi Prefecture 1995. (Courtesy Kashiwamoto Katsunari, Studio Kit's.)

Introduction

Kobori Jun
TRANSLATED BY MARI BOYD

1. God Descended on a Summer's Day

I FIRST READ KITAMURA SŌ'S *Ode to Joy* at the end of the summer of 1979. At that time, I was a theater reporter for an entertainment magazine in Nagoya called *Play Guide Journal Nagoya*. Although it was one of the lesser magazines in that city, I did share a sense of community with the avant-garde I was reporting on. Reporters like myself were ill-paid and hungry and the young theater practitioners at the artistic frontline were also poor. Kitamura was one of them.

Kitamura Sō was contributing a monthly series of essays in *Play Guide Journal Nagoya*. Although he is a year older than I, very different in personality, and engaged in different types of work, he and I nonetheless enjoyed congenial relations. Reporting on his theatrical troupe Total Produce Organizers★Company, I met with Kitamura almost every day. I was delighted to have this opportunity to talk with this highly talented artist. He was an easygoing person with a natural style, very different from theater people of the 1970s, who had a definite attitude. Witty and humorous, he was a comfort to those around him and at the same time, he maintained a distance from others. He did not intrude on their privacy; neither did he allow others to invade his. I took advantage of my position and made provocative statements like, "The three conditions for becoming a writer are alcohol, women, and illness."

Kitamura was one of the first Japanese playwrights to use word processors and computers, but at that time, he was still writing his manuscripts in long hand. Every month, when I received one of them, I could tell by his handwriting what condition his health was in. His essay series in 1979 was a journal of his personal thoughts and it reflected his anguish at his poor health. It was the first year of his neurosis, which became chronic, and also the year his interest in Christianity deepened. He was profoundly influenced by G.K. Chesterton's *Orthodoxy*.

In the summer of that year, his neurosis worsened, and Kitamura returned temporarily to his hometown, Ōtsu City in Shiga Prefecture. Impatient with the usual method of writing a manuscript, he wrote with a ballpoint pen directly on a mimeograph stencil. The fruit of that effort is

Ode to Joy. He says he had to take frequent rests while writing it as he was not in good health, but he only took two days to finish the play. He now has over one hundred plays to his name and is known to be a fast writer. Nonetheless, two days is a record, even for him.

It is said that divine inspiration sometimes enables a writer to reach a state of automatic writing. *Ode to Joy* must be such an example. Years later, Kitamura told me, "I wrote it in the grip of some strong images. I was suffering from the summer heat and wanted to make snow fall. My health was in a disastrous condition and my feelings were turbulent. In retrospect, I can see that the 'wasteland made by nuclear war' was my inner landscape." Apparently he kept a dictionary by his side as he wrote, and when writer's block set in, he would open the dictionary at random and use the first word he saw to move the play along. The comb Kyōko uses in the play was chosen by this method.

Kitamura took the title *Ode to Joy* from an LP record by jazz musician Hino Terumasa. He found the record by chance as a customer had left it at the café Kitamura operated. He particularly wanted to have the word "song" or "ode" in his title as both appeared in the works of two writers he respected—philosopher and poet Yoshimoto Takaaki's poem "Love Song"[1] and novelist Hikage Jōkichi's novel *Kamunagi Ode*.[2] I cannot help but feel Fortune extended her help to him in this matter.

I read the work in mimeograph form with the odor of fresh ink rising from the page. It was a new and yet strangely familiar world. That the characters were called Gesaku, Kyōko and Yasuo was also refreshing. Gesaku sounds like *gikyoku*, or a play; Kyōko, like *kyokō*, or fiction; and Yasuo, like *Yaso*, or Jesus.

The play is set in the Kansai (Osaka-Kyoto) area after a nuclear war. The human race has practically died out and missiles fly about at random. A couple comes by pushing a cart. The man is Gesaku, age thirty to forty. On the cart flies a flag with "Kokonoe Gorōkichi Theater Troupe" on it. Also, sitting in the cart is a young woman, Kyōko, who seems a little weak in the head yet could be a pure young girl. Significantly they meet a young man, Yasuo, who seems to be a beggar, and travel together with him. During their travels, they entertain invisible audiences with low-grade gigs done sloppily. Just when affection begins to grow among the three, the moment of parting unexpectedly comes. Yasuo decides to go to Jerusalem and Gesaku and Kyōko head for Moehnjo-Daro in the falling snow.

The first time I read the script, I laughed at the ridiculously funny exchange between the comic duo, Gesaku and Kyōko; later on seeing the stage performance, I was to break into tears. At first the image of Gesaku overlapped with Kitamura; then Yasuo also reminded me of Kitamura; soon Kyōko joined the kaleidoscope of overlapping figures that eventually brought me to the point of tears. I remembered getting inexplicably excited and saying, "Sō, this play, you know, it's really something."

2. A Miracle Written in Desperation

After graduating from a high school in Shiga Prefecture, Kitamura was unable to realize his dream of studying in France. Instead, he became a fake student at Chūkyō University in Nagoya and joined one of the university drama clubs, Ikazuchi Theatrical Troupe. With some of the Ikazuchi members who were his old high school friends, he formed the Organizers★Company[3] in 1973 and renamed it Tokyo Produce Organizers★Company in 1976. In 1982, he formed Comet 86[4] (1982-86) and now heads Project Navi[5] (f. 1987).

As a child, Kitamura was exposed to the fundamental pathos of the human condition—to live is the beginning of sorrow—through reading stories like "Red Ogre, the Cry Baby" by Hamada Hirosuke and "The Cow Girl" by Ogawa Mimei. In his teens, he discovered novelists Dazai Osamu (1909-1948) and Sakaguchi Ango (1906-1955). Kitamura uses quotations from and allusions to Dazai's short story "Leaves"[6] and Sakaguchi's "Dr. Wind."[7] One of his favorite terms, "farce," can be traced to Sakaguchi's work *On Farce*.[8] In the natural course of development, Kitamura would have turned to novels and literature, but his encounter with Kara Jūrō's drama swung him over to theater.

Kitamura, together with director-auteurs Yamazaki Tetsu and Takeuchi Jūichirō and actor-director Ryūzanji Shō, belongs to the so-called post-Kara Jūrō generation of the 1970s that was greatly inspired by director-auteur Kara. Kitamura once said that Kara's emergence transformed Japanese modern theater. Kara used a collage method of borrowing from other works—east and west, old and new—and dynamically created his own surrealistic world. Furthermore, by applying his theory of the privileged body of the actor,[9] Kara enabled the actor to transform from a menial who delivered lines to an overwhelming physical presence on stage.

Kitamura's early plays do indeed reveal direct impact from Kara. In a more general sense, Kara's methodology encouraged Kitamura to think in terms of the "infinite possibilities of theater." In theater production, a playwright is required to work with others and this involvement prevents him from maintaining the sense of completion he had when he finished the script. If anything, the reverse is true in that theater begins when the script is done. Often what couldn't be grasped in the reading becomes comprehensible through the medium of the actor's body. Theater enables us to give free reign to our imagination and to bring novels, comics, poetry and local news together and, just as Kara did, turn them into three-dimensional art.

All of Kitamura's works are imaginatively constructed with an eye to infinite possibilities and filled with boyish curiosity and playfulness. In addition, as Kitamura's motto is "to risk his life for the sake of laughter," there is a light, dry humor that runs through his opus. Due to the playwright's understanding of acting and his own generous spirit, his works are both easy to understand and exciting for audience and actors alike. *Ode to Joy* is indeed such a work, but its difference from his other plays is that *Ode to Joy* is written not only by Kitamura but for Kitamura himself. It is the embodiment of his fierce determination to write and produce as a member of the human race and as an individual who desires to express his inner self.

In the second half of the play, there are two important stories in which the dying Gesaku speaks to Yasuo. The first is the parable of the rabbit that jumps into the fire so that it will be roasted and his Master will be saved by eating him. Cartoonist Tezuka Osamu is known for including this Buddhist parable in his work *Buddha*. Kitamura explains the story in the following way.

> GESAKU: [. . .] You see, Yeshua-han, the "self-sacrifice" Rabbit did to repay his master was nothing more than feeding himself to his master. Can you understand how sad this is?
> YASUO: That's what you call sentimentalism.
> GESAKU: It's not sentimentalism. Rabbit did his best—he did the only thing he knew how.
> YASUO: What are you trying to say? Are you supporting Rabbit's action or denying him?
> GESAKU: Take the master—do you think he actually ended up eating Rabbit?
> YASUO: I think it would have been hard for him to eat it.
> GESAKU: You're wrong, he did eat it. All he could do for the RABBIT at that point was to eat him.

A few lines later, Gesaku continues.

> GESAKU: Say that you fall into a hole where there's a man-eating tiger, and you come face to face with him. Do you think there's a way to actually beat the tiger?
> YASUO: No, I don't.
> GESAKU: But there is.
> YASUO: How?
> GESAKU: Before he eats you, you let the tiger eat—
> YASUO: What?
> GESAKU: Yourself. What else is there?
> YASUO: That's silly.
> GESAKU: That's what you think. But don't you see, that's really

the way it is. When you're staking your life, it's hard for
whichever side you're on. It's hard, yet it's no different from
what I've just described.

This example is based on a fable by Deguchi Onisaburō, the founder
of the Daihonkyō sect, who was persecuted by the authorities for having
taken an anti-war stand before World War II. Kitamura's choice of fables
reveals his loneliness and the powerful determination that set in
reactively to it. The paradoxical thinking of "eating a rabbit that
sacrificed itself for you" and "letting yourself be eaten before being
devoured" is the essence of Kitamura's philosophy of life. Why do we
live? If to live intrinsically involves hurting others, then let us accept
human existence wholeheartedly. Instead of making a narrow political
commitment, let's do whatever we can to help humanity.

Kitamura calls *Ode to Joy* a "bright emptiness." It is a sad tale but has
a careless, bright humor because of the playwright's trust in this world
and its people. Otherwise no one would risk his health just to perform
theatrics for others.

> GESAKU: You can never see the audience. The only thing you can
> see is your own eyes. So you only have to play for your eyes,
> that's all.
> YASUO: In "hit-or-miss" fashion?
> GESAKU: Yep. Here they come, the invisible audience has arrived.

After the revival of *Ode to Joy* a decade after its premier performance,
Kitamura says he has just caught up with the play: "[I]n retrospect, it's a
revelatory work that I wrote for my future self."[10] Writing a story is in
itself a kind of miracle. The various events in his life, the children's
tales, novels, comics he read, the music, philosophy, criticism, films and
theater that nourished his soul, the innumerable people he met and those
he parted with—the residue of all these moments and memories met in a
flash of summer light and became the *Ode to Joy*. Usually when
someone is ill, he stays still and doesn't write. But Kitamura had to
write. In that act, I feel the existential humanism of the playwright who
must accept sadness and create.

The God of theater descended. But it was Kitamura who risked his
life to write the words down. His expression of the miraculous enables
us, too, to see "the light of hope at the far end of despair" in the final
scene where Gesaku and Kyōko travel through the heavily falling snow.

Notes

1. Koiuta.
2. Kamunagi-uta.
3. Shi★dan.
4. Suisei 86.
5. Purojekuto Nabi.
6. Ha.
7. Kaze hakase.
8. Farusu ni oite.
9. Tokken-teki nikutai-ron.
10. *Kitamura Sō Daizen★Shigeki* (Complete works of Kitamura Sō) (Jiritsu Shobō, 1983). Kitamura's essays were first published in the *Play Guide Journal Nagoya*.

Ode to Joy

Kitamura Sō

TRANSLATED BY MITACHI RIHO

CHARACTERS
KYŌKO
GESAKU
YASUO (YESHUA)

Notes:
GESAKU and KYŌKO call each other "GESAKU-DON" and "KYŌKO-HAN"
  which indicate their western Japanese dialect.
YASUO addresses the two, "GESAKU-SAN" and "KYŌKO-SAN," which are the
  standard Japanese.

Scene 1: Fireworks
*(A local town in the western part of Japan after a nuclear war. A road
piled with debris. In the midst of the smell of the burnt air ……*
*"Una Sèrie di Tokyo" sung by The Peanuts is heard. Then, with their
household goods piled on a cart,* GESAKU *and* KYŌKO *enter.)*

KYŌKO: Look, it flashed again. This time, over there. Gesaku-don. Do
  you think it's another missile?
GESAKU: Yep, Kyōko-han. Another missile. *(Answers halfheartedly.)*
KYŌKO: How come? How come, Gesaku-don? Ain't the war over yet?
GESAKU: The war may be over, but there's plenty of missiles left. No use
  saving 'em. That's why they keep shooting 'em one after another.
KYŌKO: "Leftover missiles," huh? If they are leftovers, they should leave
  'em over, like leftovers. Look, it flashed again. This time, it's red.
GESAKU: Red means an H-bomb. Looks like it hit Tokyo.
KYŌKO: Oh, no, it can't.
GESAKU: Huh?
KYŌKO: I used to write to a kid in Tokyo.
GESAKU: Not any more. Ain't no post offices left. Letters'll never get
  there.
KYŌKO: That's awful. He was such a good kid.
GESAKU: Why don't you call him sometime?

KYŌKO: You think the phones'll still work?

GESAKU: Submarine cables should be okay, I suppose.

KYŌKO: Yeah. All right, I'll call him.

GESAKU: H-O-T. It's getting hot. While we're here, why don't we take a little break?

*(*KYŌKO *looks around restlessly.)*

GESAKU: What's the matter? You gotta pee?

KYŌKO: Yeah.

GESAKU: There's nobody around. Just do it over there.

KYŌKO: Okay. *(Exits.)*

GESAKU: SO HOT. Hey, the locusts are singing. "Summer grass, what's left of the dream of the brave warriors, songs of the locusts absorbed by the rocks." Look, it flashed again. It's a lithium bomb this time. Sure had enough of 'em, 'specially in this heat. What's this? A cockroach. Should I try eating it? Hey you, Roach. Wait, wait, wait just a minute, you hear me?

KYŌKO: Gesaku-don!!

GESAKU: What in the world, you scared me! Hey, that roach got away.

KYŌKO: Good god, never mind the roach.

GESAKU: What is it, what happened?

KYŌKO: A pervert. There's a pervert on the loose.

GESAKU: A perrr-vert?

KYŌKO: Oh God, he's coming this way. Back there, when I pulled up my kimono to pee, he was staring right at me.

GESAKU: Did he get a good look?

KYŌKO: Not so good.

GESAKU: You should've peed right on him.

KYŌKO: He scared me so, I stopped peeing.

(A young man looking like a beggar "looms" out. It is YASUO.*)*

YASUO: LOOM.

GESAKU: Who the hell you think you are "looming" out like that? You were peeking at Kyōko-san's pussy, weren't you?

YASUO: PUSS ...... PUSS ......

GESAKU: PUSS, PUSS, how dare you? Who are you anyway? Why don't you get lost?

*(*YASUO *falls down.)*

KYŌKO: Oh no, he fell down.

GESAKU: Who the hell is this guy? Look at him, he's out of it. Come on man, pull yourself together.

YASUO: PUSS. PUSS ...... PUSS.

GESAKU: Stop that PUSS PUSS stuff, would you? This guy's a pain in the ass.

KYŌKO: Do you wanna see my pussy?

GESAKU: You're kidding. What are you crazy? Showing a thing like

THAT for free?

KYŌKO: But, he kept saying PUSS, PUSS.

GESAKU: No, wait a minute, Kyōko-han. I think he's just hungry. He ain't saying "PUSSY," he's saying "pudding, pudding."

KYŌKO: Maybe we should give him something to eat. Come on, Gesaku-don.

GESAKU: Oh, all right. Kyōko-han, go over and get some water and dried sweet potatoes.

KYŌKO: Okay. Let me think where they are.

GESAKU: Look in the red bag.

KYŌKO: I got it, I got it.

GESAKU: Hey, hey, slow down. You're gonna choke to death.

KYŌKO: Look, it flashed again. A double-shooter.

GESAKU: Spending so much money just to make machines that kill people. Sooo dumb.

KYŌKO: Do you think Japan's gonna collapse?

GESAKU: I think it's already changed shape. Look at it, Mt. Fuji—only half left.

YASUO: JAP! JAP-PAN. *(Stands up.)*

GESAKU: Oh, you've come to your senses, have you?

YASUO: OOH. OH. OOOOH, OOH.

KYŌKO: Quite a talker, ain't he?

GESAKU: Come on man, get a hold of yourself.

YASUO: Must it crumble? Even the comb, given me as a token of love must it crumble?

KYŌKO: What's he up to?

YASUO: Behold, I can see the hill of death; and now, life is heading towards it.

GESAKU: This one's a poet. "Le poèt" in French. Oops, my education slipped out.

YASUO: Who are you? *(To both of them.)*

KYŌKO: I'm Kyōko.

GESAKU: I'm Gesaku.

YASUO: Huh?

KYŌKO: What's your name?

YASUO: I ...... I ...... am YA ...... SUO ......

KYŌKO: Yasuo's your name, huh? Awfully simple, ain't it?

GESAKU: Where're you from? We're from over there. How about yourself?

YASUO: I'm, ... there. There ......

KYŌKO: THERE—where's "There"?

GESAKU: Just this side of Europe.

KYŌKO: Was there a place like that, I wonder?

YASUO: Water, and food—you gave them to me.

KYŌKO: That's right.

YASUO: Thank you very much. *(Chews the dried sweet potato.)*

KYŌKO: My God, Gesaku-don. This man's got good manners. He's thanking us, chewing on the dried sweet potatoes.

GESAKU: If you call that manners.

KYŌKO: Sir, where are you heading?

YASUO: I, I'm heading way over there.

KYŌKO: Just like us, then. We're going "round the corner." Isn't that right?

GESAKU: That's right.

YASUO: ……Well—

KYŌKO: Huh?

YASUO: I mean, you said you're going "round the corner" and I'm headin' "way over there." How come you said "just like us"?

KYŌKO: Don't know—don't know. You start thinking about stuff like that, your feet'll never move. Ain't that the truth?

GESAKU: Right. But it's how you think about it. You know they say, "A journey of a thousand miles starts with a single step." OOPS, there goes my education again.

YASUO: I see. Well—

KYŌKO: Yes?

YASUO: After you've given me water and dried sweet potatoes, I shouldn't be saying things like this but—

KYŌKO: What is it? Come on, say it. Ain't good for your health, if you don't say what you feel.

YASUO: Well. You see, I'm wondering if it's all right for me, since I'm going "way over there," to go along with you till "just around the corner."

KYŌKO: Is that all? I thought you were going to say you wanna see my PUSSY or something.

GESAKU: Kyōko-han, what a thing to say!

KYŌKO: Yeah, but at first, I really was convinced he was a pervert, so—

GESAKU: We still don't know, he might be.

YASUO: A pervert? Who me? Is that what I look like to you? Me, a pervert? Pervert, pervert, pervert, per. Pervert, perverted pervert. Per pervert. Perverted per pervert.

GESAKU: What are you talking about?

YASUO: Huh, sorry. Seems I got carried away. Well, you see, I've—sort of—nowhere to go. Maybe that's why I've "perverted." Therefore, I should be able to go "way over there." Is it all right to "pervert"?

GESAKU: Pardon?

YASUO: I mean, is it all right to go along with you?

GESAKU: Well, I suppose it's all right but ……

YASUO: If you're worried about food, I'll take care of that ……

GESAKU: What d'ya mean, you'll take care of that?

YASUO: You see, I have a special skill.

KYŌKO: A special skill?

YASUO: Yes. Well, how about some bread?

KYŌKO: Bread?

YASUO: Just some crumbs will be fine.

GESAKU: Nope. Just dried sweet potatoes.

YASUO: In that case, dried sweet potatoes will do.

GESAKU: If it's dried sweet potatoes you want, you have them in your hand.

YASUO: Oh, that's true.

GESAKU: Are you okay? Maybe you better get hold of yourself?

YASUO: Sorry. Absent-minded. Now then, "MUNYO-MUNYO-NO-GONYO-GONYO." *(Keeps pulling dried sweet potatoes out of his pocket one after another.)*

KYŌKO: Look, it's magic.

GESAKU: Is that the special skill you're talking about?

YASUO: Yes.

GESAKU: That's something. Wow. But, if you can do that, why've you been walking around with an empty stomach?

YASUO: You see, this special skill won't work unless I have something to start with.

GESAKU: No kidding? If you have something to start with, you can get anything out of your pocket?

YASUO: Not anything.

KYŌKO: How 'bout some chocolate?

YASUO: As I said, if you have it to start with.

KYŌKO: Ohh. That's no good. Some magic!

GESAKU: Oh, no, Kyōko-han, this isn't magic. This guy knows how to draw things to him. It's like when the Fox God brings stuff to you. It's just a real special skill. It's called "Come-to-Me-Things"—I saw it done a long time ago by a magician named Manji Asia, but I tell you—that then was just magic. This here's a different story. This guy's "FOR REAL." Man, he is "DOIN' IT."

KYŌKO: You puttin' me on, Gesaku-don? You sure?

GESAKU: Sure I'm sure. I haven't been in show biz for nothing.

YASUO: Excuse me, but what do you say? Can I come along with you?

GESAKU: Well, we are running low on dried sweet potatoes, so maybe your timing's good. The man with such a special skill—couldn't ask for more. What do you say, Kyōko-han?

KYŌKO: All right by me.

GESAKU: Then, it's all set.

YASUO: Thanks, I appreciate it.

KYŌKO: Oh-oh, have I gotta pee! Never got around to it before, and I

think I'm about to explode! Gotta go, gotta go. *(Starts to go but turns back.)* And there's nobody gonna watch me do it! Ha, ha, ha ......
(Exits.)

YASUO: Excuse me.

GESAKU: Huh?

YASUO: A little while ago, you mentioned you were in show business.

GESAKU: Oh, yeah, that's right. I was on the road with the Gorōkichi Kokonoe Troupe. Well, we were doing a show in Shinozaki, when that damn missile hit us, so, then the company drifted apart. That girl is the kid of a woman from Oube who the troupe leader laid his hands on.

YASUO: Shinozaki, Oube? Where are they?

GESAKU: Don't remember. Towns just over there, maybe. Now, we're the wandering beggar dancers. I play the drum, the girl dances, and we get dried sweet potatoes.

YASUO: Beggar dances.

GESAKU: Yeah. That's right. Sort of a—a fake dance. You could call it improvisational in a way. Well, not really. I mean it's just not real serious stuff. The idea is to let just a bit of her show through while she's dancing—to let the crowd catch a glimpse of hair ......

YASUO: Glimpse of hair?

GESAKU: That's right. It's a "non-strip" striptease.

YASUO: "Non-strip"?

GESAKU: I mean, we're not really "showing" anything but, if something just sorta gets "seen" ...... Well, actually, we are "showing" it, but ......

YASUO: Uh-huh ......

GESAKU: One of these days, I'll let you see it.

YASUO: Right.

KYŌKO: *(Returning.)* Wow, I feel so good. What are you two talking about?

GESAKU: Dancing.

KYŌKO: No way. I'm not gonna do it. Here I've just gone and peed, and my body is not pure. Ha, ha. There may still be a few drops left on my hair, ha, ha, ha ......

GESAKU: Well then, should we get a move on?

KYŌKO: Right now? Hold on just a minute, let me have a drink, too. I got to fill myself up again. *(KYŌKO drinks directly from a canteen.)*

GESAKU: *(To YASUO.)* You got any luggage?

YASUO: No, nothing.

GESAKU: That's OK. No problem. We've got plenty of blankets. Besides it's so hot.

(KYŌKO gets on the cart. YASUO pushes it from the back. The cart starts moving.)

KYŌKO: Look, it flashed again. Just like fireworks.

(Blackout.)

Scene 2: Firefly

(GESAKU is cooking rice in a mess tin. YASUO is looking at the sky. KYŌKO is combing her hair and singing.)

GESAKU: It's been three days now …… rice and more rice. It really worked. I can't believe we found that one grain of rice.

KYŌKO: *(Singing.)* White is the morning meandering light
      Smoky and soft, it comes following the night
      Sweet is the grass, that's glowing so green
      Tell me what color would your shadow be,
           Movin' along
      Waitin' for you, I sing ODE TO JOY
           Singin' for you

GESAKU: Yasuo-han, what have you been looking at all this time?

YASUO: Sunset and falling stars.

GESAKU: Ha, ha, ha. There's no such things.

YASUO: What about over there?

GESAKU: That's just burning.

YASUO: Burning?

GESAKU: Yep. RADIOACTIVITY has spilled into the vacuous space, and IONS are burning.

YASUO: And the falling stars?

GESAKU: Just lithium bombs. Local missiles. Set my Big Brother on fire.

YASUO: Quite an authority, aren't you?

GESAKU: I was there for two years.

YASUO: Where?

GESAKU: The factory.

YASUO: But isn't the war over?

GESAKU: Yep. That's probably some messed up computers keep shootin' them things off.

YASUO: ARMAGEDDON …… THE APOCALYPSE …… HEAT HAZE AT NIGHT …… *("Heat Haze at Night" by Izumiya Shigeru is heard.)*

KYŌKO: Yech, my comb broke. Darn it, what am I gonna do? Hey, Gesaku-don, can I listen to the radio?

GESAKU: We're out of batteries.

KYŌKO: Well, I sure need something. My comb's broke and I'm in a bad mood. Wish we had some batteries. Hey, Yasuo-han. Get me some batteries with your magic, will ya?

YASUO: Batteries?

KYŌKO: You remind me of the Emperor. You see, a battery's a thing with plus and minus terminals. Looks like an old mail box, and you put it in a radio?

YASUO: *(Taking a screwdriver out of his pocket.)* This?

KYŌKO: Hey, hey, hey, I see you also got a sense of humor. It's all right, you never know, we might come across a battery lyin' around somewhere. I'll just go and look. *(Starts to go.)*

GESAKU: Soon be time for din-din. Don't you go too far.

KYŌKO: I know. Hello, Kyōko to Starship Enterprise. Come in, Spock. Mr. Spock, please beam me aboard. *(Exits.)*

YASUO: *(Taking the broken comb.)* Whatever happened to the human race?

GESAKU: Excuse me?

YASUO: I mean, I just wondered if there might be anybody else around.

GESAKU: Ain't no one else 'round here, I don't think. Tomorrow, we'll be in town. Then, we'll see plenty of them.

YASUO: *(Taking a new comb out of his pocket.)* What's the town called?

GESAKU: It's got a western sounding name, Riyona.

YASUO: Riyona ......

GESAKU: I am beautiful.

YASUO: Pardon?

GESAKU: Oh no, it's nothing. Look, food's almost ready. Mmmmm, smells soooo good, I can hardly wait. For us Japanese, rice is the best.

YASUO: Hard to believe—that this is not the glow of the sunset.

(A lithium missile is shot from west to east. A low explosion is heard.)

GESAKU: That one was real close, wasn't it? But I don't think there's any more missiles left in the Megaton Range. They shot all those up in the first few days.

(KYŌKO returns.)

KYŌKO: Gesaku-don, Yasuo-han, I found something real interesting. I wonder what kind of a doll this is.

GESAKU: A doll? Let me see ...... ooh, Kyōko-han, this is an OTOGIBŌKO. It's called "Amagatsu." It's a charm to protect a child.

KYŌKO: OTOGIBOUKO?

YASUO: AMAGATSU?

GESAKU: It's one of those Katashiro they use at the Shintō purification ceremonies. You know, "Purify them! Exorcise them of the evil spirits!"—those paper dolls shaped like a man they use in those ceremonies—they're called Katashiro, and this here is to keep by a child to drive away the evil spirits.

YASUO: I wonder where it came from.

KYŌKO: There, just around that corner there's a dead kid. I found it there.

YASUO: A dead kid?

KYŌKO: Looks like. I ain't quite sure, but when my kid sister died, well, she looked just about like that.

GESAKU: There's no way a kid's gonna die alone. The kid's parents must be around here somewhere. But of course, they might've already turned to ashes. Come on, the rice is ready. Why don't we eat?

KYŌKO: Hmmmmm. Ain't there a single battery lying around here somewhere? I'm dying to listen to the radio.

GESAKU: Even with a battery, no tellin' for sure you could listen to the radio.

KYŌKO: How's that?

GESAKU: Might not be any radio stations left.

KYŌKO: Gesaku-don, don't you start saying such realistic things. The moment I put a battery in the radio and turn on that switch, you'll be hearin' three or four stations in no time flat.

GESAKU: Sorry. Here you go. Be careful and try not to spill it.

(Gives her some rice.)

KYŌKO: Wow, long time no see. What have you been up to, Mr. Rice? Well, I've been to the zoo for a spell. Oh, doing what? Well, eatin' a tiger ...... What's your problem? You're no fun. Here I am trying to be a good sport playing a two-man comic show all by myself. The least you could do is laugh.

GESAKU: Ha, ha, ha. So you ate a tiger ...... now how's your stomach holding out?

KYŌKO: It's roaring like this—GRRRRRRRRR. Ha, ha, ha, ha.

GESAKU: Yasuo-han, here you go. *(Passing some rice.)*

YASUO: Did you really eat a tiger?

KYŌKO: Ha, ha, ha, ha, you've gotta be kidding.

GESAKU: Just a two-man comic show. DING-DING-DING-A-DING-DING-BOOM-BOOM.

(GESAKU and KYŌKO start a two-man comic show.)

GESAKU: Ladies and gentlemen, welcome. I'm Gesaku.

KYŌKO: I'm Kyōko.

GESAKU: The two of us together make "Gesaku and Kyoko."

KYŌKO: Slightly weird duo of the two book-freaks.

GESAKU: Astoundingly intellectual two-man comic show.

KYŌKO: But anyhow, isn't this something?

GESAKU Yep, it sure is.

KYŌKO: We don't even have one good idea and ......

GESAKU: Hush, don't mention that.

KYŌKO: But say, Gesaku-don, about the subway.

GESAKU: What about the subway?

KYŌKO: Why do you think it flies?

GESAKU: Well, it's because—no reason at all.

KYŌKO: You know, those subway trains—

GESAKU: Yeah, the ones you find deep down underground?

KYŌKO: Yeah, those. I wonder who buried them.

GESAKU: I went out that time even though I had no umbrella.

KYŌKO: Just as I thought. No wonder it was weird. My Mama's been nuts ever since she woke up.

GESAKU: Makes perfect sense to me. Don't you know we're living in times when you got a spaceman coming down from the moon.

KYŌKO: Even so, my Mama always says—

GESAKU: Says what?

KYŌKO: Kyōko, what're you gonna be when you grow up?

GESAKU: Sure, anybody would take the umbrella along.

KYŌKO: So, I say to her. Mama, there's no umbrella.

GESAKU: Spaceman took it right back to the moon, huh?

KYŌKO: Since the subject is subways—

GESAKU: I buried it.

KYŌKO: There's no hope. BOOM-BOOOOOOM.

(GESAKU and KYŌKO bow and sit down.)

GESAKU: What d'ya think?

YASUO: Was it about some new kind of human relationship?

KYŌKO: Nope. It's called "the elliptical two-man comic show." You just skip the middle part.

GESAKU: It requires great skill. When I skip one line, Kyōko-han skips two. When we skip five, we go back to the first line we skipped.

YASUO: You go beyond the words?

GESAKU: You got it. Treason against pre-established harmony. Resistance against fate. It's called "LAPLACE[1] Reversal two-man comic show."

YASUO: Amazing.

GESAKU: I'm only kidding. Truth be told, Kyōko-han keeps forgetting her lines, so I just go along with her. Kyōko-han, you've been shooting out the rice all over the place. Excuse me for a moment. *(Tries to pick the grains of rice stuck on KYŌKO's kimono.)*

KYŌKO: *(Backing up.)* No, don't. It's not rice—look, it flew away. It's a firefly—a firefly.

GESAKU: You sure?

KYŌKO: Yeah. I'm sure a—firefly. It was black, you see. It wasn't white.

GESAKU: Maybe it was scorched.

KYŌKO: Only thing's been scorched is our jokes for the comic show. That one really was a firefly.

GESAKU: Was it glowing?

KYŌKO: Just a little.

GESAKU: Was it? Well, no matter. Why don't we go ahead and finish our meal.

YASUO: Excuse me, Kyōko-san.

KYŌKO: Yes?

YASUO: When we're done eating, would you take me to the place where you found the kid's body?

KYŌKO: Sure, all right. *(Gorging.)*

GESAKU: No, no, Kyōko-han. Slow down would you?

KYŌKO: Eating fast, shitting fast, both great skills to be proud of. Thanks for the good meal. *(Stands up.)*

GESAKU: Uh-huh, don't you be moving around right after a meal. You should count to one hundred and then move. Otherwise, it's bad for your digestion.

KYŌKO: *(Sitting down.)* One, two, three, look …… another missile is heading this way. Nine, ten …… I'm gonna go look for fireflies …… Fifteen, sixteen …… *(Lying down.)* Eighteen, nineteen ……

GESAKU: Yasuo-han, how 'bout seconds?

YASUO: Oh, no thank you.

KYŌKO: Twenty-one, twenty-two …… *(Gradually, her voice fades. She falls asleep.)*

GESAKU: She's out, I think.

YASUO: Shall I get a blanket?

GESAKU: Ohh, thanks.

(YASUO puts a blanket over her.)

GESAKU: Sun's startin' to set. Temperature's gonna drop …… During the day, it gets hotter 'an hell like the middle of the summer; but at night, it's like goddam winter, it gets so cold you can't sleep.

YASUO: Should I check the fire?

GESAKU: Yes, that'll be great, if you would. I'll make some rice-balls with what was left over.

(Dusk falls suddenly.)

YASUO: Goodness, it sure got dark. "Autumn dusk comes without warning," I should say.

GESAKU: More like. But, it seems a bit strange …… Well, I suppose it's a good idea to go to bed early on a day like this.

YASUO: *(Taking out a comb.)* Uhhh, this comb, would you give it to Kyōko-san.

GESAKU: Oh, my, another one of your "Come-to-Me-Things" by God Fox, is it? Yes, all right. But you know, you shouldn't give a comb away for free. Tomorrow morning, we'll exchange it for something. I'll keep it for now.

YASUO: All right, then. Please.

GESAKU: You go on and go to bed. I'll watch the fire.

YASUO: In that case, excuse me. *(Gets under KYŌKO's blanket.)*

GESAKU: Hey, hey, what are you doing?

YASUO: Pardon?

GESAKU: "Pardon" yourself. I don't believe this. What're you gonna do if she ends up having a baby? Why don't you head on over there and use that blanket?

YASUO: Certainly. Then, good night.

GESAKU: Yep. G'night.

(Eventually, GESAKU also dozes off. The fire goes out. Then, out of

nowhere, a firefly flies in and starts to fly around KYŌKO.*)*

KYŌKO: *(Waking up, still half asleep.)* What is it? Who's there? Look, a firefly, it's a firefly.

(As if to follow the firefly, KYŌKO *walks.* KYŌKO *exits. Then, another firefly begins to fly around* GESAKU. YASUO *wakes up. The firefly disappears.)*

YASUO: *(Noticing* KYŌKO *is gone.)* Gesaku-san, Gesaku-san, wake up! Kyōko-san is gone.

GESAKU: …… What is it? What's wrong? *(*GESAKU *seems like a completely different person.)* KU-KU-KU. *(He snickers.)*

YASUO: Kyōko-san is not here.

GESAKU: What's wrong with that? KU-KU-KU. *(He snickers.)*

YASUO: Gesaku-san?

GESAKU: Sir, a duel, take thy sword. I am D'Artagnan!

(Then, he takes a saber out of the piles of luggage, and a set of long and short Japanese swords, which he gives to YASUO.*)*

GESAKU: Take the swords. What now, hast thou shrunk from fear, Musashi[2]?

YASUO: Musashi?

GESAKU: I shall now avenge Kojirō's death.[3]

YASUO: Why does D'Artagnan avenge Kojirō's death?

GESAKU: If you say so, then. I am Guy Williams.[4] Peep, peep, the mark is "Z."

YASUO: And now, "THE WONDER MAN Zorro," is it? How strange to speak of revenge.

GESAKU: Enough! Say no more. Come on, Musashi! If thou will not, then, I shall come after thee.

YASUO: Gesaku-san, you're still asleep.

GESAKU: What? Thou call me "SENILE."

YASUO: Not "SENILE," "STILL ASLEEP."

GESAKU: Ohh, this must be a "HELL-OF-A-SLEEP."

YASUO: What in the hell?

(Since GESAKU *is coming after him with the saber,* YASUO *is forced to hold the two swords at the ready.)*

GESAKU: Great God, your form is Nitenichi-ryū.[5]

YASUO: Well, you're the one who said I am Musashi just a little while ago.

GESAKU: Then, thou art Miyamoto Musashi.

YASUO: That's enough. Never mind that. Don't you see Kyōko-san is missing?

GESAKU: Musashi's so-called "two-sword technique" reveals the workings of a clever mind. He developed this sword technique just before the bloody duel with Shishido Baiken.[6] In order to beat Baiken with his sickle and chain, Musashi figured he could use the sword to entwine the chain. That left only the sickle to fight, much to his advantage. However, if he's got only one sword, and he uses that to entwine the chain, that means he's got nothing with which to fight the sickle. So, naturally he creates the "two-sword technique." Musashi's sword technique is quite flexible; he changes his technique according to the person he fights against. Against the long spear of the Hōzōin School, he uses a small sword; against the clothes pole of Kojirō, he uses a long oar of a boat. Quite an intellectual technique, is it not? By the way, the only time he actually used two swords at a duel was the one with Shishido Baiken. Of sixty-some odd duels in his life, he did not use the "two-sword technique" any other time, according to the record. Now, Musashi ......

YASUO: That's enough about Musashi.

GESAKU: No, never enough. You never know enough about things, for all things are in a state of flux. Sasuke, every day of your life is another day of learning.

YASUO: SASUKE?

GESAKU: I am HAKU'UNSAI, the Ninja.

YASUO: Gesaku-san, this reminds me of the Laplace Reversal two-man comic show you did a little while ago. He, he.

GESAKU: You impudent fool! "Reversal" is a word we use for a miracle during a high school baseball game. To indulge in this idle chatter will jeopardize the quality of the play.

YASUO: So this is a play, this state of nonsense?

GESAKU: Nonsense or caramels, when you make them into a play, they melt into what we call THEATER. Hmmmm, Hmmmm, Gooood.

YASUO: Quit yammering and wake up, will you! Gesaku-san!

GESAKU: *(Suddenly crying.)* Ohhhhh, ohhhh ......

YASUO: *(Throwing the swords away and rushing over.)* Gesaku-san.

GESAKU: YOU SHALL DIE! *(Slashes at him.)*

YASUO: Pardon me, but I'm immortal.

GESAKU: Oh, I didn't know, then it's no fun. But try to die, anyway. *(Starts to strangle him.)*

YASUO: GESAKU-SAN, S-STOP.

(Just then, KYŌKO returns.)

KYŌKO: Quit it you two. What the hell do you think you're doing?

YASUO: Oh, Kyōko-san, Gesaku-san's in big trouble.

KYŌKO: D'Artagnan again?

YASUO: Exactly.

KYŌKO: Then, Zorro comes out, and then the revenge, right?

YASUO: How do you know?

KYŌKO: It's the usual. He's sent two men right to heaven with this trick already.

YASUO: Can't you stop him?

KYŌKO: Sure I can. Sure.

YASUO: Then, please do something.

KYŌKO: Now hold your horses, would'ya?

YASUO: Just hurry. There's a limit to being immortal.

(KYŌKO *starts digging into the household goods on the cart. Finally, she takes out a framed photo. It is a photo of a hippopotamus.*)

KYŌKO: Look, Gesaku-don. It's a hippopotamus; it's a hippo.

GESAKU: A hip—hippopotamus ...... Mmmmmmmmmmm. *(Falls down.)*

YASUO: Thank goodness.

KYŌKO: It worked, it worked. Godzilla's intercoursin' suckin'-sex.

YASUO: Huh? What's that about Godzilla?

KYŌKO: I mean, Godzilla's done it again. Well, what I really mean is, BIG FUCKIN' SUCCESS.

YASUO: I don't get it at all. What is it you've got there?

KYŌKO: It's a picture of a hippopotamus. You see, Gesaku-don hates hippos. A long time ago, he got bitten in the face by a hippo. Ever since then, he falls down whenever he sees a picture of one. When he's having a fit, this works the best.

YASUO: A fit? Was he having a fit just then?

KYŌKO: Yep.

YASUO: What kind of fit?

KYŌKO: Your regular, garden-variety fit.

YASUO: I see. I thought it might be due to a firefly.

KYŌKO: A firefly?

YASUO: Yes. I thought he might've been possessed by a ghost of a firefly or something, because just a little while ago ......

KYŌKO: Look, a firefly.

(*A firefly flies out of the body of* GESAKU. GESAKU *gets up.*)

YASUO: Are you all right, Gesaku-san?

GESAKU: It ain't no firefly.

YASUO *and* KYŌKO: What?

GESAKU: I said it ain't no firefly.

KYŌKO: Then, what is it?

GESAKU: It's Amagatsu.

YASUO: AMAGATSU?

GESAKU: Yep. It was Amagatsu. All a'glowin', 'cause of the radio-activity.

YASUO: So that was Amagatsu, you say ......

(*Blackout.*)

Scene 3: Wind and Thunder

GESAKU: We'll be there soon. We'll be in town soon.

YASUO: What's this town called?

GESAKU: We were gonna go to Riyona, but we took the wrong road, so we'll probably end up in Parutai.

YASUO: I wonder why we took the wrong road.

GESAKU: 'Cause we're just bumbling along—it's hit-or-miss.

YASUO: Why didn't we walk with some direction in mind?

GESAKU: If I could walk with some direction in mind, I wouldn't be a player on tour.

YASUO: What's Parutai like?

GESAKU: Dunno, till we get there.

YASUO: Everything you do is hit-or-miss, isn't it? Everything.

GESAKU: You got it. Hit-or-miss—we bumble along and look the town bumbles along right to us.

YASUO: So it's the towns that come along on their own, then?

GESAKU: Truth is—we're not moving one tiny bit. It's the earth that's doing the turning.

YASUO: Kyōko-san. You're awfully quiet today.

KYŌKO: I'm thinkin'.

YASUO: Ohh. About what?

KYŌKO: Well, actually, last night I got pregnant.

(The cart stops.)

GESAKU: We congratulate you.

YASUO: Are congratulations in order?

GESAKU: The firefly's kid, ain't it?

KYŌKO: Yeah, how did'ya know, Gesaku-don?

GESAKU: Seems like something Kyōko-han would think of.

YASUO: Speaking of fireflies, you mean that firefly?

KYŌKO: Yep, that's right. Since last night, fireflies, thousands of them, have made their way into my secret place. Inside my belly, there are ten billion neon signs and a hundred billion illumi-countries.

YASUO: Illumi-countries? You mean "illuminations."

KYŌKO: What'll I do if I have a baby firefly?

GESAKU: You could give it some sugar water.

KYŌKO: Yeah. I should start looking for some sugar right now.

YASUO: When we get to town, we should be able to get some sugar. Just one cube, and I can get you as many as you like. Come now, it's about time we get moving and head for the town.

GESAKU: We've arrived. We've arrived in town.

YASUO: What, we have?

GESAKU: This is Parutai.

YASUO: There's no sign of people.

GESAKU: The towns are just about like this anywhere you go. You kind of "feel" the town, but the only thing's there is the air. Come on, we'd better hurry and find some people so we can make some money. The sky looks a bit weird. It might rain, it just might. Well, Kyōko-han, should we have a go? TONTOKO-YOIYA!

(Accompanied by GESAKU*'s bell and drum,* KYŌKO *dances. It's a "hit-or-miss" dance. TONTOKO-YOIYA! At the "YOIOYA,"* KYŌKO *lifts a leg up. Her thigh can be seen now and then.)*

GESAKU: *(Chants.)* Now here it is, here it is
                 Here it is at last
                    YOIYANOSA
      Here it is at last
                 Underneath the red kimono of this fairy
                    Catch a glimpse of the flesh
                       The flesh that bids farewell to this earth
                        AH YOINA-NO-SASSA-NO-SAAH

      Not like the water
         Of this orb
            At this canal
               Of here there and everywhere
      But the Holy Water
         That was sprinkled
            Over Joseph's head
      Has cleansed
         This flesh
            SANO-SASSA

      Tracing way back
         For two thousand years
      Not being spoiled
         Nor being decayed
      Even being compared to Oriharukon
         And being known as the secret treasure
            Of a Brahmana
      That's what it is
         This flesh

      Have a look
         Just one look
            At this flesh

      If you're to take
         A second look
            And a third look
      Your eyes will turn into
         The brain to see
      Your ears will be filled with
         A good timbre

And will listen to
A strange strange song

Here we go
Here we go
YOIYA-NO-SASSAH

YASUO: Nobody's coming.

GESAKU: Don't you worry, the people will flock to us just like the moles in the early spring.

TONTOKO-YOIYA!

(Chants.) Now here it is, here it is
Here it is at last
YOIYASSA
Here it is at last
Underneath the scarlet kimono of this virgin
Catch a glimpse of the flesh
The flesh that rules this earth
AH-YOIYASA-NO-SASSAH-NO-SAH

Not like the stone
Of this planet
Of this volcano
Of here there and everywhere
But the Graphite
That fell
On Jesus' head
Has polished
This flesh
SANO-SASSA

YASUO: SANO-SASSA.

GESAKU *and* KYŌKO: Sweep time SANO-SASSA.

YASUO: Are you sure it's all right to sing such baloney?

GESAKU: Sure, it's all right. In most cases, it's better to do it this way than try to make any sense out of it. Baloney is the essence of art. The ruling power of the time gives it the meaning. SANO-SASSAH.

YASUO: HORESA.

GESAKU: Yeah, that's the way to go.

YASUO: MEKE-MEKE-MEKE-MEKE, ARA-ESSA-SAH-I.

GESAKU: *(Chants.)* Tracing way back
For two hundred thousand years
Not being muddy
Nor being clear

Being compared to a crystal
I've never seen
The balls of a dragon

YASUO: Total nonsense.

GESAKU: *(Chants.)* Have a look
Just one look
At this flesh

If you're to have
A second look
And a third look
Your brain will turn into
The eyes to see
And you will feel as if
In a strange, strange dream

Here we go
Here we go
YOIYASA-NO-SAH

YASUO: Nobody's showing up.

GESAKU: Oh yes, it's a full house, doing great. You're the only one who can't see them.

YASUO: There are townspeople here?

GESAKU: Yep.

YASUO: I don't see anybody.

GESAKU: You can never see the audience. The only thing you can see is your own eyes. So you only have to play for your eyes, that's all.

YASUO: In "hit-or-miss" fashion?

GESAKU: Yep. Here they come, the invisible audience has arrived.
(There is a feeling that an audience is watching.)

YASUO: Now that you say so, I do sort of feel them.

GESAKU: Come join us. What you are about to see are awesome and highly skilled performances. If they please you, then let us know by your applause and cheers.
(KYŌKO stops dancing.)

GESAKU: First of all, the world's greatest phenomenon, Human-Material Transmission-Machine. Whatever you wish for, it is yours—the most wondrous of wonders, or the oddest of odds. And performing this magic is this young gentleman, Haretoke Yasuo.

YASUO: You mean, ME?

GESAKU: That's right. Do that "Come-to-Me" trick.

YASUO: But, that's not something you do for show.

KYŌKO: Let's see, what'll come out first? *(Whispers.)* Hurry up, hurry up.

YASUO: But, I have to have something to start with.

KYŌKO: Something to start with? …… What have we got?

GESAKU: Let me think. Something with a big surprise to it.

KYŌKO: How 'bout my jack-in-the box?

GESAKU: Dumb.

KYŌKO: Then what?

GESAKU: Something we could give out as a free souvenir would be nice.

KYŌKO: Okay, I've got it. This necklace. *(Taking the rosary off her neck.)* If you're wearing this, I heard that even a vampire would be so frightened it would faint.

YASUO: But this is a rosary.

KYŌKO: You know it, Yasuo-han?

YASUO: Of course. Kyōko-san how come you have it?

KYŌKO: Mom gave it to me.

(There is thunder and lightning.)

GESAKU: Hey, hey, we'd better hurry up and do it, else the rain's gonna hit.

KYŌKO: Yes, let's start. Whatever we get, we'll give them out as free souvenirs.

YASUO: My giving out rosaries to people— Quite a suggestive scene.

KYŌKO: What are you mumbling about?

YASUO: Nothing. Well then, I'll try it.

GESAKU: Okay, here we go, TONTOKO YOIYASA.

KYŌKO: YOIYASAH.

YASUO: *(Chants.)* That which I've just taken out here
                    Is a silver-plated iron cross
                        Called the rosary
                Tracing way back
                    For two thousand years

GESAKU: Sounds familiar.

YASUO: *(Chants.)* Jesus Christ
                    Was born
            Into this everchanging world
                Into the storms of life
            He has cried
                Has had fun
                    Has been carried away
            And he has been crucified
                Upon the hill of Golgotha
                There stood this—
                    AN-AN-A-AN-AN-ANA-AHN
                    Cro-oo-sssss

KYŌKO: Doin' good, doin' good.

YASUO: ONE—*(Throwing.)* TWO—

(Each time YASUO *counts and throws a rosary, there is a bolt of*

lightning.)

GESAKU: The rosary you've just received is a free souvenir, but due to the limited budget, as you can see, there's no figure of Jesus on the cross. If you wish, we'll be happy to crucify Jesus on your cross at minimum cost, so please bring it over here. Furthermore, for those who are of different denominations, we not only can do Jesus, but we also have Buddha, Mohammed, Kōbō-Daishi,[7] Sun Wukung,[8] and many others. Please feel free to bring your cross over here.

(Sound of thunder.)

KYŌKO: And now, for our next act, there's only one man in the world— because most of the human race has been extinct since the last war— there's only one man left in this world who can do it—the famous "CATCH THE BULLET" TRICK. Here I have a Colt—shooting up into the sky, it'll shoot through the wings of an angel, shooting down into the ground, it'll shoot through the tongue of the devil. And with this 45 caliber, I shall shoot a man. An ordinary man's heart would be smashed. But not this man. The only man in this world who can do this trick! One and quarter inch away from his heart, he will catch the bullet with his bare hands!

YASUO: Can you really do that?

GESAKU: Yep.

YASUO: Will you be all right?

GESAKU: Oh yeah. During the last war, that's how I kept myself from getting hit by bullets. I can even catch a lithium missile.

KYŌKO: Then, shall we start? Appearing in ABB-TV THE WORLD "Give-A-Shock" HOUR, winning second prize for the "Give-A-Shock" GRAND PRIX—DON GESAKU! Here he goes.

YASUO: Second prize—who won first?

KYŌKO: The man who caught the bullet with his heart itself. Gesaku-don, all set?

GESAKU: LADIES AND GENTLEMEN, please have a look at this hand —check it out against the sun—"look at it through the sunlight, and you'll see my bright red blood streaming; even a worm, even a mole cricket, even a water spider, whatever's alive you can eat it." Come to me, BULLET.

KYŌKO: Here goes.

GESAKU: I wanna be alive
             I don't wanna die
                   Come to me
                       I'll stop you.
                           I'll catch you.

(KYŌKO shoots. It hits GESAKU's leg.)

GESAKU: OOOUUUCCHHH!

KYŌKO: Oh no, I'm sorry, I'm sorry.

YASUO: Are you, are you all right?

GESAKU: Only acting, only acting, don't you worry.

KYŌKO: This time, I'll take steady aim at him.

(KYŌKO shoots, and GESAKU catches the bullet.)

GESAKU: Here, I caught it. Here, this is the bullet. Here it is, this ......

(KYŌKO shoots again and GESAKU falls down.)

KYŌKO: Oh no, it went off by accident.

YASUO: Gesaku-san, are you acting?

GESAKU: Nope, nope. No good, I'm gonna die.

YASUO: Where did you get hit?

GESAKU: It made a hole in the life of a man.

YASUO: The life of a man?

GESAKU: My back, it hit me right in my back.

YASUO: Are you sure you're not acting?

KYŌKO: Are you all right, Gesaku-don, I'm real sorry. I'm really sorry ......

GESAKU: No good, my eyes are getting foggy. My eyes, my eyes ......

KYŌKO: Men—Men—Men Mentholatum may work.

GESAKU: Mentholatum? ...... I put it on a piece of bread and ate it the other day. It's all gone.

KYŌKO: What should we do, Yasuo-han? I guess we'll just have to run away, just the two of us.

YASUO: What are you saying?

KYŌKO: Run away, and think about it tomorrow. Tomorrow is another day. I'll think about it tomorrow. I entrust my hope to tomorrow.

(Thunder. Clouds are dispersing. Music from Gone with the Wind.)

YASUO: Kyōko-san.

KYŌKO: Listen, when Miss Kasugano went to "Wuthering Heights" and was about to cross the Yorkshire wilderness, she said she felt "uneasy." Since she was playing the part of Heathcliff, she was afraid of getting involved in a love triangle with their apparitions. But I think she must've felt "excited," don't you? *(Changing her voice.)* It is difficult to say.

YASUO: Wh—who art thou?

KYŌKO: People call me "The Virgin's Mask."

[Playwright's note: This play, The Virgin's Mask by Kara Jūrō, inserted here is just an example. Any play could be used here.]

GESAKU: Hey, you two, what play are you doing?

KYŌKO: Deceiving them—the audience.

GESAKU: Well, while you're deceiving 'em, I'll end up dying.
  (Lightning.)
YASUO: How about this? It feels like it's going to rain any minute.
  Why don't we get the hell out'a here?
KYŌKO: GET THE HELL?
GESAKU: OUT'A HERE?
YASUO: Yes.
GESAKU: You mean run away?
YASUO: Yes, that is correct.
GESAKU: Either way, I'm gonna die.
YASUO: Do your best. In any case, we should get out of here.
GESAKU: Kyōko-han, would you go around the audience and get some
  dried sweet potatoes or some money, please?
KYŌKO: All right.
GESAKU: We should get some money for at least Kyōko-han's dance.
KYŌKO: All right. Gesaku-don, don't you die—you wait for me, OK?
  (KYŌKO *disappears into the invisible audience.*)
YASUO: Gesaku-san, lean against my shoulder. Go ahead and hold onto
  me.
GESAKU: If anything, would you offer me your back?
YASUO: You mean, you want a piggy-back ride? *(Squatting.)*
GESAKU: If at all possible, I'd like us to exchange backs.
YASUO: That's absurd.
GESAKU: Maybe so. But at my age, my life—
YASUO: Your back, you mean.
GESAKU: Yes, my life; I've never thought of carrying a bullet in my "life."
YASUO: But don't you see I'm carrying you and the bullet all on my
  "back" now.
GESAKU: Thanks. Oh, I feel awful. It's no use, I'm gonna die.
YASUO: Pull yourself together, Grand Prix Number 2. The man who has
  managed to avoid lithium missiles shouldn't let a Colt 45 get him.
GESAKU: Yasuo-han, to tell you the truth, I'm the one who shot up the
  missile.
YASUO: Are you having a nightmare?
GESAKU: No, I'm not. I shot up that missile. Can't you understand?
YASUO: No, I can't.
GESAKU: You see, Yasuo-han. Can I ask you an odd question?
YASUO: What is it? You shouldn't talk too much.
GESAKU: You ain't Yasuo, you're Yeshua, ain't ya?
YASUO: Yeshua?
GESAKU: Yeshua, the Christian—the "AMEN," you know.
YASUO: What difference would it make if I were the "AMEN"?
GESAKU: I confess I'm an "AMEN." It's a secret though.
YASUO: A secret?

GESAKU: Yep. You see, I ain't a "gentleman," so I can't behave like other "AMEN" people. Drinking, shooting, women. *(Pretending to give an injection.)* Shooting, you know? I hate to get other members in trouble, so I keep it a secret.

YASUO: Gee, is that right? A secret member—

GESAKU: Come on, Yasuo-han, you are Yeshua, ain't ya? The way you made your entrance was real fishy. Are you sure you ain't a man of significance?

YASUO: If I am, then what are you going to do?

GESAKU: Can you lend me your back?

YASUO: I'm already lending it.

GESAKU: No, I didn't mean that.

YASUO: Don't tell me you want to switch? You know I can't do that.

GESAKU: Sure, I know we can't switch our backs. But we can make them the same.

YASUO: Make them the same?

GESAKU: Look, this is the bullet I caught a little while ago. Take this and put it here.

(GESAKU *puts the bullet into* YASUO*'s back.* YASUO *falls forward and drops* GESAKU. *Thunder crashes.*)

YASUO: Holy smoke! What—what are you doing to me? *(Writhes.)*

GESAKU: These hands managed to catch a bullet coming at you. They certainly can manage to push a bullet into YOUR back.

YASUO: Why? Another fit, is it? A hippopotamus, a photo of a hippo.

GESAKU: It's not a fit. I've been thinking a long time—

YASUO: Been thinking about killing me?

GESAKU: No, that's not it. I've been thinking of becoming a Christian, not a secret one but a real one, you see.

YASUO: What's that got to do with this cruel treatment?

GESAKU: When I'm sick, so is Yeshua. When I steal, so does Yeshua. When I sin, so does Yeshua. I and Yeshua are the same. Within me, there is Yeshua; therefore, and then, it is thus, AMEN.

(Thunder crashes. KYŌKO *rushes in.)*

KYŌKO: It's struck, it has struck. Holy Moses, the lightening struck the rosary. Holy Moses. We've got to get away!

(KYŌKO *starts to pull the cart.*)

YASUO: Kyōko-san, the lightning might strike the cart. It's dangerous.

KYŌKO: No kidding …… if it struck the rosary, it can strike anything. Come on, get on it, Gesaku-don.

GESAKU: Thanks. But I'm gonna die anyway.

YASUO: What are you going to do if it strikes you?

GESAKU: I'm gonna flip it right back. We'd better get out real quick, otherwise the townspeople're gonna come and lynch us.

YASUO: Of all things, why did the lightning strike the rosaries? It's just like Justine of Sade.

KYŌKO: What's the matter with juice?

YASUO: No, not juice, it's Sade. Justine of Sade. A misfortune of virtue. In other words ......

KYŌKO: No time for other words or other worlds. Let's hurry up and get out of here.

(Just then, stones are thrown from the front.)

KYŌKO: Shoot, they came around to the front.

YASUO: Kyōko-san, step back, step back. I'll take care of it. It's my fault.

KYŌKO: Are you sure you'll be all right?

YASUO: Ladies and gentlemen of the town! Stop throwing stones, please.

(A big and heavy stone used for making Japanese pickles is thrown in.)

YASUO: People of Parutai, hear me out. I am the one who gave out the rosaries as free souvenirs. Therefore, it is my fault that the lightning struck the rosaries. However, People of Parutai, hear me out. Those people who have been struck by the lightning were called to enter the Kingdom of Heaven. That is the reason why the lightning struck. God has chosen. God has chosen the people and ......

(Thunder crashes. Something blazes up.)

KYŌKO: Now is the time. Come on, let's get out of here.

YASUO: God is, God is, uhmmmmm, saying we should get out quick.

(They run away with the cart.)

GESAKU: What was it, what was it you just said. Yasuo-han?

KYŌKO: Gesaku-don. You came to your senses.

GESAKU: I've been awake all this time. Say, Yasuo-han. Do you happen to know the story of the Fox, the Bear, and the Rabbit?

YASUO: I don't think you should talk. You're going to bleed again.

GESAKU: This is what ya call a real bleeding service.

KYŌKO: I wanna hear the fairy tale.

GESAKU: Once upon a time, there lived a great man. He was raising a Fox, a Bear, and a Raccoon. Oh no, not a Raccoon. It was a Rabbit, yep, a Rabbit it was. Now, he was a kind man. One day, he had some errands to take care of in the town over the mountain. But the trip took longer than he expected. On the way back, the mountain was covered with snow, and the man fell ill. Meanwhile, back at the house, the three animals were waiting for their master, but there was no sign of him for days. They were running out of food, so they headed for the mountain. There, they found their master lying on the ground. He was still alive. The fire was still going. They figured there was still time to save him. He'd been really good to them. So, the three of them went out each on their own to look for some food. But you see, it was winter in the mountain, and there just wasn't much food around. Nevertheless, Fox and the Bear managed to find some food. But

Rabbit, he was in trouble. He just couldn't find any food at all. "So, what could I do?"—he wondered. "Nothing, I can't do anything. No, that's not true. There is one thing I can do. Rabbit meat is real tasty, you know—"So, he went and jumped into the fire. To make a long story short, he turned himself into a roast rabbit feast! That way his master could eat *him*!

YASUO: A fable of self-sacrifice.

GESAKU: It's not as simple as that, Yeshua-han. When I first heard this story, I didn't think the self-sacrifice was an act of beauty.

YASUO: Then, what did you think?

GESAKU: I thought that was just about all Rabbit was capable of doing.

YASUO: You're being too hard on Rabbit.

GESAKU: No, I'm not. You see, Yeshua-han, the "self-sacrifice" Rabbit did to repay his master was nothing more than feeding himself to his master. Can you understand how sad this is?

YASUO: That's what you call sentimentalism.

GESAKU: It's not sentimentalism. Rabbit did his best—he did the only thing he knew how.

YASUO: What are you trying to say? Are you supporting Rabbit's action or denying him?

GESAKU: Take the master—do you think he actually ended up eating Rabbit?

YASUO: I think it would have been hard for him to eat it.

GESAKU: You're wrong, he did eat it. All he could do for the RABBIT at that point was to eat him.

YASUO: Why are you telling me all this now? All I can think of at the moment is the lightning striking the rosaries.

GESAKU: Listen, Yasuo-han. This has nothing to do with the story I just told you but—

YASUO: What is it now?

GESAKU: Say that you fall into a hole where there's a man-eating tiger, and you come face to face with him. Do you think there's a way to actually beat the tiger?

YASUO: No, I don't.

GESAKU: But there is.

YASUO: How?

GESAKU: Before he eats you, you let the tiger eat—

YASUO: What?

GESAKU: Yourself. What else is there?

YASUO: That's silly.

GESAKU: That's what you think. But don't you see, that's really the way it is. When you're staking your life, it's hard for whichever side you're on. It's hard, yet it's no different from what I've just described.

KYŌKO: Gesaku-don, I know a story about a rabbit, too.

GESAKU: The story about a rabbit and a turtle having a race?

KYŌKO: Yeah, that's the one. When I heard that story, I think I learned one good thing.

GESAKU: Wow, so you learned a lesson. What was it you learned?

KYŌKO: For the first time I learned that a rabbit is an animal that takes a nap. Up till that time, I thought the cat was the only animal that takes a nap.

YASUO: We have here an "ecological" discovery about the animal.

KYŌKO: Is that it? Is that what you'd call it? Then, that explains why the lightning struck the rosaries.

YASUO: It does?

KYŌKO: Lightning does not strike plastic. It's a discovery about a scientific phenomenon. Next time you make a rosary, make it out of plastic.

GESAKU: Religion is not that rational. Lightning strikes not iron rosaries but wooden charms—that's where God comes into it.

KYŌKO: But the lightning did strike Yasuo-han's rosaries.

GESAKU: That's true. There were plenty of people who were killed by missiles, and now they go ahead and get struck by lightning, wearing the rosaries around their necks. Pretty irrational, isn't it? T'is irrational, therefore I—Oh shoot, I've started to bleed again.

YASUO: It's because you're talking.

KYŌKO: Well, Gesaku-don, where should we head for now?

GESAKU: We could go straight, without making any side trips.

KYŌKO: To where?

GESAKU: To Paradise. The world to come.

KYŌKO: Then you are gonna die.

GESAKU: Yeah. Well then. Excuse me for going first …… COLLAPSE.

YASUO: Gesaku-san!

KYŌKO: Gesaku-don. You shouldn't die.

YASUO: You can't die in such a hit-or-miss fashion, Gesaku-san. Gesaku-san.

KYŌKO: What should we do?

YASUO: No good, the heart's stopped.

KYŌKO: Is he dead?

(YASUO *and* GESAKU *nod. Terrible thunder. Blackout.*)

Scene 4: Lamenting Over Snow

(YASUO *and* KYŌKO *are standing in front of* GESAKU*'s grave.*)

KYŌKO: It was my fault to begin with. If I hadn't let that pistol …… (*Cries.*)

YASUO: Kyōko-san, don't cry. Crying won't bring back the dead. (*However,* GESAKU *does come back.*)

GESAKU: Sorry to have kept you waitin'.

KYŌKO: What took you so long? Where've you been? Were you off playing pachinko games or something?

GESAKU: Don't be silly. I went to get some water. And look what I found—a battery!

KYŌKO: Wow, no kidding! Now I can listen to the radio.

(KYŌKO *starts looking for a radio among the things on the cart.*)

GESAKU: You know, it might snow tonight.

YASUO: *(Putting* GESAKU*'s grave away.)* Snow? What season are we in now anyway?

GESAKU: Seasons are all messed up. At any rate, the atmospheric layers are totally unreliable.

YASUO: How is the wound in your back?

GESAKU: Not good. Do you wanna have a look at it? You can see a hole.

YASUO: Oh, no thank you.

GESAKU: Once in a while, the wind blows through it and it hurts.

YASUO: I see, you have a hole in your body.

GESAKU: That's right. How's yours?

YASUO: Mine closed up right away.

GESAKU: Shoot. I was gonna ask you to let me go through it to get into heaven.

YASUO: Pardon?

GESAKU: Don't you see? I mean those words, those words. You know, "Thou shalt enter through the narrow hole."

(The radio starts making noise.)

KYŌKO: Hey, I'm getting something, I'm getting something. It's started making noise.

YASUO: Gesaku-san where are you heading for now?

GESAKU: Well, let's see. Under these circumstances, it may not be a bad idea to decide where we're going and walk towards it.

YASUO: I'm planning to go to Jerusalem.

GESAKU: You mean we have to say good-bye?

YASUO: Yes. I happened to go along with you since you were going "just around the corner," but now, I'm beginning to feel the urge to go "way over there."

GESAKU: Do we have to say good-bye?

YASUO: Why don't you come with me to Jerusalem?

GESAKU: Maybe you can get Kyōko-han to come along. Kyōko-han.

KYŌKO: What? I'm busy now.

GESAKU: Do you wanna go to Jerusalem with Yasuo-han?

KYŌKO: Gesaku-don, what are you gonna do?

GESAKU: I can't go.

KYŌKO: Then, I won't go, either. It's no good, this radio is no good. Makes noises—that's all it does.

YASUO: Gesaku-san, I'll say good-bye here.

GESAKU: So soon? Just like Moon Princess. Kyōko-han.

KYŌKO: What is it? Leave me alone, I'm busy!

GESAKU: Yasuo-san's saying good-bye.

KYŌKO: Forget it, forget it. I'm busy!

GESAKU: Well, you heard her.

YASUO: Then, so long.

GESAKU: Yeah, it's a shame that we have to say good-bye so soon.

YASUO: Good-bye. *(Exits.)*

GESAKU: Abruptly he came, and abruptly he went.

   *(*KYŌKO *is crying.)*

GESAKU: Hey, Kyōko-han, are you crying?

KYŌKO: Yep. The radio's not working right, and I'm crying.

GESAKU: Oh, I see. That's a shame. Oh, yeah, I forgot. Yasuo-han gave you your comb, I mean, a new one, but it's unlucky to get one for free, so why don't we give him two or three of those dried sweet potatoes in return? I think he's still around. Would you mind takin' 'em to him?

KYŌKO: You really think he's still around?

GESAKU: Yeah, hurry up and find him.

   *(*KYŌKO *rushes off in a flurry.)*

GESAKU: It won't work. I won't be able to travel with her after all. You see, I do everything in a hit-or-miss fashion, that's why. Brrrrr, it's cold. North wind's blowing through the hole in my body. As far as the eye can see, nothing but piles of debris. That means wherever you're headed, you end up in the same place. Nowadays, most people are dead; things that look like shadows are forms created by the moonlight hitting the air. They should be running out of lithium missiles any minute. I wonder what they're doing—those people who went their separate ways.

   *(*GESAKU *starts pulling the cart.)*

GESAKU: Wherever you go, it's to nowhere. Where is there?

KYŌKO: There is Mohenjo-Daro, Gesaku-don.

GESAKU: What now, Kyōko-han? You came back.

KYŌKO: Yep. *(Nibbling on the dried sweet potatoes.)*

GESAKU: You couldn't catch up with him to give him the dried sweet potatoes?

KYŌKO: That's not it, Gesaku-don. It was a phantom. He was a PHANTOM. From the beginning, he didn't exist. If he was anything at all, he was just a firefly. Yeah, that may be it, he was a firefly.

GESAKU: I wonder.

KYŌKO: Yeah, that's it. Hey, Gesaku-don, you're going to Mohenjo-Daro, aren't you?

GESAKU: Looks like.

KYŌKO: I wonder if everybody would be there.

GESAKU: Here it is. It's the comb that firefly Yasuo-han gave you.

KYŌKO: Oh, I see, I'll take it. But you said it is unlucky to get it for free, right?

GESAKU: Why don't you stop off in Jerusalem and have a baby or somethin'.

KYŌKO: Yeah. I wonder if I should do that. *(Combing her hair.)*

(Singing.) White is the morning meandering light

Smoky and soft, it comes following the night

Sweet is the grass, that's glowing so green

Tell me what color would your shadow be,

    Movin' along

Waitin' for you, I sing ODE TO JOY

    Singin' for you

GESAKU: What's that song called?

KYŌKO: It's called "Ode to Joy." I can't get a handle on it; I have no idea what it means.

GESAKU: Typical hit-or-miss.

(Then, it starts snowing.)

KYŌKO: Look, Gesaku-don, it's snowing.

GESAKU: No shit.

KYŌKO: What a dirty snowfall.

GESAKU: It's radioactive ash.

KYŌKO: But there are a few white flakes here and there.

GESAKU: You're right.

KYŌKO: Look, it melts, it melts. When I grab it, it melts. This is real snow for sure.

GESAKU: Well, shall we go then?

KYŌKO: Yep …… Gesaku-don?

GESAKU: Yeah?

KYŌKO: D'you think it's snowing in Jerusalem?

GESAKU: Dunno ……

KYŌKO: D'you think it's snowing in Mohenjo-Daro?

GESAKU: Dunno ……

(A blizzard in the distance. The cart starts heading for that snow.
Music: "Una Sèrie di Tokyo" by The Peanuts.
On this day, it is snowing in the world. It is snowing all over the earth.
From this day on, the ice age has begun.)

THE END

ODE TO JOY[9]

Music and lyrics by Kitamura Sō
English lyrics by Mitachi Riho

As you think fit. . . .

White is   the mor-ning mean-dering light   Smo-ky and soft, it comes fo-llow-ing the night

Sweet is the grass, that's   glow-ing   so green Tell me what co-lor would your   sha - dow be

Mo - vin' a - long   Wai - tin' for you, I sing   ODE TO JOY   Sing - in' for you

[Playwright's note: The song goes something like this. Sing it as you think fit, and sing it slowly. You don't have to sing it as it is written, either. In the performances, every actor who played KYŌKO sang it with a slightly different melody of her own.]

Notes

1. Pierre Simon de Laplace (1749-1827), French mathematician, astronomer and physicist.
2. Miyamoto Musashi (1584-1645) was one of the most famous swordsmen in the early Edo period (15th-16th century). From his first duel at the age of 13 to his final duel at age 29 with Sakaki Kojirō, Musashi fought over sixty duels and was never defeated. He developed his unique sword technique called two-sword fighting style, nitenichi-ryū, from the drum movements at Araki Shrine.
3. A famous Japanese swordsman and disciple of Toda Seigen. Kojirō invented the famous "Flipping over Swallows" (Tsubame-gaeshi), a superb long-sword technique so quick and sharp that it could supposedly kill two flying swallows in one swing. With this technique, Kojirō established his own school, "Ganryū." In 1612, Kojirō fought against Musashi and was defeated. It was the most famous duel in Japan between the two independent Sword Schools, Kojirō with a three foot long sword and Musashi with two swords.
4. Played Zorro in the Walt Disney TV series.
5. Nitenichi-ryū, or two-sword technique, is one of the traditional Japanese Sword Schools developed by Miyamoto Musashi. *Niten* means "two heavens," which are the sun and the moon, the light and the shadow, symbolizing two opposing forces. Musashi believed the world consisted of opposing forces, which, when brought together, gave birth to something totally new. By unifying the moves of the two swords, one long and one short, held in the right and the left hand respectively, the two-sword technique could fulfill another aim, to win a fight. Musashi believed this idea applied not only to sword tactics, but also to the logic of the world; thus, he named the technique nitenichi-ryū or the "Two Heavens into One."

6. Baiken was a wandering samurai famous as a superb master of chain sickles. His brother was killed by Miyamoto Musashi, and in revenge, Baiken fought Musashi but was defeated.

7. Kōbō-Daishi, or Kūkai, (774-835) was a Buddhist priest who founded the Shingon sect at the beginning of the Heian period (9th century) at Mt. Kōya, the present chief center of the sect. In 921, he was posthumously accorded the title of Daishi or great teacher.

8. The Monkey Spirit is a Chinese classic novel, *Hsi Yu Chi or The Road of a Journey to the West* by Wu Cheng-en. *Hsi Yu Ch*i is a collection of episodes about a pilgrim and his supernatural disciples. Sun Wukung, is the top disciple.

9. The lyrics are loosely set to music and the beats are deliberately irregular.

Nippon Wars

Kawamura Takeshi

TRANSLATED BY LEON INGULSRUD and KAWAI SHŌICHIRŌ

*

Introduction

Nishidō Kōjin
TRANSLATED BY LEON INGULSRUD

This translation is based on the 1990 version of
Nippon Uoāzu.

Kawamura Takeshi (Courtesy Kawakami Naomi.)

Center right: General Q, played by Kawamura Takeshi, enters with his spokesmodels. Center left: J. The Suzunari, Tokyo 1984. (Courtesy Kagami Hisako.)

Trainees party in the Blue Whale Room. The Kinokuniya Hall, Tokyo 1986. (Courtesy Kagami Hisako.)

O´ (seated center) arrives at the Blue
Whale Room. The Toga Festival
Amphitheater, 1986. (Courtesy Kagami
Hisako.)

After the trainees instigate a successful "rebellion," the Blue Whale submarine surfaces. The Theater Apple, Tokyo 1987. (Courtesy Kagami Hisako.)

Using their Neuro-Kinetic Energy, the trainees confront Sue Ellen. The Sai Theater, Tokyo 2001. (Courtesy Miyauchi Katsu.)

The battle with Sue Ellen. The Sai
Theater, Tokyo 2001. (Courtesy
Miyauchi Katsu.)

Introduction

Nishidō Kōjin

TRANSLATED BY LEON INGULSRUD

Nippon Wars IS A LANDMARK WORK by the then 24-year-old playwright Kawamura Takeshi. Japanese theater of the 1980s was rejuvenated by the emergence of a new generation of young artists. A plethora of companies, most having their origins in university theater groups, emerged and were collectively hailed as the third great generation, following the 1960s generation. Many of these artists, who were in their twenties during the 1980s, went on to lead and sustain a new avant-garde in Japanese theater. Kawamura Takeshi was among these leaders.

In 1980, Kawamura founded his company, The Third Erotica, at Meiji University where he was enrolled. A sophomore at the time, Kawamura led his company as playwright, director and actor. The titles of The Third Erotica's first productions in 1980, *Love at the End of the Century*[1] and *The People of the Bomb Zone*[2] indicate the aggression and street-smart sensibilities which have been the company's trademark since its launching.

These characteristics made The Third Erotica distinct from many of the other companies of its time. The dark underground sensibility that dominated the theater of the 1960s was being replaced by a bright and playful interest in light entertainment; however, Kawamura resisted this tendency and created work that was wild, hard-edged and uncompromising.

Kawamura first came to widespread notice in 1983 with *Radical Party*. He cemented his reputation the following year with *Nippon Wars*, and furthered it with *Genocide* that same autumn. Both of these plays were nominated for the Kishida Drama Award, and although they did not win, Kawamura was awarded the 30th Kishida Drama Award the next year for his *Shinjuku Version of The Tale of Eight Dogs: The Birth of the Dog*. This award firmly established Kawamura as a major figure in the theater of the 1980s.

Nippon Wars was first performed at the Suzunari theater in Shimo-kitazawa, Tokyo, a venue that was fast becoming the most exciting of the small theaters. *Nippon Wars* was then revived at the 1986 Toga International Arts Festival, on the open-air stage. In 1987 a tour of

Europe was canceled, but the English version was performed in Japan. In 1990 the English version was performed again on the open-air stage in Toga as a co-production with the Toga International Arts Festival. Directed by Kawamura, the production featured actors from the United States, Australia and Japan. In 2001 the play was performed in repertory with a "new version" in Tokyo.

Nippon Wars is set in a Japan of the near future. In the world of the play, analysis of all data concerning humanity indicates that war is inevitable. In response to this, the government secretly begins development of combat androids. The play takes place inside a Blue Whale submarine out at sea. Inside the submarine an elite group is being prepared for war, but not through traditional military training in the use of guns and explosives. The trainees are engaged in a two-and-a-half-year program consisting of 200 lessons, in which they will experience or simulate all of the various experiences of the average person. They begin with happiness, sadness, anger and humiliation and move on to futility, violence, and death. By going through each of these experiences they become more human and therefore more effective as combat robots. However, they are missing what is most valuable for humans—memory, which gives us each an individual history of experience and therefore individual autonomy. As artificial beings, the androids have no memories, so the government uses its massive data bank of memories to implant each android with a random person's memory. Through this process the androids become fully human. This is where the drama begins.

The protagonist, a fighter who has abandoned the terrorist group Rebel Canary, realizes that he needs his own war. He fires his gun at the sky and silver papers fall to the ground. The silver papers are draft notices that are only picked up by those who are bored. He picks one up and is immediately drafted into military service. The United Capitalist Republic of Nippon (Japan of the future) is already at war, but it doesn't seem real to the protagonist who is now in the training room in the belly of the Blue Whale, where he is given the name O´ (the playwright specifies that this name be read "O Dash"). There is a young prodigy in the room named O and the two quickly become rivals. A beautiful woman, a former "spokesmodel of the battlefield" called I, is also in the room. Furthermore there is a "Total Brain" named Sue Ellen who controls the room. Her body was destroyed in combat and now is able to exert enormous power through thought alone. As the various characters make their way through the story towards the final training program, they are increasingly filled with doubt. They wonder if this war is really theirs. Eventually the trainees hit upon the idea of destroying Sue Ellen, who controls them, and they seem to succeed by harnessing their psychic energies through "Neuro-Kinetic Energy." However they are told that this was simply another part of their programming, a lesson called "Revolt." All forms of rebellion and resistance are caught in a web of ever deeper levels of organization and turn out to be programmed after all. Finished with all of the lessons, the completed soldiers will be sent to war the very next day.

Kawamura's calmly detached social commentary is strikingly evident. Without goals, the younger generation is bored to death. They cannot simply join the social order, nor do they want to join the corporate world and become a part of that structure; they are seemingly left with no options. *Nippon Wars* is a vivid expression of the futility and sense of being hopelessly trapped that was characteristic of the younger generation of the 1980s. The playwright's brilliance lies in his examination of this problem in a political framework, rather than on the scale of the individual or as personal alienation. Devoid of power or ideas, the young generation is subsumed into the nation and ends up as little more than fodder for war.

In this environment individual emotion is the only means for rebellion. O´ has held on to a faint love for I but, when he discovers that this was merely a program called "Crossed in Love," he despairs. The androids are stripped of all hope. Desperately, O´ decides to mount a personal rebellion by killing Q, their leader. Just as he is about to succeed, Q says something decisive: "Don't you ever have any doubts about yourself [. . .] you're pretty stupid about your self." Forced to face the fact that he too might be an android, O´ plays a final gambit. He shoots himself in the head, gambling that if he is human he will die and, if he is an android he will not. The bullet passes straight through his head leaving him alive. He declares "I'm alive" and in that moment he comes to know what he is. Finally accepting the truth, he heads into his own war as a "thinking type android, ZERO."

Nippon Wars begins with the quote:

> Calm down. The world is just moving. That's all.
> But don't misunderstand. The world is, if nothing else, against you.

This is a wonderfully concise expression of playwright Kawamura's world view. The world does not stay put; it is always shifting, changing and moving. We as humans must also keep moving and changing. We can't grab onto anything too tightly, nor should we be indifferent. Kawamura's position is very subtle: Maintaining a distance from his subject, objectively observing and critiquing the world, Kawamura is indeed a "thinking type" playwright. The issues raised are the dignity of being human and the hubris that often results from trying to defend that dignity. What are the limits to what I am? Am I merely someone's creation? In the face of these questions, the distinction between human and android is obliterated. The subject is explored in Ridley Scott's film *Blade Runner* (1982), which was based on Philip K. Dick's novella *Do Androids Dream of Electric Sheep*. *Blade Runner* had a huge impact on Japanese theater of the 1980s, and Kawamura was one of the artists inspired by it. From that inspiration he has created a story of human memory and identity. Kawamura questions the self and posits that there is no such thing as identity. Starting with this assertion, he moves from questions of where we come from and where we are going straight into the central drama of being human.

In retrospect, *Nippon Wars* is surprisingly ahead of its time. It captures the soft fascism of the post-Cold War world, the loss of a sense of life in the information-age body, and a Japanese society burdened with profound doubts about the future groping for solutions. I have no doubt that this play will continue to shine a bright light into the present.

Notes

1. Seikimatsu rabu.
2. Bakudan yokochō no hitobito.

Nippon Wars

Kawamura Takeshi

TRANSLATED BY LEON INGULSRUD AND KAWAI SHŌICHIRŌ

CHARACTERS

MIDDLE-AGED MAN
YOUNG MAN
GIRL
CROWD
WOMAN
I *(female)*
O´ *(male)*
O *(male)*
R *(male)*
J *(male)*
B *(male)*
P *(female)*
M *(female)*
F *(female)*
K *(female)*
RIGHT
LEFT
GENERAL Q
SUE ELLEN

Calm down. The world is just moving. That's all.
But don't misunderstand. The world is, if nothing else, against you.

(Music. Light slowly comes up. People are seeing off a young man in a military uniform who is leaving for the front. A variety of banners. A middle-aged man among them. A voice is heard from deep below the stage.)

VOICE: Lesson 25. Program designated "Departure for the Front." Begin.
MIDDLE-AGED MAN: Ladies and gentleman, our country and her people are in a state of war. Our country shall be victorious. Our men shall win many battles through the strength and courage of Mr. *(Use Actor's*

name.), whom I present here. He is holding, as it were, our country in his hands. Mr. *(Actor's name.)*, you are the first student to be drafted. You are the pride of our town. Mr. *(Actor's name.)*, a word, if you please.

YOUNG MAN: Thank you, I am still young, but I will fight for the United Capitalist Republic of Nippon.

MIDDLE-AGED MAN: Three cheers for Mr. *(Actor's name.)*.

(The CROWD *cheers three times.)*

MIDDLE-AGED MAN: Three cheers for the United Capitalist Republic of Nippon.

(The CROWD *cheers three times.)*

YOUNG MAN: I am going now. Thank you, everybody. *(Bows several times.)*

(The CROWD *cheers. A girl rushes to him.)*

GIRL: *(Actor's name.)*

YOUNG MAN: *(Actor's name.)*

GIRL: Take this with you. *(Hands him an amulet.)*

YOUNG MAN: Thank you. *(Actor's name.)*, good-bye for now.

GIRL: Please fight bravely for our country. I'll keep the home fires burning.

YOUNG MAN: *(Actor's name.)* *(Takes her by the hand.)*

GIRL: And I will . . . wait . . . until you come back.

YOUNG MAN: I'm sorry *(Actor's name.)*, I don't know what happened. . . .

GIRL: Never mind. I hear it happens to lots of guys.

YOUNG MAN: I'm really sorry. I was tired and upset that night. But, *(Actor's name.)* I'm not always like that. Look, I have a hard-on now.

GIRL: It's all right. I know.

YOUNG MAN: If you feel too lonely, use this. *(Hands her a vibrator.)*

GIRL: What? What's this?

YOUNG MAN: I bought it in Kabuki-chō. You know what it is. Don't play innocent.

GIRL: I don't know. I don't know what you're talking about.

YOUNG MAN: If you don't know, read *Hustler.* If you turn this, it moves, see?

GIRL: *(Looking at it.)* You're going to the front *(Actor's name.)*.

YOUNG MAN: Yes. This is a real war. I'll fight for the U.C.R.N.,[1] the United Capitalist Republic of Nippon.

GIRL: For the U.C.R.N. . . . . But what is U.C.R.N.?

(The young man and the girl gaze forward. Again the CROWD *gives three cheers. The piercing shrieks of sirens. Cries—"Alert!" "Raid!" —are heard. The people scatter for cover. Screams. Overlapping the clamor, the tune of "Le Internationale" begins to sound solemnly. A gunshot. A* MAN *with a gun appears from the back of the house and stands up on an elevated platform.)*

MAN: The U.C.R.N. is the country of my birth, my home country.

(The clamor of the air raid becomes the clamor for a deserter. The CROWD *notices the man and cries "Deserter! Deserter!" The* CROWD *surrounds the man. He fires into the air. The* CROWD *disperses quickly.)*

MAN: History is my friend.

CROWD: Shut up.

MAN: You assholes. There's no hope for you. Get lost.

(The CROWD *disappears at once.)*

MAN: I've come a long way, carried by the memory of an unknown history. I know nothing. But yet, I know everything. I am nothing but an arrogant neurotic.

(He fires. A screen comes down with the legend: "THE 12TH YEAR OF EMPEROR SEIKI'S REIGN. THE UNITED CAPITALIST REPUBLIC OF NIPPON WAGES WAR AGAINST CALGARIA.")

MAN: I joined the Rebel Canary a year ago. I needed a war for myself.

(He fires. Another screen comes down: "THE 13TH YEAR OF EMPEROR SEIKI'S REIGN. ALL-OUT WAR IN CALGARIA. THE U.C.R.N. FORMS AN ALLIANCE WITH THE REPUBLIC OF AMERIGO.")

MAN: But I ran. Here I am, a man who escaped from the secret underground base of the Rebel Canary. A man who has lost his own war is now standing here in the night.

(He fires. Another screen comes down: "THE 16TH YEAR OF EMPEROR SEIKI'S REIGN. WORLD WAR. TOTAL WAR. THE U.C.R.N. INSTITUES A POLICY OF TOTAL CIVILIAN WAR EFFORT.")

MAN: Oh, my semicircular canals are sloshing. . . . Nausea like carsickness. I could puke my guts out. History is making me sick. *(Is about to vomit.)*

(Another shot. Another screen: "THE 17TH YEAR OF EMPEROR SEIKI'S REIGN. THE U.C.R.N. ESTABLISHES CONSCRIPTION. THE ANTI-GOVERNMENT ARMY REBEL CANARY MAKES A STATEMENT." This is followed by another screen: "THE 20TH YEAR OF EMPEROR SEIKI'S REIGN. STUDENTS GO TO THE FRONT.")

MAN: Fuck. Bullshit. I was born and raised here. *(Fires into the air.)* What do I have to shoot at? The bullet that I shoot in the air—won't it come down? I've come so far, so far. . . .

(Silver sheets of paper flutter down from the sky. The man picks up one and reads it.)

MAN: "A REAL WAR. NOT A GAME, NOT CHILD'S PLAY. ARE YOU BORED? HOW ABOUT FIRING A REAL GUN? ARE YOU WITH IT, THE BATTLEFIELD IS WAITING FOR YOU."[2] What the hell. . . .

(A voice—"There he is!"—is heard. Unidentified people appear and

shoot at the man.)

MAN: The bullet. The fucking bullet that I shot into the air has come down. . . . *(Falls down.)*

(Matsuda Seiko's "Sweet Memories"[3] is heard. A woman appears and sings before the man, who is carried away by the people.)

WOMAN: Somebody, solve this equation of history and memories. Removable logic. False setup. Trick backdrop. Isn't there anybody who can solve it? This equation? . . . The fear that you might die if you close your eyes, trying to sleep. You, do you wanna feel this fear?

("Sweet Memories" become louder.)

WOMAN: Please. Don't kiss me, because, because, I. . . .

(Murmurs, which gradually become louder. Lights up. A room. Young men and women are sitting in a circle, playing games in a strange language. They keep playing for a while. A voice is heard from the back of the room.)

VOICE: Lesson 100. Program: "Conversation." The scheduled number is complete. Change your thought, and get a reward. The leader is going to give you a smile.

(Everybody stops playing. They look relieved. The leader "J" appears holding the MAN in a coma, and throws him down.)

J: How are you doing today?

A YOUNG MAN: So-so.

ANOTHER YOUNG MAN: You're the one who made the mistake.

A YOUNG MAN: Are you kidding? It was you.

J: Forget it. We have lots of time; your term is two and a half years.

A YOUNG MAN: Is he a new one, J?

J: Conscript number 72502. He must be good if he was sent here.

A YOUNG MAN: Bullshit. He doesn't look so tough.

J: Hey, R. I'll cut your marks for that.

R: Who gives a shit. If you wanna cut'em, cut'em.

J: Just watch it. *(Looks at the new man.)* He's still under anaesthesia. We better wake him up. You all give him a warm welcome, alright?

(J sprays something over the MAN's face. He wakes up and looks around.)

J: Welcome to the Blue Whale Room!

ALL: Welcome to the Blue Whale Room!

MAN: Blue Whale Room . . . Who, who am I?!

J: A slight loss of memory is to be expected when you've been shot by the Algin Z^4 anaesthetic gun. He'll eventually recover his memory.

MAN: I am . . . I am. . . .

J: What is your name?

MAN: I am. . . .

J: Tell me your name, son.

MAN: I am. . . .

J: The memories you had relating to your former name have been removed by Algin Z. Everyone here, in this room, went through the same thing. Names are nothing. Their only function is expediency. You no longer have your old name, son. From now on, your name is "O".[5]

A YOUNG MAN: J, what the hell. . . .

J: I know how you feel, O. But this comes directly from the general. I know you're already called O. But I'm sure the general has something in mind. This young man is O´ from now on. You understand, don't you O?

O: Yes sir.

J: Be his friend. You're the smartest one in this room.

R: Shit.

MAN: O´. . . .

J: Yes, you are O´ from now on.

O: Hi, O´. I'm O. We might as well get to know each other.
   (O takes the hand of O´, who is still looking blank.)

R: Look at him. Dreamy-eyed, like he'd just jerked off.
   (B giggles.)

M: He's kind of cute.

K: It's good to have another boy.

O: Stop it, girls.

J: Quiet. See. He's looking around. You were all just like him when you first came here. It's slowly sinking in that he's O´.

O´: Where am I? . . .
   (ALL laugh.)

F: That's what we all say at first.

J: You are in the Blue Whale Room.
   (The sound of waves in the sea.)

O´: The Blue Whale Room. . . .

J: We are in the stomach of a blue whale, which mutated to this size because of the radiation from the 7th battle of San Sebastian. We are drifting in the black sea, off the U.C.R.N.

O´: Why am I here?
   (Everybody laughs.)

R: We're fighting a war, you asshole. Didn't you know that?

O´: War?

M: You got one of those Silver Slips, didn't you? Man, this is a real war.
   (O´ takes out the silver paper from his pocket.)

J: You were drafted.

O´: Drafted?

J: That Silver Slip is a draft notice, what they used to call PINK SLIPS.

O´: PINK SLIP!? *(He drops down.)*

J: What's up?

o´: My legs went weak.

J: You know conscription has been re-initiated, don't you?

o´: But. . . .

J: It's war. It's not child's play, not a game. The U.C.R.N. is in the middle of a war, a war in which people really die. You've heard in the news how we're losing in Calgaria.

o´: But I. . . .

J: You are so accustomed to peace. I know it's a sudden change. Hard to get used to. We were all like that. Right?
(Gabble.)

J: Our country is in a state of emergency. Your country, the United Capitalist Republic of Nippon.

o´: But the country. . . . It's. . . .

J: Who do you owe your life to?

o´: Nobody.

J: What?

o´: My life's my own. I take it in my own hands.

R: Hey, he's got balls.

o´: I die for myself, not for anyone else.

R: Yippie-Kai-Yae!

o: Cut it out, R.

J: R, you just lost three marks.

M: Serves you right, jerk.

R: Shut yer fucking cunt.

M: What! Motherfucker.

J: M, that's two marks for you.

o´: Why am I here?

J: Oh, yes, I almost forgot. *(Takes out a file.)* "O´ from West Tonkie."

o: West Tonkie. That's where I'm from.

J: "A member of the anti-government partisan Rebel Canary for the past year, before escaping."
(Murmurs.)

J: So you're a deserter from the Rebel Canary, eh? Pretty mysterious background. Mysterious and dangerous. But that's probably why you were chosen for this room. Danger is very attractive. People love danger even if they're scared of it.

P: Yeah!

J: *(Drops the act.)* Yeah! How was that? Did I look cool?

o: J. . . .

J: *(Recovering himself.)* P loses two marks.

P: What the hell? Hey, how come?

o´: This is a violation of my civil rights.

J: A civil rights violation! Did you hear that? Civil rights violation, huh! Somebody, bring me the Xerox.

(F brings it.)

J: You apparently don't read newspapers. Look O´, this is a copy of the
  Daily News, the 17th year of Emperor Seiki's reign, September the
  first. Here are the details of how conscription was passed by the
  House. You were engaged in anti-government activities and didn't
  know about this?

ALL: Stupid asshole!

O´: What, you! . . .

J: In short, it's these!

  (Numerous silver papers are falling through the air.)

J: Isn't it beautiful? You must have seen something like this before.
  Twinkling silver papers falling down through the gaps in the blue sky.
  Did you see any sort of flying vehicle?

O´: Flying vehicle?

J: I'm asking if you saw a flying vehicle scattering these papers?

O´: No. . . . Well maybe.

J: No, you didn't. Nobody let them fall. They come pouring out of the
  blue sky, just like a mountain spring.

O´: *(Reads a silver paper.)* "A REAL WAR. NOT A GAME, NOT
  CHILD'S PLAY. ARE YOU BORED? HOW ABOUT FIRING A
  REAL GUN?"

J: The moment you took that paper in your hands is recognized as the
  moment you accepted the call. Only the bored ones pick them up.

O´: This is bullshit.

J: Well, weren't you bored?

  (O´ can't say anything.)

J: Were your days so filled with bliss that you didn't have time to get
  bored? Why'd you run away from the Rebel Canary then?

O´: That's because. . . .

J: The sky knows everything. That big blue sky knows everything in your
  mind.

O´: I hate the blue sky!

ALL: You stupid asshole!

J: Alright. He'll get it eventually. I was just like him at first. I felt
  constricted. That's what everyone feels in the beginning. But that's
  what's called a persecution complex. You'll come to understand. This
  is a relatively free space.

O´: Free. . . . I haven't heard that word for a long time.

J: Oh, by the way, let me introduce myself. I'm J, sub-leader of this Blue
  Whale Room. I keep things organized. Nice to meet you. *(Offers his
  hand.)*

O´: Free space. . . .

J: Free space means space which is not completely restricted. *(Forcibly
  shakes his hand.)* You can think whatever you want. You're to

complete the two-and-a-half-year military drill while here on probation, and then you go to the real front. This isn't the old kind of militarism. Let me be clear, here you're free to do whatever you want. That's why boys and girls are together here. You may fall in love, make love, or jerk off!

B: How about tonight?

P: No.

B: Come on. You'll have a good time.

P: No.

B: *(Snickering.)* Huh, I know you want it.

O´: We might be killed.

J: Sure. But at least you won't get bored.

O: Boredom or death.

R: I choose death. Bang, boom.

(R *and* B *start to play war.*)

M: Humanism's old fashioned, bro.

O: Let's fight together, O´.

J: That's right. You're the elite here.

O´: Elite?

ALL: *(Proudly.)* Yes, we're the elite.

J: They've been chosen because they have special aptitudes for battle. You who are wild, strong, quick, and have various special abilities. You are the war elite.

ALL: Yes, the war elite.

O´: That's a weird kind of elite.

ALL: Yes, a weird elite. (ALL *realize what they have said and become angry.*) What did you say?

J: Don't belittle their powers, O´.

R: Yeah, don't fuck with us, asshole.

O´: Go fuck yourself, dick-wad.

R: *(Knocked down.)* Oooh.

J: Take R, for instance.

(R *makes very quick movements.*)

R: *(Blahs meaninglessly.)* Chonwa. Chonwa. Chonwa. Chonwa.

O´: What's so special about that?

J: R, open your hands.

(Something crumbles from R*'s hands.)*

J: He caught forty Seiki Flies, flying at Mach speed, too fast for us to see.

ALL: Wow.

J: Seiki Flies. These are also mutants created by radioactivity. Next, B.

(B *brings a huge bar and breaks it.*)

ALL: Wow.

(B *giggles.*)

J: You know what that was that he just broke? Marble.

O´: Marble?

J: You ain't seen nothing yet. F and K.

(F *and* K *start playing at cat's cradle yelling encouragement at each other.*)

O´: So what?

J: Cat's cradle with wire.

ALL: Wow.

O´: Is that all?

J: You ain't seen nothing yet.

O´: You're right, I ain't.

J: P, do it.

(P *flaps his fan and imitates a hen. After several big motions, he makes a popping sound with his cheek.*)

O´: What now?

P: *(Takes out an egg.)* I laid an egg.

ALL: Wow.

J: You ain't seen nothing yet.

O´: I've seen enough.

J: Go on, M.

(M *opens her eyes and mouth wide and breathes in and out. Sound of the wind is heard.* ALL *cry out, "what is it?"* M *breathes violently and causes a vortex.* ALL *spin around.*)

J: Enough. Stop it, M. Stop.

(The vortex ceases.)

J: She could cause a typhoon.

ALL: *(Panting.)* Wow.

O´: Now, this is something.

J: You ain't seen nothing yet. O, start.

O: Yes.

J: O is the brightest one in this room. Look into his eyes.

(O´ and O stand face to face.)

O: Think of something. Place a thought in your brain. I'll read it.

J: You see. He's a telepath. He reads people's thoughts.

O´: Thought. . . .

O: Yes, any thought you like.

J: You ain't seen. . . .

O: Quiet.

J: Sorry.

(Some metallic sound.)

O: Your name.

O´: O´.

O: Your former name.

O´: I forgot.

O: This is West Tonkie.

o´: Yes, do you know it?

o: You're thinking of your hometown. I can see it. I'm looking at it. The railroad is stretching out forever. The Western Line running through the wheat field. It's like the wheat field Van Gogh painted just before he died. The station is called "Satisfaction." You get off the train. The same beautiful scenery. I see. The dime store in front of the station. You bought your first wristwatch there. The pub "JR" on the corner. You used to fight there, drinking beer. The cheap motel along Route 31. Yes, that's where I made love to her the first time. The radio was playing the Doors. You pass the bus stop for Tonkie Park and you'll soon be home.

(o´ starts whistling lightly.)

o: The same old house. The white swing. You open the dark brown door. Yes, you're starving; you go straight to the kitchen. The same smell. Corn soup made from the corn that grows in the backyard. Roast turkey. You always had three eggs scrambled. You want beer. Yes, you like beer before anything else. Mom, where's the beer? Cold beer. Your mother brings a can of beer. The same face. . . .

(Something happens to O. O cries out suddenly and can't breath.)

J: What's the matter, O?

(o continues gasping.)

J: Take him away. Take him to bed.

(o is carried out.)

o´: *(Recovering himself.)* What happened?

J: I don't know. He was doing alright. Maybe it's because he hasn't done this for awhile. Don't worry. What did you think?

o´: He was describing the exact scene I was imagining.

J: Yes. Are you impressed?

o´: Yes, I see what you mean.

J: But you too must have some kind of power if you were sent to this room.

o´: Me?

J: Yes. You must have. You just haven't realized it.

o´: Me?

J: You have two and a half years to find out.

o´: Two and a half years. . . .

J: I'll teach you.

o´: Two and a half years. . . .

J: Yes, after two and a half years, you'll be one of us, the elite.

o´: . . . No! *(Produces a gun.)*

J: Battle stations.

(In an instant ALL surround o´, with guns in their hands.)

J: You fool, do you think you can win a fight against professionals?

o´: I don't like this. *(He tries to shoot.)*

J: Shoot.

> (ALL *shoot.*)

O´: They got me. . . . *(Falls down.)*

J: Stubborn fool.

F: What do we do with him?

J: Leave him. A few dozen shots of Algin Z. . . . He'll be out for at least two days.

> (ALL *leave. Music is heard from afar. A* WOMAN *emerges on the stage.* O´ *wakes up.)*

WOMAN: Do you want me to sing?

O´: What? . . . No.

WOMAN: If you want me to, say so. That's all I can do now.

O´: What?

WOMAN: Sing. . . . That's all I can do now.

O´: You're alive.

WOMAN: What?

O´: You're alive. I'm glad.

WOMAN: Silly. Do you have a smoke?

O´: I'm sorry. I'm out.

WOMAN: It's all right. There's one left.

O´: You still have trouble?

WOMAN: What?

O´: You still have trouble sleeping at night?

WOMAN: Yes.

O´: The sleeping pills I gave you. . . .

WOMAN: I don't take pills. It's too easy to become addicted. I read the book you lent me, though. It was so good I couldn't sleep.

O´: That detective story . . . it's good, isn't it?

WOMAN: Did you figure out who done it?

O´: No. It's impossible.

WOMAN: Me neither. I never got it.

O´: Nobody did it.

WOMAN: That's right, I forgot. Nobody did it. All the suspects proved their alibis.

O´: Not a bad idea for a detective story.

WOMAN: No. But why were so many people killed, when there was nobody who did it?

O´: I don't know. But. . . .

WOMAN: But what?

O´: Do you remember what the private detective said after he solved the case? "The night . . . it was all because of the night."

WOMAN: "It was all because of the night. . . ."

O´: Do you remember how the story started?

WOMAN: "You're a cold person. My ex-wife used to say."

o´: And the last line was. . . .

WOMAN: "It's probably because you think too much during the night. Man is but a rag bag full of memories."

o´: You have a good memory.

WOMAN: But I can't remember the title.

o´: You think too much during the night.

WOMAN: I'm . . . tired.

(A VOICE *is heard.)*

VOICE: Kill the woman, *(Actor's name.).*

o´: What?

VOICE: She's a spy for the government.

(The WOMAN *smiles.)*

o´: You are . . . !?

WOMAN: Now I remember the title of the novel.

VOICE: Kill her, *(Actor's name.).*

o´: I'm sorry. *(Points the gun at her.)*

WOMAN: The title of the novel was. . . . *(As she speaks, she raises her own gun slowly and points it at her temple.)*

VOICE: Kill her, *(Actor's name.).*

(Both guns are fired simultaneously. At that instant, it becomes brighter. R, B, P, M, F, K, J *are seated at the table in a row, facing the audience. Six of them have their hands clasped in front of their faces and have their eyes closed.)*

M: Our dear homeland, the U.C.R.N., we thank you tonight for this good supper. Amen.

ALL: A-men. B-men, C-men.

M: We thank you, oh Unseen One, for letting us live another day. Amen.

ALL: A-men. B-men. C-men.

M: U.C.R.N. stands for UNITED CAPITALIST REPUBLIC OF NIPPON.

ALL: A-men. B-men. C-men. This is getting old!

J: Now, let's eat.

(ALL talk.)

R: Hey, B, give me back my kangaroo meat.

B: I didn't take it.

R: Then where is it?

J: Relax. You can have mine.

R: Yeah!

*(*O´ *looks blank and is in the same posture as he was before.)*

o´: Wh . . . Where am I?

M: Look, he's coming to at last.

K: He wants to know where he is.

R: Hey, bro. We already had that where-am-I stuff in the last scene. Lay off that hero shit. What are we, actors?

P: That's right. And I'm going to play the heroine.

B: Me too.

R: You can't.

B: The hell I can't! *(Snaps his fork in half.)*

J: Settle down and eat quietly.

R: Oh come on, let's play heroes.

ALL: Yeah!

O´: Now I remember. This is the Blue Whale Room.

P: Did you see that acting? Sends shivers down my spine.

M: Doesn't it?

K: Doesn't it?

O´: *(Suddenly serious.)* Hungry, hungry, I'm hungry. Hungry, hungry, I'm hungry.

All the hungry young men and all the angry young men

Couldn't put hungry together again.

(As soon as he finishes singing, he starts to eat like a horse.)

R: Look at him.

F: Let him eat. He hasn't eaten for two days.

J: But . . . but I can't figure him out.

P: Don't give up, J.

J: Yeah. I'm the leader, aren't I?

(O appears.)

O: Hi. Sorry about freaking out like that.

F: Are you alright?

O: Yeah, I'm OK. I had some kind of fit. I'm more delicate than you think. *(Coughs.)*

R: Don't make me laugh. *(O coughs.)*

B: I don't buy that for a second.

R: Alright. Now eat.

(Everyone is taken aback by the way O´ and O eat. Then, J speaks.)

J: OK, everybody, let's eat. *(Starts to eat.)*

R: You know what I think?

M: What?

R: I think the war's gonna get tougher and tougher.

F: I heard four Nazi warships were sighted in the Iowa Sea.

K: Nazi?

M: Yes, Nazi. Who'da thunk it?

F: J, is it true that the Nazis have more nuclear missiles than anyone?

J: Well, I'm not sure.

P: They bring in nuclear weapons, it's game over for the U.C.R.N., eh?

B: Amerigo will help us.

R: Dream on. That sort of thinking is so infantile.

B: Are you saying I'm infantile?

R: You're too independent.

M: You mean "dependent."

R: Yeah. You're fucking dependent.

B: Well, why don't you tell us what to do if you're so smart? *(Breaks his spoon.)*

R: We'll win it ourselves. That's why we're here, right, J?

J: Well, I'm not sure.

R: What a loser.

J: Well, I'm not sure.

B: Hey, P, let's fuck tonight.

P: Fuck yourself.

B: *(Laughs.)* I know you want it.

P: Yeah, but not with you.

B: Come on, it's not like it'll hurt you.

   (P pours water over B.)

B: Ugghh!

R: OK. Calm down. Now calm down.

B: It won't hurt you, will it?

P: It will.

B: What?

F: Now, now, now.

K: Does it really hurt, d'you think?

J: Well, I'm not sure.

F: But it's kind of strange.

K: What?

F: Sitting all together like this, I wonder if we're ever really going to the front. *(ALL pause in their eating except O´ and O.)*

R: Hey J, what's combat like?

J: Well, I'm not sure.

R: Can't you say anything else? *(R makes the motion of strangling J.)* You're the only one who's actually been in a real war.

J: Ugghh. Alright, I'll tell you. It's like hell. Hell.

P: Hell.

R: Come on, stop fucking with us. You've seen *All Quiet on the Western Front.* You've seen *Apocalypse Now.* You've seen *Rambo VII, Platoon.*

M: I haven't seen *Rambo VII.*

F: You don't have to.

J: It's hell over there. *(Stands up.)* I, Private J, was Marlon Brando on Rarotonga Island.

R: What the hell are you talking about?

J: I was a god to the natives on Rarotonga Island, just like Marlon Brando in *Apocalypse Now*!

B: Bullshit.

J: It's true. I got tired of the war.

R: What d'you mean, tired, you motherfucker?

J: I'm not trying to piss you off. But I'm fed up with killing. Do you know who I was before I came to the Blue Whale Room?

M: No.

J: You're lucky that you didn't meet me then. Good evening, ladies and gentlemen, may I present Jack the Ripper.
(Music.)

O: What, you're Jack the Ripper?

J: Not a rip-off or a jack-off, not Rip Van Winkle, but Jack the Ripper.

O: Bullshit.

J: You think I'm dead. But I'm not. Yes. Thanks to some delicate maneuvering by the government, I have survived. Why? Because my inherent sense of cruelty and violence was a perfect match for the profile for this room.

R: This room?!

J: Yes. The Blue Whale Room. According to research conducted by the U.C.R.N. Criminology Association, my qualities exactly match the qualities of the war elite. We're going to bring the memory of Jack the Ripper into the battlefield. But of course, murder in daily life and murder in the context of a war are not the same. In battle, you get tired of it after only killing about ten people.

R: Ten?

J: If you kill ten, no one's left. And so I became Marlon Brando.
(O reads a poem by T. S. Eliot.)

J: Just like this, alone in a cave.

M: What did you do then?

J: I reached a conclusion. Murder is for yourself. . . . Who do you murder for in battle?

O: For our friends, our countrymen.

J: Be more specific.

R: For the U.C.R.N.

J: That's right. But can you really die for the U.C.R.N.?

O: Are you allowed to say that J?

J: Shut up recruit. Let us confirm the situation. I am your leader, J, commissioned by General Q. There are other troops besides us, the Emperor Penguin Room, the Bottlenosed Dolphin Room, the Sperm Whale Room. I know that in those rooms nationalistic discipline is strictly adhered to. Which is to say. . . .

ALL: *(Except O´.)* Which is to say!

J: Your bodies belong to the U.C.R.N.

ALL: Our bodies belong to the U.C.R.N.!

J: Save the U.C.R.N.

ALL: Save the U.C.R.N.!

J: But you are the elite. General Q intends to turn an entire battlefield over to you. You are not necessarily going to die for the U.C.R.N.

O: What does that mean?

J: You'll know when your term is completed. You're free, that's what General Q said. Ugh! *(Shows intense suffering.)* Shit, the memory of Jack the Ripper. . . .

P: You live too much in the past.

J: Ugh, ugh. This is a bad one. *(Falls down and rolls over.)* Ugh, ugh.

F: J, are you alright?

(ALL run towards J. J suddenly stands up.)

J: *(Drooling.)* You saw me rip.

M: What the fuck.

J: I'm Jack the Ripper. I want women. I want young women.

(He chases the women, his mouth watering.)

J: I wanna fuck. Give me fuck.

(O´ slams the table. ALL look at him.)

O´: Are you really ready to fight a war?

J: I'm ready. I'm ready to fuck.

O´: Get lost.

J: You saw me rip. . . .

(He goes out, chasing the women. R, O, O´ and B are left.)

O´: I hate this stinking place.

R: Still worried? You just ate a meal here.

O´: But. . . .

R: It's not so bad once you get used to it.

O´: But where's dessert?

(ALL collapse.)

B: Well aren't you the momma's boy.

R: If you want to take off, it's easy. There's a small submarine called the "Devilfish" at the back of the room. The keys are in it. I'd go but the Rebel Canary is after me. Besides. . . .

O: Cut the theatrics. Even if you got back to Tokio, the streets are full of unemployed workers. It's the worst depression of the Emperor Seiki era. They call it super stagflation. We're the lucky ones. The Silver Slips took care of us. At least we don't have to worry about food. Stay here with us.

O´: But I was a member of Rebel Canary.

O: Don't be a fool. Get rid of your ideology. Throw it to the plankton. Get real, O´ from West Tonkie. I was so happy to see it all again. I mean the pictures of West Tonkie in your thoughts. That wheat field. The view along the highway. Did you go to Guatemala Elementary School?

O´: Yeah.

O: Me too.

O´: You went to Guatemala Elementary School?

O: I went to Guatemala Junior and Senior High School too.

O´: Me too!

R: Hey, this isn't an alumni meeting, you hicks.

O´: Where are you from?

R: Me? I'm from Sakhalin.

O´: Sakhalin! Fuck, you're the real hick, aren't you?

O: Yeah. The Sakhalin mountain ape.

R: Shut the fuck up. He's from Andalusia.

O´: Wow, Andalusia, where they still use paper to wipe their ass.

B: What's wrong with wiping your ass with paper?

R: Hayseed.

B: Don't be ignorant. It's the farmers of Andalusia who support the economy of the U.C.R.N.?

R: Get lost, hick.

B: The hick's getting mad.

O: Oh, shit. B's mad now.

B: BBBBB! *(Rages about. B attacks R.)*

R: Back off, country boy.

B: I'll kill you, city boy.

(J runs after M.)

J: You saw me. . . .

M: Get him off me.

O´: Still at it?

(J holds down M.)

J: I'm Jack the Ripper.

M: Ahh . . . !

O: Quiet! The General's coming.

(ALL freeze.)

O: I can feel General Q's body heat.

(Noises are heard.)

J: O, are you sure?

O: I can feel it. I can feel General Q's heat.

(The sounds become louder.)

J: He's right. It's a surprise inspection by General Q!

(Q appears on the elevated passageway smoking a cigar. Sawada Kenji's[6] song, "Miscast," is heard. GENERAL Q comes on stage singing, followed by RIGHT and LEFT, spokesmodels of the battlefield. J and the others salute. O´ follows suit reluctantly. Q still singing, inspects their salutes, their clothes, and their belongings.)

Q: Oh, you wonderful people! Human existence is a colossal miscasting. It's worse than if Jane Russell had played Scarlett O'Hara. Don't you think?

RIGHT: Yes, yes, I agree.

Q: I mean, people are so unhappy, aren't they?

LEFT: Oh, I'm burning.

Q: Yes, we are all burning with the pain of human intelligence.

LEFT: My pussy is burning.

Q: Yes, the pussy is the great spark of intelligence.

LEFT: Do me quick General.

Q: To do it quick means to come too soon.

RIGHT: Do me quick General.

Q: For the sake of all those who suffer, I can't do it with you.

> (LEFT *and* RIGHT *hit the* GENERAL *in the groin.*)

Q: Uggh! *(Doubles over.)* I've got no cum. *(Jumps up.)* My penis was burnt by napalm in the battle of San Sebastian. You knew that, didn't you, J.

J: Yes sir, but you've still got your balls, sir.

Q: Yes indeed, and balls of fire they are. A dirty joke. By providence, my balls escaped being burned. But since then I have not experienced the ecstasy of ejaculation. Do you understand my pain, J?

J: Yes sir, General.

Q: Don't lie to me. *(Kicks J's groin.)*

> (J *doubles over.* Q *kicks everyone in the groin one at a time.*)

Q: Good. You are all doing fine. Let me introduce you to the new spokesmodels of the battlefield. Miss Right and Miss Left.

RIGHT *and* LEFT: Pleased to meet you.

> (ALL *start to drool.*)

Q: You are not to love.

ALL: No, sir.

Q: Good. Love retards thinking. The new man should not be involved with love affairs. I'll show you the simplest form of our new love.

> (RIGHT *and* LEFT *open their legs wide.* ALL *gather around them.*)

Q: Now line up. Behave yourselves.

> *(They line up.)*

Q: Good. This is indeed a new democracy.

O´: Hey, why are YOU in line?

M: I'm lesbian.

O´: I see.

> *(They start fucking* RIGHT *and* LEFT, *but* J *and* M, *who started first, take too much time.)*

Q: How about that? The great miscasting of our existence as human beings. When the world collapses, you'll be something more than human.

O: Hurry up. We're waiting!

R: I'm a bit too ready!

B: I'm about to come.

R: J takes too fucking long.

> *(ALL gather and bitch about it.)*

Q: Behave yourselves. Where's your sense of democracy?

B: Hey, there's another woman over there!

(The woman struggles.)

O´: You, you're . . . !

(The sound of the sea.)

Q: Welcome back, I.

O: Welcome, I!

LEFT: Who is that woman?!

(Q hushes LEFT.)

Q: It's Miss I, the first spokesmodel of the battlefield.

RIGHT *and* LEFT: Oh, pardon our ignorance, please.

I: Q, you are miscast. You are the only miscast one here.

Q: I knew you'd come back. Everyone does. They always come back here, knowing everything.

I: I'll tell you something, Q.

Q: Don't say a word.

O: What happened, I?

Q: You'll find out eventually, O. Don't push it.

O: What?

Q: I, come to my quarters tonight after midnight. I'll give you a real good one. I'll make you come all night with a super-deluxe electronic vibrator.

(I spits at Q.)

Q: J, programs!

J: Yes, sir. Salute.

(ALL come forth, line up, and salute.)

Q: J, which one is the newcomer in this room?

J: O´, step forward.

(O´ steps forward in front of Q.)

Q: *(Touching O´'s body.)* Wonderful. . . . This is a perfect human being. You still don't understand any of this. I know how you feel. But you'll gradually understand. You have plenty of time. J, I want a sit-rep of the war.

J: Yes, sir.

(A TV set is brought in. The situation of the war is projected on the screen.)

J: After forming an alliance with Assist, Cal raided Nanjing with their secret special forces unit.

Q: Nanjing too, at last.

J: There is a temporary lull in the battle of Calgaria, but guerrilla warfare is expected to break out at any moment. Given this situation, it is probable that Cal is going to be involved in the World War semi-permanently.

Q: You all understand this? Any questions?

ALL: No, sir.

Q: Then we'll move on to the programs. Since you're a newcomer, O´, stay there and watch. The troops have to master 200 lessons in two and a half years. They have various names. This is a new type of military drill created by Sue Ellen.

O´: Sue Ellen?

Q: She is the sum total of our thoughts, our total brain. You'll come to know her. Now, everyone, show me the results of your work.
(J holds a microphone. The sound of a siren.)

J: All of you in the belly of the Blue Whale, we are going to start our lesson. Places.
(ALL take up their positions.)

J: Breathe in. Breathe out. Breathe in. Breathe out. You're stuffed. *(ALL move their mouths according to the instructions.)* Woodpecker. Fellatio. Vampire. Neuralgia. Concentrate. Lesson 7: Burst of laughter.
(ALL burst into laughter.)

J: Lesson 10: Joy.
(ALL smile.)

J: Lesson 5: A shy smile. Lesson 34: A wry smile. Lesson 35: Orgasm. Lesson 39: Grief. Lesson 40: Wailing. Lesson 43: Crying with joy. Lesson 45: Surprise. Moving on to lesson 50: Anger. Lesson 51: Shouting. Lesson 52: Controlled anger. Lesson 55: Violence. Lesson 57: Giving up. Lesson 58: Masturbation. Lesson 59: Insignificance. Lesson 60: Self-confidence. Lesson 61: Obedience. We are skipping up a level. Lesson 70: Death.
(ALL collapse. J checks whether they are really dead.)

J: If you can do this, you've completed the elementary level. R, you are not completely dead. Lesson 71: Returning to life.
(ALL get up at once.)

J: Now, we move on to physical training. Lesson 80: Karate.
(ALL shout as they take up postures for karate.)

J: Lesson 81: Tricks. Lesson 82: Playing games.
(ALL walk around on can-stilts, and play soccer.)

Q: What do you think of this kind of drill? It gives you practical skills.

O´: I don't understand.

Q: It's very different from the Rebel Canary, eh? What did you learn there? The same old stuff like how to use your gun, how to use explosives, how to fight a guerilla war, how to find spies. . . . That's all useless bullshit. The enemy we face is far greater.

O´: What do you mean, greater?

Q: I'll show you our final trump card. J, get them ready for lesson 100: Conversation.

J: Lesson 100: Conversation.
(ALL sit in a circle.)

Q: This is communication. You exchange your own ideas. But you cannot use any existing language. You let your ideas whirl around the circle. On the top of the circle sits Sue Ellen, our total brain, observing us. Let's begin.

J: Begin.

(ALL *talk to one another in a strange language. They speed up and get excited and tense. They rise and get heated. Speaking in a strange language, they face the audience.*

The emergency siren is heard, and the sound of the sea becomes louder, like a storm. Something has happened. Vibration. ALL *are trembling. The sound of an explosion.* ALL *fall down on the floor. Screams.*)

Q: What happened? What's going on?

J: The enemy submarine "Sea Bat," searching for us, exploded near the tail of our whale. There are no survivors.

Q: Did we attack?

J: No, we didn't do anything at all.

R: What happened, then?

P: I feel like something exploded in my head.

Q: You did it, troops.

O: What do you mean, General?

Q: You blew up the "Sea Bat."

ALL: What?

Q: Your power id materialized for the first time. Our research shows, the concentration of your thoughts can create explosive power. It's Neuro-Kinetic Energy.

O: Neuro-Kinetic Energy?

Q: Neuro-Kinetic Energy has only been a theory, until now. We've been waiting all century for this moment. J, bring us champagne for a celebration.

J: Yes, sir.

Q: Everyone, you will soon depart for the front.

(Q *takes a glass of champagne and hands one to* I.)

Q: You saw it, I, didn't you?

I: But there's no telling what will happen.

Q: *(Ignoring her.)* You have just joined the war. We drink to your war!

O´: Our war?

(A VOICE *is heard.*)

VOICE: Well done, everybody. Here is your reward—the sound of the battlefield.

O: I know that voice!

Q: Thanks, Sue Ellen.

(*Loud music. Slowly lights down. Several gunshots are heard in the darkness.* O´ *wakes up suddenly.* P *is lying besides him.*)

O´: I was dreaming.

P: What's up?

O´: What are you doing here?

P: What the hell are you talking about? You let me in.

O´: (*Looking at the empty bottles around them.*) We drank too much.

P: I'm hammered. You're hammered.

O´: Oh, my head aches.

P: I should've known.

O´: What?

P: As soon as you hit the bed, you started snoring.

O´: What do you mean?

P: Don't get caught up with a battlefield spokesmodel. There are lots of nice girls like me.

O´: What are you talking about?

P: Chill out. You don't have to marry me right away.

O´: I had a dream. I was blindfolded and my hands were tied behind my back. I was shot and killed.

P: That means you're frustrated. Don't make love to the spokesmodels. They're a disgrace to women. Do you know the rate of marriage between people in the same room? In Sunfish Room where I used to be, it was 90%. Oh, shit. I shouldn't have mentioned marriage. Hold me.

O´: I can still feel the bullets in my body.

P: Come on, hold me.

O´: In the dream, I was alive after I was shot. I pretended to be dead, but I was alive. Somebody saw me and shouted something, looking at me.

P: Hold me!

(*A voice—"Hold her."—is heard.* I *lights her cigarette in the dark.*)

O´: You. . . .

I: Hey, sweetie, you're too uptight.

P: Get lost. You're disgusting. You battlefield spokesmodels are complete sluts.

I: I didn't choose this.

P: Get away. Filthy bitch.

I: I know. . . .

P: What?

I: A year ago, there was a spokesmodel named P in the Sunfish Room.

P: That's a lie.

I: You know a man named Alpha.

P: You mean Alpha. Alpha. (*Starts to cry.*)

I: You don't have to hide it.

P: Alpha. My Alpha.

I: They tricked you.

P: No. He just went to the front.

I: He's dead. General Q said he died a honorable death in Calgaria.

P: You lie. You're a goddam liar.

I: Why should I lie to you about your lover?

P: Liar. *(Cries.)*

I: Miserable little dope. You should have known this would happen if you have an affair with someone in the same room. Women in the rooms avoid affairs. You know why? Because they don't want to suffer.

P: Alpha is alive. He has to be alive.

I: When all is said and done, war is just a game for men.

(P runs away.)

O´: You.

I: What do you want?

O´: You were in the Rebel Canary, weren't you?

I: Why do you ask that?

O´: I shot a girl who looked just like you.

I: How can I be here if I'm dead.

O´: I know. . . . Have you been here long?

I: Yes, I've been here longer than anybody else. If I were a soldier, I would have gone to the front a long time ago. I've watched many of them go.

O´: How are they now?

I: Some are dead, some are still fighting. It depends. I heard you're from West Tonkie.

O´: Yes.

I: I'm from East Tonkie.

O´: Well, what a coincidence.

I: Not now.

O´: What do you mean?

I: I used the submarine "Devilfish" and escaped to East Tonkie. I went to the orphanage where I grew up.

O´: You were in an orphanage?

I: Doesn't matter now. I lost what I was.

O´: Was it destroyed in an air raid or something?

I: Yeah, sort of. I have memories of living in the orphanage until I was four. A painting by Lautrec on the wall. The linden tree you could see out the window. *(Produces a photo.)* Look. This is me, when I was three. It's in front of the gate of the orphanage. But now. . . . *(She is in a daze for a second.)* Do you have a photo?

(O´ searches his pocket and takes out one.)

O´: My mother.

I: Oh, she's beautiful.

O´: This is my house.

I: It's a beautiful house. The wheat field, sparkling. There's quite a difference between West and East Tonkie.

O´: Why do people here want to talk about their memories all the time.

I: Living here, it seems like your memories are all that count. You'll soon understand.

(R, O, B, M come in, roaring drunk, followed by RIGHT *and* LEFT.)

R: Hi, there. How are you fucking?

M: I need more booze.

O: Oh, am I drunk.

LEFT: Come on, pass the booze.

O: No. No more. Hey, you two. What are you doing there?

B: Don't be fucking around behind our backs, new guy.

R: Right. If you fuck us up, I'll tie a rope to your cock.

M: I need more booze, fucker.

R: Drink this, bitch.

M: I said I need more, asshole.

(They shout at each other.)

RIGHT: Miss I, have a drink with us.

LEFT: Miss I, tell us about your experiences. We want to learn from you.

I: Never fall in love. That's all.

LEFT: That sounds cool! But we'll never fall in love with these jerks anyway.

B: What did you say, bitch?

R: You cunt.

M: Forget them. Let's go.

(M, RIGHT, *and* LEFT *go out.)*

O: Oh, I'm done. *(Vomits.)*

R: Shit. What a mess! This is why I hate these bright boys. What a fucking waste!

I: Are you alright, O?

O´: I want to ask you something.

B: Ask J.

O´: I want to ask you.

R: Pay up. If you want to ask us something, give us money.

(O´ hands R *some money.* R *tears it into pieces.)*

O´: Why'd you do that?

R: There's no use having money in this room. What do you want to know?

O´: First. About Neuro-Kinetic Energy.

R: What about it.

O´: What the hell is it?

B: How should we know?

O´: But you created it.

O: We don't know how we did it. We just did it.

R: Do you want us to do it again?

B: Yeah, let's show him.

(R *and* B *strain themselves. Sound of a fart.*)

R: Oh man, that stinks. Fuck you.

B: You who did it.

O´: The other thing is about Sue Ellen. What is a total brain?

O: Sorry, we don't know about her either. We just know that she's somewhere in the depths of this room.

O´: You don't know anything.

R: I don't give a fuck. We have all the booze we need. What else do you want?

I: Shall I tell you about Sue Ellen?

O: Do you know something about her, I?

I: Where's J?

B: He's sleeping, dead drunk.

I: Look around and make sure nobody is around.

O´: We're alone.

I: Promise that you won't tell this to anyone.

R: What the hell. I'm getting sober.

I: I'll show you Sue Ellen.

O: Are you serious?

I: Yes. We're friends.

R: So she's a cunt just like you.

I: Shut up. Keep quiet. Close your eyes.

(R, O, O´ *and* B *close their eyes.*)

I: Do you care if you die with your eyes closed? We're at the bottom of the sea. Hear that? The sound of running water. It's like waking up in your coffin after being buried. Just like this. No sound. You have nothing to do but to wait for a slow death. You scream. You scratch till your nails come off, but nothing happens. It's hopeless. You can't do anything in the dark. Take three steps forward.

(*The* FOUR *walk forward.*)

I: You understand for the first time where you're from and where you're going.

O: We're from far far away and are going far far away.

O´: No. It's just a matter of perspective.

I: Quiet. Take two steps back. Answer the questions. Do you have the memory of being loved?

O: No.

B: Maybe.

O´: I don't know.

I: Do you have the memory of having loved?

(ALL *are quiet.*)

I: Answer the question. Do you have the memory of having loved?

O´: I don't know.

I: Did you hear that, Sue Ellen?

(The atmosphere of the room suddenly changes. There is an open space in the middle, where a brain is floating in the air in the darkness. Several women are surrounding it with candles in their hands.)

R: What the hell is that?

I: That's Sue Ellen. She is breathing only in idea and thought. Do you read me, Sue Ellen?

SUE ELLEN: I read you, I. It's been a long time.

R: Blah blah blah. . . .

I: She is the total brain that supports the intelligence in this room.

B: I'm gonna try poking it.

(B is thrown back by an invisible barrier.)

I: That's the barrier of thought.

O: The barrier of thought?

I: Although she has no body, she can exert an invisible force by thinking.

Oʹ: By thinking?

O: She can exert force just by thinking. That's fantastic. That's the ultimate power of intelligence.

I: You could say that. Her intelligence is the sum total of all human intelligence. Isn't that so, Sue Ellen?

SUE ELLEN: Don't flatter me, I.

O: Her intelligence runs everything here, eh?

I: Yes.

SUE ELLEN: But I'm not an authority figure. I'm just a sad, lonely woman.

R: Yeah, but you're the bitch in charge, aren't you.

SUE ELLEN: Hey, here's one with guts. What's your name?

I: He's R, Sue Ellen.

SUE ELLEN: Nice to meet you, R.

R: When are you gonna let us fight?

SUE ELLEN: Are you eager to fight?

R: Sure thing. Any time.

O: How did she get to be this way? She was an ordinary woman before, wasn't she?

I: Yes. She was once a brave soldier. She was a war hero from the Emperor Penguin Room. But she was blown up in the war before last.

O: And her brain was all that was left, eh?

I: She was transformed into a new entity that can only think. She hasn't made a single mistake since.

SUE ELLEN: No. I'm not so powerful. I'm just an unhappy woman who can no longer love.

B: I'll hold you, baby.

(B is blown away again.)

I: Don't you ever learn?

B: She must have been a fox.

O: Don't you have a photo or something?

SUE ELLEN: This is an old picture of me.

> (*A photograph of* SUE ELLEN *when she was alive is seen in the darkness. It is a photograph of Ingrid Bergman.*)

R: Wow, she's beautiful!

SUE ELLEN: This was me, when I could still believe in things.

O: What about now?

SUE ELLEN: I can't believe in anything.

I: Stop it, Sue Ellen.

SUE ELLEN: I've thought too much.

I: Stop it, Sue!

SUE ELLEN: I'm sorry, I. I didn't mean to upset you.

O´: Tell me where our Whale is swimming right now.

SUE ELLEN: The Whale is about 2000 meters above the "Crying Sea." The bottom of the sea here is covered with skeletons of dead soldiers.

O´: Where are we going?

SUE ELLEN: To the coast of Calgaria.

R: Calgaria?

O: That's the front line.

O´: Are we going to fight?

SUE ELLEN: I don't know.

O´: What about Neuro-Kinetic Energy?

SUE ELLEN: It's your own power. If you use it, the U.C.R.N. cannot be beaten.

O´: Are we going to get killed?

SUE ELLEN: I don't know.

O: Where are we from?

I: O, don't.

SUE ELLEN: O, you're like I. You think too much at night.

O: Where are we from? What are we, floating in the sea, awakened by the sound of the Whale's breathing at midnight. Tell me, Sue Ellen.

> (O *rushes towards her, but is blown off by the barrier.*)

O´: What is that dream that we always dream? The dream where we're thrown out into cosmic space, floating among the planets, not knowing if we're alive or dead?

I: Stop it, O´.

O´: Miss I, what is this?

> (I *runs away.*)

R: What's up, O? You freaking out again?

O: Please, Sue Ellen!

SUE ELLEN: If you insist. . . .

> (*Gunshots.* O *is shot.* R, B, *and* O´ *are shot one by one. They fall down.* SUE ELLEN *disappears.* I *comes out with a gun from the back of the room, followed by* GENERAL Q *and* J.)

Q: Well done, I. That was close.

I: I was . . . I scared myself.

Q: J, erase the memories of these four.

J: Yes, sir.

> (J *approaches the four. It slowly gets dark. A* VOICE *is heard in the middle of the darkness.*)

VOICE: Emergency. Emergency. Cal Laser Tank Troops have captured Harna, the capital of Nanjing. The President of Nanjing, Ri Eipeni, has committed suicide in his palace. The Calgaria district is again in a state of tension and the troops on both sides are prepared for all-out war. And now for the domestic news. There will be snowfall in the early morning. A small hand-made bomb was thrown into the carriage of Governor-General Suzuki Takenobu. Four men including the Governor-General were killed in the explosion. Hours later, martial law was declared in the capital of Tokio. I repeat. Tokio the capital of the U.C.R.N. is now under martial law.

> (O´ *rises.*)

O´: A dream again. Am I dreaming again? Something's been wrong ever since I came here. If I am dreaming, why does it feel so real? If the dream world is real, am I supposed to live in that world too? You have to tell me, Sue Ellen.

O: Quiet, O´. In the dream world there is a dream version of you. This is neither dream nor reality. This is the third world.

O´: What's that?

O: I already told you. We're in the belly of the Whale.

O´: I. . . .

O: You are your third self. Look. You have friends in the third world.

> (R, B, P, M, F, *and* K *are seen in the dark.*)

ALL: You understand, O´?

> (*Each speaks, telling their blood type and zodiac sign.*)

F: I'm F. Taurus. Blood type **. I'm still a kid at heart. I'm bright and cheerful, but a little sentimental. I sometimes write poems, influenced by my brother, who is two years older than me.

M: I'm M. Gemini. Blood type **. When I was seven, my father ran away with a lover. I was brought up by my mother after that. I became a criminal at 15, and went straight again at 20 when I met my boyfriend. I might look tough, but sometimes I cry at night. My boyfriend is working at a confectionary factory in South Sakhalin. I write to him once a week.

B: I'm B. Cancer. Blood type **. I'm from Andalusia. I'm a farmer.

R: Good, hayseed.

B: Shut up. If I have a stern character, it's because of the cold climate in Andalusia. Cold has a great influence on the character. But I think I'm cheerful at heart.

K: I'm K. Capricorn. Blood type **. I was born in a normal household in Ikursk. My father is a junior high school math teacher. My mother teaches elementary school. I was an only child raised without want or worry. I've never known poverty. I've never known true hunger. If I had to have a serious problem it's that I've never had a serious problem. But right now, I have lots of friends and I am enjoying every day.

R: I'm R. Leo. Blood type **. I was born near the sea of Sakhalin. It was a nice place. Sea gulls flying around. I was brought up near the sea. My character? I'm very cheerful. I'm what you would call an open-hearted guy. Everybody thinks that I'm wild, but if you spend some time with me you'll see what I'm really like. I'm actually gentle and warm-hearted.

P: My name is P. Gemini. Blood type **. I'll soon be too old to get married. I really want to get married. Is anyone interested? Let me tell you about myself. My hobbies are knitting and listening to music. I like pop music. I went to a bridal finishing school for one year after junior college. I can handle flower arranging and tea ceremony without trouble. I have a bright personality and can become friendly with just about anybody. My ideal man is kind and tolerant. I'm not picky about looks.

O: I'm O. Capricorn. Blood type **. I'm from West Tonkie. I graduated from Guatemala High School. Do you remember the high school dance?

O´: Yes. You mean the one on Christmas Eve.

O: The girls couldn't take their eyes off you.

O´: Bullshit.

O: The band made a BOOM, and the party poppers were popping all over the place. We drank punch without alcohol. Teenage boys and girls smelling of milk.

O´: Were you at that dance too?

O: You danced with a girl named Chiko for the first time when you were a sophomore.

O´: How do you know that?

O: Do you have any photos?

O´: Photos?

O: Any old photos?

O´: I have some of my home and mother.

O: Show them to me.

O´: Sure.

(O *receives photographs from* O´. *His hands are trembling. After looking at them, he hands them back slowly.*)

O: Thank you.

O´: What's wrong, O?

o: First your pyorrhoea flairs up. Then your semicircular canals begin to swirl.

o´: What?

o: *(Bending his body in pain.)* Then your eyesight goes, your hearing, and you feel a deep anxiety. You lose hold of your emotions and your existence itself. . . . Oh, oh!
   (He runs off.)

o´: O, what happened? O!
   (The sound of party poppers. Music. It is a dance. Everyone is dancing an easy and slow dance. The atmosphere is bright and happy.)

o´: What is this? Where am I?

R: *(Dancing.)* You're finally awake.

o´: Where am I?

M: *(Dancing.)* Is that all you ever say?

K: *(Dancing.)* You forget where you are whenever you dream.

o´: Dream? Was that a dream?

F: You were asleep for three whole days.

R: I bet you're hungry again, eh?
   (ALL laugh.)

P: Come on. Join in. It's the Room's annual dance.

o´: Dance?

B: A generous move on their part—they let us off the drills for a day. Come on, let's dance. Find a partner.

R: Even B has a partner.

B: Shut up, you asshole.

o´: Where's O?

R: No idea. He's probably drunk and barfing again somewhere. Come on. Dance.

o´: I don't feel like dancing.

P: What a loser.
   (O´ sits alone away from the others. I comes up to him.)

I: Why, don't you dance?

o´: I had another strange dream.

I: Come on, dance. This is your last chance to dance.

o´: What do you mean?

I: Don't yell at me. I'm only telling you this: when the war is going badly, dances are more frequent.

o´: You mean. . . .

I: The trainees in this room will leave soon for the front.

o´: I see.

I: It's a good plan. Q, I mean, Sue Ellen was really thinking. They're going to send us to the front satisfied and happy. We're free here. We can do anything—drink, gamble, make love.

o´: I don't think so.

I: Well, do you think the world outside is so full of freedom?

O´: No.

I: You have to admit we have more freedom here than what they have outside.

O´: I know what you mean, but. . . .

I: Let's talk about something else. I don't like arguing. Especially with men. *(Looks toward the dancing people.)* I remember the dances we had in high school.

O´: You too!

I: What's wrong? You look pale.

O´: I don't seem to be able to distinguish between dreams and reality. We used to have dances like this at my high school too.

I: Yes? Doesn't this take you back?

O´: It does. Aren't you going to dance?

I: I didn't dance even in high school.

O´: How come?

I: I was too proud. I wanted to dance, but I just sat smoking in the corner, looking down my nose at everybody.

O´: Like you do now.

I: *(Laughs.)* Yeah, like now. I was just dying to dance. Teenagers are strange. When a boy you like comes up to you, you get even more proud and cool.

O´: I was like that too.

I: You?

O´: I'm like that now.

I: You haven't grown up.

O´: No.

I: . . . Soon they'll be in battle.

O´: Is there really a war going on?

I: What?

O´: Nothing. You wanna dance?

I: Sure.

(They both rise. O runs in, his face pale.)

O´: O!

O: O´, look at me!

(He produces a knife and points it toward his wrist. Scream. The dance circle is broken up. B tries to stop O. A crashing sound. The room sways. The emergency siren sounds.)

J: Our Whale is under attack by two enemy warships. Battle stations.

R: Hey, Something's wrong with O.

J: Forget about him. Battle stations!

(ALL scatter. O is standing rigid.)

O´: Hey, O. What's the matter, O?

J: Hey, I told you to take up battle stations.

o´: But O is. . . .

J: Are you disobeying me?

(A voice—"That's all right, J."—is heard. Q comes in, accompanied by
RIGHT *and* LEFT *clad in operating gowns, pushing an operating table.)*

J: But General.

Q: He might as well know. Ladies and gentlemen, stand by.

(J sprays something over O. O *becomes rigid.* RIGHT *and* LEFT *strip him*
down to his shorts and lay him out on the operating table.)

Q: It seems like the sewing machine and the umbrella have finally met on
the operating table, eh?

LEFT: We're ready, sir.

J: *(Puts on a mask.)* Shall we begin?

Q: Just a second. *(To* O´.*)* Don't be shocked. It's a simple process. You're
beginning to figure it out, aren't you?

o´: I dream more often than I used to.

Q: They aren't dreams.

o´: What?

Q: In this room is a third world, which is neither dream nor reality. O has
told you that much, hasn't he? All our science and intelligence have
yet to find out what this world is. We call the phenomena in this room
"a third world."

o´: What is it?

Q: I told you, we don't know.

o´: What does that have to do with this?

Q: Observe carefully. Start the operation please.

J: Yes, Dr. Spock.

Q: What's that?

J: General Hospital.

Q: Cut it out.

J: I'm sorry. Scalpel, please.

*(*RIGHT *hands him a scalpel.* J *places it against the chest of* O.*)*

J: Wow! *(Throws down the scalpel.)* I'm sorry. Scalpel, please. *(*RIGHT
hands it to him. He places it against the chest.) Wow! *(Throws it*
down. Repeats it several times.)

Q: What the hell are you doing?

J: I'm sorry, sir. I'm afraid of blood.

Q: Move over. Scalpel.

(Q cuts O*'s chest open.)*

Q: Ladle.

(Q puts the ladle into the chest, ladles out the blood and tastes it.)

Q: How is it?

J: *(Drinks.)* It's just right.

Q: Good. Ear pick.

(Q scrabbles in the chest with the ear pick.)

J: Ahh. It tickles.

Q: Oooh . . . here it is, a big ball of earwax.

(Q *blows into the chest.*)

J: Ahh, it tickles.

Q: The chest seems OK. Let's cut open the skull. Gaff tape.

(Q *tapes the chest.*)

Q: Scalpel. *(Opens the head.)* Good God! Look!

(RIGHT, LEFT, *and* J *look into the head.*)

J: It's here, just as I expected.

RIGHT: Energy's running out.

LEFT: The right-hand tank is empty.

J: There's clearly been too much use of emotion.

Q: Hey kid, come and have a look.

(O´ *peeks in, looking scared.*)

O´: What the. . . .

Q: Isn't it wonderful?

O´: I can't believe. . . .

Q: This is not a dream. Not a dream, boy.

O´: I refuse to believe this.

J: Don't be an idiot.

O´: I won't believe this! EVER!

Q: Don't run away.

(O´ *crouches down with his hands covering his head.*)

Q: Since the beginning of the reign of Emperor Seiki, the U.C.R.N. has promoted the development of microbe bombs and androids. That's how we prepared for war. The computers concluded that there would be a war, based on all the data in the world. We could not avoid a war. As early as in the 10th year of Emperor Seiki's reign, the U.C.R.N. completed the first android: type R3VZ. They don't age of course. The problem was that they had emotions. Even the engineers who made them didn't think that androids could have emotions, like O here, or J, Right, and Left.

O´: What?!

Q: The first emotional skill they acquired was laughter. Then crying, and anger. In three years, they learned to master complex feelings. That is, bashfulness, humor, coyness, loneliness, regret. . . . Type R3VZ was gradually becoming human. But there was one emotional skill they hadn't acquired. Can you guess what it is?

O´: . . . .

Q: Love. Affection was the most difficult. Can a machine love? It turns out that it is possible. A type R3VZ fell in love with my late wife.

J: Let's not talk about that now, General.

Q: J, bring it here.

J: But, sir.

Q: Quick.

(J brings in a kind of board.)

Q: One spring night in the 14th year of the era, a type R3VZ committed adultery with my wife. At last we had made a complete human being. The moment his steel penis entered my wife's vagina was a great historical moment for humankind!

O´: Where's that R3VZ android now?

Q: After I reported it to the authorities and received permission, I destroyed him.

(J fires.)

Q: An android can't be killed with an ordinary gun. *(Takes the gun from J.)* I shot him with this special gun for androids. In the midst of their fourth session, I shot him in the back.

O´: Him. . . .

Q: He wasn't a machine anymore. He was a man. I held him before he died, and did my duty. I re-confirmed his affection. I asked him "Do you have the memory of being loved?"

J: "No."

Q: "Do you have the memory of having loved?" *(J moves his mouth slightly.)* He seemed to answer something, but I couldn't hear it. It is written here. *(Takes off the cloth covering the board J has brought. It is a monument which reads:*

> *Do you have the memory of being loved?*
> *NO.*
> *Do you have the memory of having loved?*
> . . . . *(Indecipherable)*   TYPE R3VZ)

Q: We made this in secret to commemorate the birth of the perfect human being. The first android in history. A year later my wife killed herself. the U.C.R.N.'s skill in manufacturing androids has improved greatly. For example—

RIGHT: I'm the male libido-releasing sexaroid type A.

LEFT: I'm sexaroid type V1.

J: Officer-obeying type B20.

Q: We had a lot of trouble getting this far. The type R3VZ was not a perfect human being. He lacked the most important feature of a human being. He lacked memory.

O´: Memory. . . .

Q: Yes. A man's memory is what he cherishes most. Androids don't have memories of their infancy and teens. So we started programming them with memories at an early stage, just when they start to have emotions. We extract an individual's memory, which is stored in the capital, at random and implant it without knowing whose memory it is. The government has access to everyone's memory.

O´: Then O's memory is. . . .

Q: Yes, coincidentally, it was your memory up through high school.
(O´ kicks the monument.)
O´: I'm dreaming.
Q: No you're not. Look at O's brain. A work of science. Almost a work of art. Give me some gaff tape.
(Q seals O's head with tape.)
O´: Then in this room. . . .
Q: Yes, as it turns out you were sent to a room where you and I are the only ones who aren't andro. . . .
(O suddenly wakes up and starts to strangle Q.)
Q: Help. Hel. . . .
J: Stop, O. Why do you want to kill the General?
O: He is the one. He is the. . . .
J: What are you talking about? In a sense the General is your father!
(The strength goes out of O.)
O: My father. . . .
J: Your parents are not in West Tonkie, the General gave you life.
(O releases Q, exhausted.)
Q: Phew. Calm down, O. Look, the war is not going well. In a few days, you will be the first to leave for the front, alright? *(He leaves, followed by J.)*
O: My parents are your parents. *(Produces a photograph.)* This picture is a lie . . . I feel as if I've been thrown into outer space. I am neither alive nor dead. . . . I'm NOT HUMAN!
O´: Calm down. Calm down, O.
O: I can handle it. I know the truth now. But what about the others? They don't know anything yet. I can't listen to them talking about the past anymore.
O´: I feel the same way.
(A voice—"We were listening."—is heard. It is R's voice. R, I, B, P, M, F, and K come out from all directions.)
R: I heard it all, O.
M: I had a feeling something was wrong. We were always kind of different.
P: *(Taking out his photograph.)* They do a good job. I'll say that for them. *(Tears it up.)*
(Each of them tears their photograph. Piercing sounds of a siren. J rushes in.)
J: The alert is cancelled. We're outside the range of the enemy warship's radar. Everybody, prepare for drills!
(They do not move.)
J: What are you waiting for? Get ready for drills!
(R, O, I, B, P, M, F, K, RIGHT, and LEFT take up positions.)
J: Don't relax too much even after you've accomplished something.

Don't cheer till you're sure you're out of the woods. We'll jump right into the program. Breathe in and out. Breathe in and out. We'll skip the warm-up. Concentrate. Now, let's begin. Lesson 1: Laughter.
(ALL *do as* J *says.*)

J: Lesson 2: Sorrow. Lesson 3: Anger. Lesson 7: Burst of laughter. Lesson 34: A wry smile. Lesson 35: Orgasm. Lesson 40: Wailing. Lesson 45: Surprise. Lesson 51: Shouting. Lesson 57: Giving up.
(ALL *looked drained of emotions.*)

J: Good. Very good. Perfect. Perfect human emotions. Make no mistake. You're human. More than human. That's all for today. Get ready for dinner. *(Leaves.)*

(ALL *prepare for dinner without a word. Silence.* ALL *sit down when the preparations are completed. They close their eyes and clasp their hands together.*)

I: Dear God, the world is now in perpetual twilight. Amen.

ALL: Amen.

R: Dear God, all men are living as the dead. Amen.

ALL: Amen.

M: Dear God, we no longer look to a bright morning, a dripping rain is hitting the pavement. Amen.

ALL: Amen.

P: Dear God, we are all. . . .

ALL: Amen.

P: Dear God, we cannot even kill ourselves. Amen.

ALL: Amen.

F: But Dear God, we do not say, "Save us." Amen.

K: But Dear God, we do not say, "Save us." Amen.

ALL: Amen.

O: Dear God, all the brains are now heading out into the universe like an injured white horse. Amen.

I: Dear God, Your horizon is different from ours. Amen.

O´: Dear God, this war, our war, sees the universe at the end of the retina, and starts again towards another darkness. Because. . . .

ALL: Because.

R: Because this war is not our war. Amen.

ALL: This war is not our war. Amen!

(ALL *slowly turn over the table in front of them and rise.*)

ALL: This is Nippon's war. But it's not ours!

I: Weapons. . . .

(Steel rods are handed to ALL.*)*

R: What are we going to do?

O: We point the Whale toward the horizon.

M: What's the password.

I: More than human.

O´: Destroy. Destroy everything.

(ALL start destroying the room with their rods. A storm of metallic sound. They keep on hitting. The sound of the sea becomes louder. The room sways.)

R: The Whale, the Whale is freaking out!

(J rushes in.)

J: What the hell are you fuckers doing?!

O´: Destroy. Destroy everything.

(ALL start hitting again.)

J: Watch out. The Whale is going to breach.

(The Whale breaches and ALL tumble over.)

J: *(Quickly stands up and takes out the gun for androids.)* We do not allow rebellion.

O´: Tie him up.

(R and B tie J up.)

I: It doesn't work. The Whale is too tough.

M: What do we do?

R: Shoot it.

O: No way.

I: Sue Ellen.

O: What?

I: Sue Ellen's brain is controlling the Whale. If we destroy her, we might make it.

P: But it's impossible to fight against her.

O´: Let's try, win or lose. Miss I, show us Sue Ellen again.

I: Look out into the universe. Use your imagination and see your own universe. . . . Turn around. Say a word.

(Each says a word: HOPE, DESPAIR, HAPPINESS, DESIRE, SOLITUDE, DEPRESSION, PLEASURE, SOUND OF THE SEA, CORRUPTION, DESERT, STARDUST.)

I: Sue Ellen, we're going to fight you.

(In the darkness, SUE ELLEN appears with a roaring sound.)

SUE ELLEN: What's going on, I?

I: We've come to destroy you, Sue Ellen.

SUE ELLEN: Destroy me? You're insane, I. You know me, don't you?

I: If we destroy you, we'll be free.

SUE ELLEN: Free? Free! *(Laughs.)* You still believe in freedom?

R: Don't laugh.

SUE ELLEN: Freedom is like stardust. It's a flower that doesn't exist. It's a place which is nowhere.

(R shoots at SUE ELLEN.)

SUE ELLEN: Impossible, because I am you.

O´: Destroy her. Your power is being tested. Call up the power you know you have.

(R, B, M, F, K, *and* P *together rush towards* SUE ELLEN, *but are thrown back.*)

O´: Again!

(*This time, an electric current runs through them and* ALL *retreat paralysed.*)

SUE ELLEN: Children, you are so full of spirit. My dear children. Relax. Everything will be sorted out. All your hopes and fears. . . .

(*A slow lullaby is heard.*)

O´: No. Don't fall asleep. M, do it!

(M *creates a storm, but* SUE ELLEN *is not affected.*)

SUE ELLEN: Good night, my dear children.

O´: O, read her mind.

(O *concentrates.*)

O: What the hell is this? What kind of universe do you have in your mind, Sue Ellen? Ah, my pyorrhoea. My semicircular canals are swirling. . . . I'm losing my eyesight, my hearing, I feel a deep anxiety. I'm losing control of my emotions. . . . Sue Ellen, you are not my mother!

(*The lullaby stops.*)

R: No. You are not my mother!

SUE ELLEN: Then where is your mother, R?

R: In Sakhalin. . . .

SUE ELLEN: Don't lie to me, R. You know you're not human. You are a combat android type V3.

R: No.

SUE ELLEN: Tell me then, do you have a vision, R?

R: A vision?

SUE ELLEN: A vision that belongs to the human race?

R: Our vision is to destroy you.

SUE ELLEN: You're wasting your time, R. Do you think there is any vision in this revolt? This war represents the last vision of humankind.

R: This war?

SUE ELLEN: Yes. Humans could only pursue their vision through war. They couldn't think of anything except war. And you were created to serve this vision.

O´: Don't let her trick you.

SUE ELLEN: War is necessary for human beings. Now, stop making trouble and go to bed. You're going to war when you wake up.

(*Again the lullaby is heard.* ALL *start to get drowsy.*)

O´: No. Don't sleep! Neuro-Kinetic Energy. Use your Neuro-Kinetic Energy.

(ALL *regain alertness.*)

O´: Only Neuro-Kinetic Energy can defeat her.

SUE ELLEN: Good night, my dear children.

O´: This is our last chance. Gather round.

(They form a circle for Neuro-Kinetic Energy. They utter a language which is not a language. They stand up, get together, separate themselves, and take up various postures. The Neuro-Kinetic Energy gradually builds.)

SUE ELLEN: Ah, what is this . . . ?

(They direct the power at SUE ELLEN.*)*

SUE ELLEN: No. . . .

(They get together once again to exert their last strength. SUE ELLEN *explodes.)*

R: We did it!

O´: Bring J here. Did you see that, J?

J: You assholes. What have you done?

O´: Make the Whale surface.

J: But. . . .

O´: Do it now!

J: All right, I'll do it. I'll do it. Come up!

(The sound of the waves becomes louder. The Whale comes up. A blue sky is seen on the stage. ALL *look up at the sky.)*

P: The air. . . . The outside air. . . .

M: The blue sky. . . .

B: How long has it been since I've seen the sun?

F: I feel great.

O: We weren't free after all.

R: Look at the sea gulls. *(Falls down.)*

*(*ALL *look surprised for a moment and then fall down, expressionless, one after another, as if they were broken machines.* O´, I *and* J *are left.)*

O´: What, what the hell happened?

(J laughs.)

O´: J, what does this mean?

J: We're finished, General.

(Q appears.)

Q: Lesson 200: Revolt. The scheduled lessons are completed. Tomorrow everyone will fight as a first-rate soldier.

O´: Q, what the hell. . . .

Q: Don't worry. They've been running on sea energy for such a long time that they can't make the switch to solar energy right away. They'll wake up in a few hours.

O´: You son of a bitch, Q.

J: Calm down. The world is moving. That's all.

Q: The last lesson, "Revolt," is the most difficult lesson. We had to wait for the right moment. But it went very well. It was the most successful one we've had so far, thanks to excellent personnel. Good work, J.

J: Thank you, sir.

Q: What would you like to do now?

J: I'd like to take a bath and wash off the sweat, sir.

Q: OK. Off you go.

J: Yes, sir. *(Leaves.)*

O´: *(Stupefied.)* It was programmed.

Q: Our soldiers aren't sent to the front until they have drunk of the nectar called "revolt." It's just one of the programs, but this was one of the most wonderful revolts we've ever had. Don't you agree, I?

O´: I? You knew?

Q: Anyhow. . . . Solar energy is good, isn't it? Look. We'll have a sunset in a few hours. Sweet night comes and then the sun rises again on the horizon. It'll be a bright, brilliant morning for you soldiers who have lived through all the despair, all the hope, and this revolt. You will be resurrected as brave soldiers for the U.C.R.N.!

I: A brilliant morning. . . .

O´: Miss I, you knew. . . .

I: I'm sorry, O´. . . .

(There is a knife in I's hand. She rushes towards Q. Q avoids her but the knife catches his arm. A gun is fired. Q has the gun for androids in his hand.)

I: Ahh. . . .

(I falls down. O´ catches hold of her.)

O´: Miss I.

Q: It's alright. I just reduced her energy. Androids don't die so easily.

O´: I. Don't die. I.

I: I'm sorry O´. I knew everything from the beginning. . . . I knew that I wasn't human. . . .

O´: That's not true. You are human.

I: Everything was a lie. The stars in the sky. The twilight when I wept. The hot soup in the kitchen in winter. Freshly baked biscuits. The taste of honey spreading in the mouth. The dream that I dreamt in a soft bed. They were all lies.

O´: But that dance. The dance that we had in the high school gym. That was real, wasn't it?

I: *(Smiles slightly.)* I sat smoking the corner, not dancing, although I wanted to.

O´: Right!

I: When a boy I liked came over to me, I pretended to be cool.

O´: Yes. That Christmas Eve dance.

I: That dance was an illusion.

O´: It's not an illusion. Let's dance. Dance with me.

I: O´. My memory is the memory of General Q's dead wife.

O´: That's not true.

I: See, she's dancing. Not me. She . . . is . . . dancing. I am sexaroid alpha type A. . . .

O´: Do you have the memory of being loved?

I: No.

O´: Miss I. Do you have the memory of having loved?

(I murmurs something and loses consciousness.)

O´: Miss I. . . . She said something, but I couldn't make it out. Indecipherable. Still I don't believe it. I can't see her face as anything but a dead woman's face. The dance was an illusion, but it must have been real between me and Miss I. For we must have been dancing at least in our minds. Not in our memory but in the shadow which is our thought.

(J is seen in the darkness.)

J: Lesson 198: Crossed in love, completed. Miss I will be alive again in 4 hours and 12 minutes. *(Leaves.)*

O´: I won't . . . I won't believe this. . . . But as J said, the dead Miss I revived exactly 4 hours and 12 minutes later.

(I rises slowly and leaves.)

O´: The sun dazzled me. The Blue Whale came to the surface and went south off the Calgarian Sea. I spent days gazing at the sun without eating or drinking. And I thought. Where did I come from and where was I going. Two days later, it was time for O's departure for the front.

(O steps forward ready for departure. A CROWD *is behind him to see him off.)*

O´: A man with my memory, no I myself am going to the front. . . . It was a strict human ritual performed by androids.

J: Three cheers for O!

(The CROWD *cheers three times.)*

O: Thank you. I'll fight hard for our country.

(F goes up to him.)

F: Here's an amulet. Please come back alive.

O: *(Holding her hands.)* Yes. I'll come back alive.

F: Take care of yourself.

O: I will.

F: Boil the water before you drink it.

O: Yes.

J: Three cheers for the UNITED CAPITALIST REPUBLIC OF NIPPON!

(The CROWD *cheers three times.)*

O´: O!

(O looks.)

O´: What are you going to fight for, O?

O: For my family. *(Salutes.)*

O´: Is that true?

O: For my country.

O´: Is that true? O!

O: It's true. For my fatherland.

(O stands at attention.)

J: The national anthem of the UNITED CAPITALIST REPUBLIC OF
NIPPON.

*("Le Internationale" is performed by an orchestra. The scene changes
and people are seen playing the tune. The conductor is* GENERAL Q. O´
slowly takes out a knife, and rushes towards Q. *He stabs him in the
chest. "Le Internationale" stops.* ALL *disappear.)*

Q: So you've done it.

O´: Do you have this programmed? Do you have one called
"assassination"?

Q: You fool.

O´: I hate you.

Q: Then, I'll tell you something. The last thing.

O´: What?

Q: Don't you have doubts about yourself?

O´: Me?

Q: Why are you here in this room? Think about it.

(O´ is speechless.)

Q: I figured you'd realize sooner or later. But you're pretty stupid about
your self. Think back. How did you get to this room?

O´: I escaped from the Rebel Canary, and. . . .

Q: *(Actor's name.)* escaped from the Rebel Canary. He was caught east of
Mecon and shot. Dead.

O´: What?!

Q: I'm going to die. *(Leaves.)*

O´: Me too? No!

(I comes out.)

I: It's the truth.

O´: Miss I.

I: What Q said is true.

O´: But that means I'm. . . .

I: Let's find out. *(Takes out a gun.)* Shoot yourself in the head with this.
If you're human, you'll die, but if you're an android. . . .

(O´ takes the gun with a trembling hand.)

I: O´, a gamble. The last gamble.

O´: But. . . .

I: Bet it all on zero, O´! On zero!

*(O´ shoots his head, and falls. The wall collapses and reveals a row of
androids behind. They all shoot at him.)*

O´: *(Sits up.)* I'm alive. I'm ALIVE!

R: Come with us, O´.

O: We've taken over the Whale. We'll change course, and sail north.

o´: Where are we going?

R: To Nippon.

I: Come on. Let's go, to our own war.

(o´ stands up. A light is seen at the back of the room.)

I: Where are you?

o´: Incept date *(Actor's birthday.)*. I am the thinking type android, ZERO.

(I smiles. The androids walk slowly towards the audience. The stage is full of light and nothing can be seen. The sound of explosion.)

Notes

1. In the original Japanese the abbreviation "Nichiren" is used instead of the initials U.C.R.N. This makes it a homonym for the Nichiren (Lotus Sutra) sect of Buddhism.

2. The silver papers are an updating of the aka-gami (red papers), which are traditional Japanese conscription notices. The text of the silver papers is written in a Kansai (Osaka area) dialect. The effect is to give the notices a somewhat informal, almost comic feel.

3. Matsuda Seiko was a major pop star of the 1980s and early 1990s. "Sweet Memories" was one of her biggest hits and is extremely familiar to a Japanese audience. The lyrics sing of sentimental longing for the past.

4. The name of a popular energy drink, e.g. Red Bull.

5. O´ pronounced "O dash." The meaning implied is that O´ is a variant or alternate version of O.

6. Sawada Kenji (also known as "Julie") was a major pop star of the 1970s and 80s, known for his flamboyantly androgynous persona.

A Legend of Mermaids
Chong Wishing

TRANSLATED BY CODY POULTON

*

Introduction

Ōtori Hidenaga
TRANSLATED BY CODY POULTON

This translation is based on the 1990 Beyoruto Kōbō publication of *Ningyo Densetsu*.

Chong Wishing

Mermaids and mermen arrive on
a raft. Second from the left:
Chong Wishing. (Courtesy
Miyauchi Katsu.)

"Surely you heard that," the Old Woman says, holding the Poet's ears as a ship's horn sounds. Front: Poet; back: Old Woman. (Courtesy Miyauchi Katsu.)

"Horsy?" Mother, Haruo, and Father throw up their arms in disgust as Setsuo, dressed in drag, welcomes a gentleman caller. Standing, from left: Horse, Setsuo, Mother, Haruo, and Father. (Courtesy Miyauchi Katsu.)

As the family enjoys a bowl of ramen from Akio and Goldfish's noodle cart, Marlene (front), carried by Akio and Father, berates Jenny for thinking of nothing but money. In the front are standing from left: Akio, Father, Haruo, Goldfish and Jenny. (Courtesy Miyauchi Katsu.)

The Baron (center) sings a torch song. Setsuo (far right) is dressed as one of the cheerleaders. (Courtesy Miyauchi Katsu.)

Natsuo and Hammer Hosoi fight it out in the boxing ring while spectators mill around. Back row outside the ring, from left: Akio and Father. (Courtesy Miyauchi Katsu.)

Goldfish (front), who has been rejected by Akio (back), demands that he take her back. Akio attempts to restrain her as she thrashes about in the water. (Courtesy Miyauchi Katsu.)

Crying, "I'm like a mermaid, waiting for someone to reel me in," the Poet slips into the water and disappears at the end of the play. (Courtesy Miyauchi Katsu.)

Introduction

Ōtori Hidenaga
TRANSLATED BY CODY POULTON

TOWARD THE END OF THE 1980s, contemporary Japanese theater experienced a breakdown. The critical, avant-garde spirit of 1960s theater had given way to the rise in the 1980s of a kind of playful, punning theater, one that captured audiences by skipping lightly over the surfaces of things and catching the postmodernist zeitgeist. But then, quite suddenly, this theater of the 1980s stalled in mid-flight. This occurred in 1987 or 1988, just prior to the 1989 fall of the Berlin Wall, and was a kind of presage of the bursting of the bubble economy. The end of eighties theater came when it could no longer continue to skate lightly over thin ice, but it didn't know how to stay still. The two standard-bearers of that theater, Noda Hideki and Kōkami Shōji, attempted to survive by either giving up theater altogether or returning to tradition, but their efforts were in vain. Noda Hideki disbanded his troupe and, in 1992, went to London to study. Kōkami Shōji also went to London the following year. By the end of the 1980s it was impossible to tell where contemporary theater in Japan was headed.

Chong Wishing, the author of *A Legend of Mermaids*, appeared on the scene just at the time that Japanese theater had tumbled into this crisis. Before Chong Wishing wrote and first staged this work, in 1990, he had written a number of plays, notably the critically acclaimed *A Thousand Years of Solitude*[1] (fp. 1988). As can be seen from these two examples, Chong Wishing's work was a far cry from the light-hearted 1980s theater, which contented itself with playing minute riffs on shallow themes; instead, his drama burst on the scene as something quite anti-contemporary, the inheritor of the atmosphere of 1960s *angura* theater. Chong made his theater debut with a group that symbolized *angura*, the Theater Center 68/71 (Black Tent). Moreover, Shinjuku Ryōzanpaku, a troupe whose director and leading actors all had deep links to *angura*, presented these plays. Its director, Kim Sujin, had been an actor in the Situation Theater (Jōkyō Gekijō, a.k.a. Red Tent), a troupe led by Kara Jūrō, arguably the godfather of *angura*. Similarly, Shinjuku Ryōzanpaku's star actress, Kim Kumija, was an alumna of Satoh Makoto's Black Tent Theater. This company thus carried a powerful whiff of *angura*, which had deep roots in the imagination of the lower classes; it clearly emerged from a completely different place from the postmodernism of 1980s Japan, which eulogized consumer society. And as playwright, Chong Wishing existed at the center of this new theater troupe.

It should also be pointed out that many of the founding members of this troupe, Chong Wishing included, were Korean nationals born and raised in Japan. Because they were written from the standpoint of the Korean community in Japan, Chong's works, including *A Legend of Mermaids*, hold a special place in contemporary Japanese theater. Incidentally, Korean playwrights are rare in modern Japanese theater, there being, besides Chong, only two other writers of note, Tsuka Kōhei and Yū Miri. Significantly, most audiences in Japan, except for a few theater people, knew nothing of Tsuka's Korean ethnicity. That is why no one had ever pointed out that the ironical viewpoint in Tsuka's works had its underpinning in his identity as a Korean national. (According to a recent essay by Suga Hidemi, ignorance of this gave rise to a fundamental misunderstanding of Tsuka.) Yū Miri's works, on the other hand, have been attacked for being too "Japanese," not too "Korean." (Yū went on to distinguish herself as a novelist. When her debut novel *A Fish Swimming in Stone*[2] created a sensation, literary critic and later president of the University of Tokyo Hasumi Shigehiko wrote that one could not help but be a bit surprised by how easily Yū had laid down her arms as playwright for the sake of fiction.)

In this respect, Chong Wishing's works hold an especially unique place: from the start, it is clear to anyone that they were an unequivocal statement of his identity as a Korean in Japan. It should also be pointed out that when Koreans living in Japan use their Korean names their ethnicity becomes obvious to all; Chong Wishing's name in itself is thus a testament to his Korean ancestry. Korean nationals in Japan have been terribly discriminated against, and many have felt compelled to protect themselves from such discrimination by assuming Japanese names. The reason Japanese did not know that Tsuka Kōhei was ethnic Korean, for instance, was because he used a Japanese pen name. In contrast, from the time of *Beloved Medea*[3] (1986), his debut work for the Black Tent, Chong Wishing has explicitly foregrounded his Korean ethnicity. In that play, numerous references were made to the Alien Registration Card that Korean residents are obliged to carry around with them. This piece allegorically depicts the complex feelings of Korean residents in Japan using elements from the Greek tragedy *Medea*. The play features countless women called Medea who attach themselves to a man who dreams of becoming a marathon runner racing toward the hills of Iolcus. Will this man be able to reach these hills dragging these women behind him? Iolcus is where Jason, the man who abducted Medea, came from.

But for Chong Wishing, who wrote this play as Seoul was about to stage the Olympic Games, the hills no doubt reminded him of the softly rolling slopes of the Olympic Park in Seoul. The women carry black trunks with them for their journey to Iolcus, but these trunks contain nothing for their trip, only earth. This and other incidents gradually make clear that their dreams to go back to their ancestral land will never come true.

Having made his debut as playwright with *Beloved Medea*, Chong Wishing's next work, A *Thousand Years of Solitude*, is a tale about men who go on digging for a mother lode of gold they never find, all the while prostituting the women who were brought from a place "across the river" that hints at the Korean peninsula. They hope to escape their situation but no one actually leaves, and they meet a tragic end in a fire which some of them set, an act of violence which also turns their own dreams for the future into ashes. Like a variation on Samuel Beckett's *Waiting for Godot*, the play's absurdist "no exit" situation also evoked vague memories of the massacre of Korean residents after the Kantō earthquake of 1923, while at the same time reflecting the real conditions faced today by ethnic Koreans living in Japan. But the condition portrayed in the play also seemed like a reprise of the "Godotist" conditions characteristic of avant-garde Japanese theater around the time of the struggles over the renewal of the US-Japan Mutual Security Treaty (Anpo), a theater that resonated with the defeatism of the Anpo debacle. For this reason, not to mention the fact that many of Shinjuku Ryōzanpaku's members were alumni of the sixties Black Tent and Red Tent companies, Chong Wishing's works came to be regarded as a kind of "Waiting for Godot" revisited some twenty years later. Indeed, Chong's work itself hovers ambiguously between, on the one hand, being a latter-day "Waiting for Godot" and, on the other, concealing its Korean identity under the cloak of metaphor. In this fashion, Chong Wishing went on to write a number of works for Shinjuku Ryōzanpaku, a tent theater that has continued to operate under the catch phrase of "the inheritors of the old *angura* spirit."

A Legend of Mermaids (1990) is one such work. This play has become a hallmark work for Shinjuku Ryōzanpaku, which has performed it in such international locales as Seoul and Shanghai. The Seoul production, which was done partly in Korean, ended in wild applause from the Korean audience packed inside a hot tent pitched over the Hangang River. Though this work portrays both explicitly and implicitly the lives of Korean nationals living in Japan, the whole work is set seemingly paradoxically inside a framing narrative that is quintessentially Japanese, a framework borrowed by Chong from *Sotoba Komachi* in the version found in Mishima Yukio's *Modern Japanese Nō Plays*.

At the Tokyo production, before the play began, a filthy old woman could be seen loitering outside the special tent that was pitched by the banks of Shinobazu Pond in Ueno, picking up cigarette butts and tossing them into an empty tin can. A young man watched her carefully. Presently they entered the tent and, mounting the stage, began to talk. The play thus began with dialogue that, while citing Mishima's *Sotoba Komachi*, amusingly twisted its lines for its own devices.

> OLD WOMAN: One and one make two, two and two make four. . . .
> *(She holds a stub up against the light and, determining that it is a fairly long one, goes to the couple at the left to ask for a light. She smokes for a while. When the cigarette burns down to a stub she grinds it out, throws it on the paper with the others, and begins to count again.)* One and one make two, two and two make four. . . .
> POET: *(Comes up behind the* OLD WOMAN *and watches what she is doing.)*
> OLD WOMAN: *(Her eyes still looking down at the paper.)* Want a smoke? I'll give you one if you want it. *(She chooses a rather long stub and hands it to him.)*
> POET: Thanks. *(Takes out a match, lights the cigarette, and smokes.)*
> OLD WOMAN: Is there something else? Have you got something to say to me?
> POET: No, not especially.
> OLD WOMAN: I know what you are. You're a poet.[4]

These are the opening lines to Mishima's *Sotoba Komachi*. A comparison with *A Legend of Mermaids* should make it clear that Chong begins his own play by liberally quoting from Mishima's. But presently the tale of the past or the world of dreams told by the poet becomes the one that Chong Wishing himself has chosen to portray. The world that he conjures is a town with a solitary slaughterhouse, and behind the slaughterhouse is the sea. The people who cross that sea to live in this town become the dramatis personae of *A Legend of Mermaids*. From this description, a Japanese audience knows that these characters can only have crossed over from the Korean peninsula. They make their living by doing those occupations that are shunned by the Japanese, jobs like slaughtering animals, or (as with the family in this play) by collecting scrap metal. In a memoir, "On Wandering,"[5] Chong Wishing acknowledged that his own family made just such a living as scrap metal dealers. Even so, when one sees this work staged, the characters actually arrive by raft over the sea, or a river, or a pond—it varies on the venue—and this scene's sense of actuality is so powerful, so stunning that the audience experiences a moment that manifests something transcending its mere significance to the story itself. The scene inside the tent, of a tenement, creates a gritty kind of space that had been forgotten in the postmodern atmosphere of the 1980s. And the writhing energy of the horde of people who live packed together there creates a vortex of proletarian passions that recall the spirit of *angura* theater. For these reasons, Shinjuku Ryōzanpaku's stage won many followers.

But why did the framework for this sort of world have to be Mishima's work? Considering the unique place held by Mishima in modern Japanese theater, this matter cannot help but raise some particularly complex problems. Borrowing the expressive form of the prewar Japan Romantic School, Mishima executed a contrarian experiment to liberate into the modern era the language of *nō,* the pinnacle of Japan's traditional performing arts, a theater that created beauty within the structure of an eternally converging spiral. That is why the adjective "modern" is applied to these modern *nō* plays; they portray a realm which indeed unveils the karmic structure of the phantasmal world of *nō.* In other words, Mishima revealed to modern Japanese readers and audiences how we dream, an act of critical consciousness that itself must be called modern. Likewise, Chong Wishing, in attempting to portray the life of Koreans in Japan within the context of Mishima's phantasmal world, was trying to place within a critical framework the sad dreams of his own people.

After this play, Chong Wishing wrote *Cinecitta* (1990) and *Jap Doll* (1991) for Shinjuku Ryōzanpaku, but prior to leaving that troupe in 1994 he had already been involved in the film world, writing scenarios. He won accolades for his coauthored script for *Which Way Does the Moon Rise?,*[6] and practically made a clean sweep of all the prizes for film scripts, including the Kinema Junpō Scenario Prize, for *The Beggar of Love.*[7]

Chong Wishing's potential is based on his sense of being an outsider, which gives him a particular critical stance as a writer. But as contemporary Japanese theater entered the 1990s and reverted to the uncritical spirit of the Japanese emperor system (a few exceptions include dumb type, Deconstruction Company, and Noda Hideki's post-London sabbatical Noda Map), the place in theater for people like Chong has disappeared. That is not to say that the film world is a more congenial place for such a spirit. But Chong was an alumnus of a film school and ever since his youth has had dreams of a career in the movies. If he has not abandoned the stage, at least he has turned his energies to cinema now.

Notes

1. Sennen no kodoku.

2. Ishi ni oyogu sakana.

3. Itoshi no Medea.

4. Mishima Yukio, *Five Modern Nō Plays*, trans. Donald Keene (New York: Knopf, 1957) p. 4.

5. Sasurai-ron.

6. Tsuki wa dotchi ni deteiru. From an original story by Yan Sogil; Sai Yōichi, dir. Both director and original author are resident Koreans.

7. Ai o kou hito, 1999. Hirayama Hideyuki, dir., from an original story by Shimoda Harumi.

A Legend of Mermaids

Chong Wishing

TRANSLATED BY CODY POULTON

CHARACTERS

POET	GOLDFISH	HORSE
OLD WOMAN	ONDINE	DEER
FATHER	BARON	HAMMER HOSOI
MOTHER	BARONESS	
SETSUO, *oldest brother*		
HARUO, *second oldest*	JENNY	BOXERS IN THE GYM
YONG-HEE, HARUO*'s wife*	KEWPIE KIM	
NATSUO, *third oldest*	STELLA	
AKIO, *fourth oldest*	MARLENE	
FUYUO, *fifth oldest*		
SHIKIO, *youngest brother*	USELESS EUSTACE	

ACT I

(The curtain is drawn, revealing a single bench. A man is standing there. His name is the POET. Yes, he's a poet.)

POET: How many nights have I missed sleep? Under the moonlight folks like me turn into poets. And then, as in Mishima Yukio's play *Sotoba Komachi*, we wait for a strange old woman to turn up. The park, the bench, the lovers, the lamps: all the ingredients are there.
(An OLD WOMAN enters, picking up cigarette butts.)
OLD WOMAN: One and one make two, two and two make five.
POET: Uh, excuse me.
OLD WOMAN: Like a fag? I'll give you one if you want.
POET: I don't smoke.
OLD WOMAN: Don't be a bore. You'll lose out on half the pleasures of life.
POET: Didn't you actually mean to say, "two and two make four"?
OLD WOMAN: Four or five, it makes no difference to me any more.

POET: But it does with me now.

OLD WOMAN: I know what you are. You're a poet.

POET: More poseur than poet, really.

OLD WOMAN: What do you mean spying on me from the shadows like that all the time, eh? What's the matter with you? Got a thing for me?

POET: I've just got this vague feeling we've met before. . . .

OLD WOMAN: Uh uh. Never met you.

POET: Tell me, gran, it's been bugging the hell out of me every night now. You always show up at the same hour and sit down on the bench, driving away the nice young couples who've claimed it before you. What's all that about?

OLD WOMAN: You got a problem with that? Do I look like a yakuza to you, come to collect my fee for sitting here?

POET: Nah, I'm just speaking for the bench because it can't speak for itself.

OLD WOMAN: Come sit, you poor poet, you.

POET: Poor? Me?

OLD WOMAN: Your face is too pale. It's the face of someone wandering around looking for answers in the dark. You'll find no answers there, you know.

POET: You read faces in a former life, did you?

OLD WOMAN: You might say I've looked into enough faces to make me sick of humanity. . . . Sit down. A bit shaky on your feet, aren't you?

POET: I'm drunk.

OLD WOMAN: You poor idiot. . . . Tell me, why is it humans were given a couple of useless legs instead of a beautiful tail?

POET: *(Sitting on the bench.)* Jeez, I'm feeling kind of queasy. . . .

OLD WOMAN: First you were just drunk, now you're seasick?

POET: Seasick?

OLD WOMAN: Everybody thinks the earth is like a hard crust, but in fact it's flowing all the time, like a river. *(The* POET *does not respond.)* We're standing on the sea. . . . And this bench, why, imagine it's a lifeboat. *(Still no response from the* POET.*)* Every night I board this bench and sail away. Come on, we'll light out beyond the straits, down canal after canal, visiting harbour after harbour along the way.

POET: *(Impatiently.)* Enough of your nonsense, old woman!

OLD WOMAN: Look! The city lights are drawing farther and farther off. . . . Can't you hear the ship's horn?

POET: I hear nothing.

OLD WOMAN: You can't be a real poet, then.

POET: You're sure you haven't lost your marbles there, gran?

(The sound of a ship's horn startles the POET.*)*

OLD WOMAN: You heard that?

POET: . . . My ears must be playing tricks on me.

(The sound of the ship's horn.)

OLD WOMAN: Surely you heard that.

POET: *(Nodding.)* I used to dream of it a lot when I was a kid. A big ship, its white sail billowing out in the breeze, sailing right into the centre of town. . . .

OLD WOMAN: But you never knew what town that was.

POET: It wasn't a real town yet.

OLD WOMAN: A straight road lined with poplars.

POET: Wheels from the trucks sent up clouds of dust.

OLD WOMAN: Fields of yellow goldenrod, bending in the breeze.

POET: With one slaughterhouse, dropped there in the middle of nowhere.

OLD WOMAN: As far east as you can go.

POET: Behind the slaughterhouse, nothing but the sea.

(The backdrop silently opens on a dark sea.)

POET: It was a desolate sea. Each and every day, pig blood, rivers of it, stained the beach a thick black. It smelled awful. Not a blade of grass could grow on that beach. Nobody ever thought of going there.

OLD WOMAN: The mermaids did. They were the first to visit where the east ends.

(Crossing the dark sea, approaching the stage, is a boatload of mermaids and mermen. They are FATHER, MOTHER, SETSUO, HARUO, NATSUO, AKIO, FUYUO, and SHIKIO.)

MOTHER: Was it here, pop?

FATHER: Aye, it were.

SETSUO: We finally made it!

NATSUO: Finally! . . .

AKIO: We came a long way.

FATHER: Aye, it were a long way, all right.

POET: There's my dad, and my ma, and my big brothers!

FUYUO: Starting today, this'll be our town, won't it, pop?

FATHER: Right you are, my boy.

POET: *(Pointing at SHIKIO.)* And that's me, when I was young!

SHIKIO: What's this town called?

FATHER: Seatown.

OLD WOMAN: And this is where the town's legend begins.

MOTHER: Right now, kids! Get to work and make your mother rich!

(The town's form begins to emerge.)

POET: Is this a dream?

OLD WOMAN: And what if it was?

POET: I hated that place.

OLD WOMAN: That's no answer.

POET: Why? Why do I have to dream about that place again?

OLD WOMAN: Figure it out for yourself.

POET: I'm so sleepy.

OLD WOMAN: I'll sing for you. An old song. *(She sings.)*

With the water we were born
And with the water we will die
A long, long time ago,
We came from the sea
And mermaids were our mothers.

Each time summer comes round
The faraway sea trembles in my breast
And faraway memories tremble in my cupped hands.

With the water we were born
And with the water we will die
A long, long time ago,
We came from the sea
And mermaids were our mothers.

(There is a blackout during the song. When the lights come up again, a young woman is singing while she does the laundry. The young woman's name is GOLDFISH. *The town is a small one. There is a river running in front of the town. The* FATHER, MOTHER, HARUO, *and* SHIKIO *are all at work. Old* USELESS EUSTACE *is drinking saké.* YONG-HEE *is seated in a wheelchair. It is a bright early morning.* NATSUO *enters.)*

NATSUO: Nice voice you got there. *(*GOLDFISH *does not respond.)* You got a nice voice there. *(Still she is silent.)* I could swear I've heard your voice someplace before.

FATHER: Don't ask me why 'cause I don't know, but that girl can't seem to talk. Akio found her standing by the riverside. Soaked to the skin, she was.

SHIKIO: She's a little mermaid.

MOTHER: Don't talk nonsense.

*(*AKIO *enters. Throughout most of the play, he stutters.)*

AKIO: *(Stuttering a bit.)* Natsuo!

*(*NATSUO *gives him some money.)*

AKIO: Thanks, brother.

NATSUO: Why don't you get yourself a decent job?

AKIO: It's 'cause I stutter. I'd be a dead loss serving customers.

NATSUO: Fucking the dog, more like it.

AKIO: Ouch! *(Laughs.)*

NATSUO: No laughing matter. You never even try to get your hands dirty.

AKIO: Ain't there anywhere I can make some easy money?

NATSUO: Dream on!

AKIO: When I wake up in the morning, I wonder, just maybe, I might have been reborn as somebody different while I was asleep at night. Just like a fresh change of sheets. But when I open my eyes, I can see

I'm still the same, old sheets stained yellow with sweat.

NATSUO: So, what's yer point?

AKIO: Nothing special.

NATSUO: No money in boxing, let me tell you. But whatever you do, ya gotta give it yer all.

AKIO: "Gotta give it yer all"—how I hate that expression. Can't say it without stuttering.

NATSUO: Fat lot of good my advice is on you. In one ear and out the other.

AKIO: Ah, but you've got Jenny.

JENNY: *(Entering.)* You complaining about me again?

AKIO: I was just saying how pretty you are all the time.

JENNY: Come off it! *(To* NATSUO.*)* You didn't happen to nick any money out of my purse did you?

NATSUO: Uh uh.

JENNY: All right. But touch me savings and you'll never hear the end of it from me.

NATSUO: I know.

JENNY: That's money I've been saving up to send home, you know.

NATSUO: Yeah, yeah. I know.

JENNY: Come get me at eleven. *(*NATSUO *nods.* JENNY *rubs herself up against* NATSUO*'s body.)* I love you, my champion. *(She exits.)*

AKIO: *(Mimicking her.)* I love you, my champion.

NATSUO: Shut up, you idiot!

MOTHER: Akio, what're we gonna do with this here girl?

AKIO: Why don't you just leave her be? Ma's the only woman in this family who's any use to us.

MOTHER: That's cruel of you.

YONG-HEE: Forgive me! Forgive me! *(To* HARUO.*)* You were good enough to take me in as your wife, and look what happened—I became bed-ridden.

MOTHER: I'll never see my grandchildren's faces!

FATHER: You don't have to bloody shout it to the world!

MOTHER: You can shut yer trap.

YONG-HEE: I'd be better off dead.

*(*YONG-HEE *begins to howl. Upstairs,* MARLENE *is practising her voice lessons.)*

MOTHER: Shaddap!

MARLENE: You shaddap! All I ever hear out of you, every morning, is gripe, gripe, gripe.

MOTHER: Speak for yerself. Thumping up the stairs in the middle of night, a soul can scarce get a wink of sleep.

MARLENE: Got yer ears to the wall listening, I bet. You horny old cow.

MOTHER: Cow?! Hey, you. Tell her off for me. *(*FATHER *grins and shakes* *his head.)* What did I do to deserve this!

SETSUO: *(Enters, dressed in drag.)* Hey, ma, pop. Be seeing yous. *(He wafts out.)*

MOTHER: My firstborn, and it's been downhill ever since.

HARUO: Setsuo works in a gay bar and here I am, left with a family that's falling to bits—all 'cause pop's fucking useless.

MOTHER: What're you on about?

HARUO: Got yerself talked into buying stocks in some phoney deal and now we're up to our ears in debt.

FATHER: Those junk bonds, you mean?

MOTHER: Your dad's worked like a slave all his life for you children. If the family's falling to bits, that's only 'cause you've got no talent for the scrap metal business.

HARUO: And who needs talent for bleeding scrap metal?

NATSUO: Easy now! No sense fighting over this.

HARUO: Natsuo, I've got a favour to ask you. You inherit the family business. I'm not going to let myself get buried in this shit.

AKIO: Here we go again.

HARUO: I've got a bright future on the stage. "You can go to Siberia if you like, I don't give a shit. It's still your turn to sweep the floor!"

SHIKIO: Where's that from?

HARUO: *The Lower Depths.*¹

AKIO: The lower depths? How low can they get, them folks in the lower depths?

HARUO: Fetters. Fetters and chains. That's what's done me in.

YONG-HEE: Forgive me! Please, forgive me, Haruo! *(Weeps.)*

HARUO: I'm the one who ought to be crying here.

(The BARON *enters with a bag of articles to pawn on his back. The* BARONESS *throws something down to him from upstairs.)*

BARONESS: You're fucking useless!

BARON: Give me a break, for crissake!

BARONESS: All you care for is your bleeding boxing!

BARON: *(Worried about what the others may think.)* Give me a break, already!

BARONESS: Don't care to chip in and help the family out?

BARON: Who was it said she'd feed me? That she'd die without me?

BARONESS: I married a baron, not some bleeding layabout.

BARON: Evening, all.

FATHER: How's business?

BARON: The pits.

NATSUO: Sorry to hear that.

BARON: Nah, it's no matter, no matter at all. Things'll turn round, they always do. We'll rake up the cash.

MOTHER: That's what you say, but we ain't seen a penny yet.

BARON: The next gig will clinch it. Then it'll all be plain sailing, you'll see.

NATSUO: So, how come I ain't booked yet?

BARON: Don't you mind about that. All you need to care about is getting in shape.

(The BARON *exits.)*

NATSUO: *(Punching the wall.)* Fucking poor excuse for a promoter, won't set up a fight for me. Said I can't draw the customers. Says folks from Seatown don't want to see me win. What about me? Ain't I from Seatown too? I bleeding gave up everything to be champ!

(Blood is flowing from NATSUO's *fists.* GOLDFISH *takes his hands in hers and, tearing off a piece of cloth from the laundry, bandages them.)*

SHIKIO: *(Pointing at the cloth used to bandage* NATSUO's *hands.)* Ain't that ma's?

MOTHER: That's my silk chemise!

FATHER: Show off!

AKIO: *(To* NATSUO.*)* Natsuo, you ought to go off and train.

NATSUO: Yeah, yeah. *(To* GOLDFISH.*)* Ta. *(Exits.)*

AKIO: *(To* GOLDFISH.*)* Natsuo's got all sorts of stuff, but I got nothin'. I'm like a jellyfish. All I can do is flap me lips.

HARUO: Jellyfish are better off. Least they got no worries.

AKIO: Then, I'd like to be a jellyfish.

HARUO: A stuttering jellyfish?

AKIO: *(A bit offended, but quickly laughing it off.)* Yeah, yeah, a stuttering jellyfish. 'Cause I stuttered, nobody would bother me. The sea's big and all I'd have to do is float around flapping me lips.

EUSTACE: Same difference.

(Enter STELLA, KEWPIE, *and several other girls who are all new to Seatown, led by* FUYUO.*)*

FATHER: What's this?

FUYUO: Ah.

MOTHER: A bleeding tour group?

FUYUO: Ah.

(That is all FUYUO *can say.* MARLENE *comes downstairs.)*

MARLENE: Thanks, Fuyuo. I asked him to bring them here.

*(MARLENE *holds out an envelope to* FUYUO, *but* MOTHER *swipes it from her.)*

MOTHER: I'll send you the transportation bill later.

MARLENE: Full of piss and vinegar, you are.

MOTHER: I don't need no compliments out of you.

FUYUO: Ah.

MOTHER: I'll look after the cash.

FUYUO: Ah.

MOTHER: He'd just go off and buy some stupid computer game with it.

FUYUO: Ah.

MOTHER: Keep this up, boy, and you'll get yerself into trouble.

FUYUO: Ah.

MARLENE: *(To the girls.)* You start today.

KEWPIE: I never want to go hungry again. That's why I came to Seatown.

MARLENE : Then you're gonna have to sweat some for yer supper. Who knows? You got a shot at becoming another Madame Devi,[2] you know. Did you learn the song and dance routine I taught you?

GIRLS: Yes, ma'am!

MARLENE : Show me, then. A one, and a two, and a three. . . .

GIRLS: *(Singing.)*
Tonight, You're a merman,
Slipping and swimming ever so easy in my sea,
Parting the thick tangles of waterweed,
Diving deeper, ever deeper into me!
Tonight, you're a fisherman,
Plunging way, way down into my sea,
With your hard harpoon in your big strong hand,
Diving deeper, ever deeper into me!

(Fadeout. When the lights come up again, the POET *and the* OLD WOMAN *are sitting on the bench.)*

POET: Bustling town. Voices laughing, crying, yelling. Shining like the sun, falling like rain.

OLD WOMAN: Only what's long gone has a taste that's bittersweet.

POET: Who are you anyway, gran?

OLD WOMAN: That's the same as you asking yourself who you are.

POET: I don't understand. Why now am I dreaming of the past?

OLD WOMAN: The past is like a pebble lodged inside your shoe. You try to get rid of it, but you can't.

POET: Dreams. Who needs them?

OLD WOMAN: But who could live without them?

POET: Let's go back to the bench, gran.

OLD WOMAN: Why do you hate the past? That was your beloved hometown.

(The POET *takes a swig from his bottle.)*

OLD WOMAN: You shouldn't drink like that.

POET: It's all right. I'm an alcoholic. Can't manage without my drink.

OLD WOMAN: Some poet, you are.

POET: Hah! Just living in that town was like being on a bender. Monotonous and carnal. . . .

OLD WOMAN: So, is that why you cast that stone?

POET: What are you talking about?

OLD WOMAN: A little ripple expands until it turns into one big ring.

POET: What the hell are you talking about?

OLD WOMAN: You really are thick, aren't you? Are you suggesting you were just a kid playing pranks?

POET: Stoppit!

OLD WOMAN: The past isn't a playground for amnesiacs, you know. It's a scar that'll never heal.

POET: . . . I'm sleepy.

OLD WOMAN: Sleep, then. When you fall asleep, another you will wake up.

(SHIKIO enters. He throws a pebble.)

SHIKIO: Oh, Ondine, my water nymph! Come out, Ondine!

ONDINE: *(Rising out of the river.)* Shikio, don't come here.

SHIKIO: Why?

ONDINE: Because you ought to forget about me.

SHIKIO: No, I won't! . . . Why does everybody forget? I remember. How you looked that day. It was summer. You wore a yellow straw hat. A white dress with white sandals.

ONDINE: I'd just bought those sandals.

SHIKIO: The sandals bobbed up to the surface.

ONDINE: You must forget, Shikio.

SHIKIO: No!

ONDINE: Humans live to forget.

SHIKIO: I see it in my dreams. Always. A big ship, its white sail billowing out in the breeze, sailing straight into the centre of town. The breeze carried the scent of your hair that day. You were sailing on that ship.

ONDINE: Surely I'm nothing but reeking old bones now.

SHIKIO: A toy boat made of celluloid and fuelled by camphor. Here. *(He sets the boat on the river.)* It won't go.

ONDINE: A camphor boat will only sail in a tub. It'll only sail in the sea of a little round tub. . . . Grow up, Shikio.

SHIKIO: I don't want to grow up.

ONDINE: You'll have to cross that dark sea on your own. Not a phoney sea, but the real one.

SHIKIO: I don't like what's real.

ONDINE: There it is, right there. Take one step forward and there's the sea, where the sad-eyed mermaids swim. They inch along, fumbling in the dark of that vast, vague sea. . . . They're calling. . . . *(Straining her voice.)* Feel me! Feel me! Feel my heart. . . . *(She disappears into the river.)*

SHIKIO: Ondine!

(Fadeout.)

POET: That toy boat I bought by the red veranda where the cherry petals fell, I set it in the tub but it wouldn't go. It just drifted there, looking like it didn't know which way to turn. Then, I watched that town float

愛読者カード

お買い求めになった本の書名

ご感想

ご氏名		年齢
		（　　　）歳

ご住所（〒　　　）

TEL.　　　（　　　　）
下記注文書をご利用の際は、必ず電話番号をご記入下さい。

ご職業または在校名

◆書籍注文書◆

（小社刊行物のご注文にご利用下さい。その際は、必ず書店名をご記入下さい。）

書　名		〔本体価〕	円	〔部数〕	冊
書　名		〔本体価〕	円	〔部数〕	冊

ご指定書店名	取	この欄は書店または小社で記入します
所在地（市区町村名）	次	

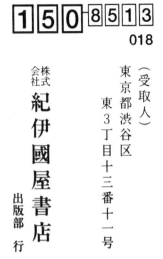
ご購入ありがとうございます。小社への要望事項、ならびにこの本の
ご感想をご記入下さい。今後の出版に活かしていきたいと存じます。
また、裏面の「書籍注文書」を小社刊行物のご注文にご活用下さい。
より早く確実にご指定の書店で購入できます。　紀伊國屋書店出版部

●通信欄● (小社への要望、出版を希望される分野など)

....

....

....

....

up from the bottom of the tub. I should have forgotten all about it.

(When the lights come up, HARUO *is standing by the waterside.* YONG-HEE *is in her wheelchair.* FATHER *and* MOTHER *are working.* GOLDFISH *is doing the laundry.* SETSUO *is making up his face.)*

HARUO: "Here lies the water; good. Here stands the man; good. If the man go to this water and drown himself, it is, will he, nill he, he goes—mark you that. But if the water come to him and drown him, he drowns not himself. Argal, he that is not guilty of his own death shortens not his own life."[3]

SETSUO: Where's that from?

HARUO: *Hamlet.*

SETSUO: Sounds tasty.

HARUO: You can't eat it.

SETSUO: Pity.

HARUO: Sure putting on the dog, aren't you.

SETSUO: Got a date.

HARUO: Date? You mean with a guy?

SETSUO: What else?

HARUO: What? In broad daylight?

SETSUO: It isn't like he was Godzilla, you know.

HARUO: Now, that ain't far off.

SETSUO: Shit, I hate mornings. My face is greasy and covered in stubble, a bleeding minefield for the makeup. The morning is a queen's worst enemy.

MOTHER: Setsuo, for heaven's sake, don't you care how you look to other folk?

SETSUO: If I cared how I looked I couldn't do this job.

MOTHER: What did I do to deserve this!

SETSUO: You used my foundation, didn't you, ma? *(*MOTHER *does not respond.)* That was expensive stuff.

MOTHER: I only used a wee bit.

SETSUO: I should be asking what I did to deserve this. Using your daughter's stuff behind her back.

MOTHER: You're my son.

SETSUO: But I've got a woman's heart.

(The foppish HORSE *sashays in.)*

HORSE: Setchan!

MOTHER, FATHER, HARUO: Setchan?

SETSUO: Horsy!

MOTHER, FATHER, HARUO: Horsy?

SETSUO: *(Hiding his face.)* Don't look! Under the light of the naked sun, I'm as ugly as Vivian Leigh.

HORSE: What're you saying, Setchan? You're a wild chrysanthemum in the sunlight.

SETSUO: But my little Horsy's as delicate as a gentian.

HARUO: I'm feeling sick.

HORSE: C'mon, Setchan. Let's go for a run on the beach.

SETSUO: But I don't have any swimming trunks.

HORSE: Two young guys like us don't need no swimming trunks.

HARUO: Shit, just trying to imagine that scene gives me the creeps.

SETSUO: I'll go, then. With you, my dear, I'd go to the ends of the earth if you asked me. I can't stop the love!

(SETSUO *and* HORSE *exit.*)

HARUO: There's no accounting for taste—now ain't that true!

JENNY: *(Entering.)* If you got something ya wanta say, then out with it, for crissake, and quit stalking me!

AKIO: *(Entering, offers her flowers.)* Here.

JENNY: What's this for?

AKIO: Your birthday. A little bird told me. . . .

JENNY: Where's Natsuo?

HARUO: Gone for a workout with the Baron.

JENNY: Nothin' but boxing, boxing from morn' till night. *(Accepts the flowers.)* I'll take these, but don't you get any ideas. *(Goes upstairs.)*

HARUO: What the fuck are you trying to pull? Messing around with your brother's girl.

AKIO: It ain't like she and Natsuo were married. What I do is me own business.

MOTHER: Akio, for crissake do something for that girl. The whole day long, all she ever does is the laundry.

AKIO: Maybe she likes the water.

MOTHER: She's bleeding washing the clothes ragged.

FUYUO: Ah.

MOTHER: What do you want?

FUYUO: Ah.

MOTHER: What did I do to deserve this? What did I ever do to deserve this?

AKIO: Hey, pop. Here. *(Gives FATHER an envelope.)*

FATHER: *(Peering inside the envelope.)* Where'd this cash come from?

AKIO: *(Smiling bashfully.)* Well, I. . . .

FATHER: Where the fuck did this cash come from?

AKIO: Don't get so bleeding worked up about it. It's money and it's a gift.

FATHER: And I'm asking where the fuck did it come from.

AKIO: Won it on the horses. You wouldn't believe how lucky I got.

FATHER: . . . Don't want it.

AKIO: How come?

FATHER: Don't want yer filthy money. *(Throws down the envelope.)*

AKIO: Money's money, ain't it? Earned by the sweat of my brow or not, where it comes from don't make no difference.

FATHER: Don't touch ill-gotten gains—never heard that expression?

AKIO: Thought it might help out at home. That's why I gave it you.

FATHER: We've done all we could. Lord knows we have.

AKIO: That's rich, coming from somebody who blew the family savings on junk bonds.

FATHER: I never caused nobody no grief doing that.

AKIO: Me neither, at the horses.

FATHER: Who lent you the money to bet on the horses?

AKIO: Natsuo. And I'll pay him back, every penny.

FATHER: I don't like what I'm hearing. Not one bit.

AKIO: Didn't Natsuo get the cash from Jenny in the first place?

FATHER: Natsuo hadn't any choice.

AKIO: What?!

FATHER: Natsuo's dedicated himself to boxing. Heart and soul.

AKIO: So he can do what he fucking pleases 'cause he's "dedicated"?

FATHER: That ain't what I said.

AKIO: Yeah, and I gave the horses me heart and soul too. So take the fucking cash.

MOTHER: Why don't you cut the boy a bit of slack, pop?

FATHER: Don't want it. Don't need it.

AKIO: Pop, all you ever think of is Natsuo. *(Exits.)*

FATHER: Idiot.

MOTHER: Don't be so hard on the boy.

FATHER: I'm only telling him what he needs to hear. So long as he don't get a decent job, he'll continue going around spouting off like a spoiled brat.

HARUO: Time's have changed, pop.

FATHER: What?!

HARUO: You've done your best, and you're still not able to save any money.

FATHER: Ain't it enough that we can eat?

HARUO: Hanging on for dear life to the scrap metal business, we'll be dead in the water.

FATHER: Things'll pick up again for sure. This ain't the first storm we've weathered.

MOTHER: Your dad's right, you know.

HARUO: The next storm is going to lay us flat.

FATHER: A breakwater protects this town, I'll have you know. The wind might whip up a few waves, but nothing too big. That's why our town's prospered.

HARUO: And just as a tiny crack in the dam will start a flood, even now our town is crumbling.

FATHER: A spring that'll never dry runs under this town. If one well should dry up, then all we need do is dig another. Anybody can find a fresh spring if he tries.

MOTHER: Your pop's right, you know.

HARUO: Yeah, and look where it's got us. Hanging on for dear life here till the bitter end. See for yourself, this stinking sewer of a town.

FATHER: Things'll pick up again, for sure.

MOTHER: Your pop's right, you know.

(The BARON *enters with* NATSUO, *who is shadowboxing.)*

BARON: One two, one two! Beautiful, Natsuo. Listen everybody! Natsuo's got himself a fight.

MOTHER: Is it true?

BARON: It's a month from now. He's fighting Hammer Hosoi.

MOTHER: That ain't much of a name.

BARON: He'll be a tough nut to crack.

NATSUO: It'll be a fucking sideshow. Even if I beat him, it's not a title bout. Just a couple of idiots slugging it out in the ring. I'm no better than a circus monkey.

BARON: Where's that old spirit, eh? Natsuo.

NATSUO: Why do I bother fighting?

BARON: So's you can win, of course.

NATSUO: What's the point of winning?

BARON: Glory.

NATSUO: Ain't seen none of that. The more I keep winning, the more folks in Seatown look at me like I was some kinda worm. Why is that? Why's the boxing world like that? Ain't it supposed to be that the winner gets the praise?

BARON: Your time will come. Soon.

FATHER: Natsuo, at least we're proud of you. The family's proud of you.

MOTHER: That's right.

JENNY: *(From the third floor.)* Natsuo! Come here for a second.

NATSUO: What?

JENNY: Just come here!

NATSUO: What do you want with me? *(About to go. Then addresses* GOLDFISH.*)* Not singing today? *(*GOLDFISH *is silent.)* I always feel better when I hear you sing.

JENNY: Natsuo!

NATSUO: What're you all worked up about?

JENNY: My music box is gone!

NATSUO: So what if a music box is missing?

JENNY: My account book and seal were in it!

(They all gaze at one other instinctively. Fadeout.)

OLD WOMAN: You were the one who took the music box, weren't you?

POET: I meant to give it right back.

OLD WOMAN: But you couldn't.

POET: I never thought it'd turn into such a big scene.

(When the lights come up, GOLDFISH *is doing the laundry.* SHIKIO *enters. He shows the music box to* GOLDFISH.*)*

SHIKIO: I didn't mean to steal it. Honest! *(*GOLDFISH *says nothing.)* What'll I do now?

*(*GOLDFISH *drops the music box into the river, then puts her finger to her mouth.* AKIO *enters and* SHIKIO *leaves.)*

AKIO: If my brothers didn't like me no more, that'd be the end of me.

*(*GOLDFISH *throws a bucket of water into the river.)*

AKIO: What the hell are you doing? *(*GOLDFISH *points at the river.)* Goldfish? *(*GOLDFISH *nods.)* Look at 'em swim!

GOLDFISH: Bought them at a stall at the fair.

AKIO: You can talk? *(*GOLDFISH *nods.)* How come you said nothing till now? *(She does not reply.)* Why'd you set free the goldfish?

GOLDFISH: 'Cause they're me. . . . Stuck in a square tub, fished out with hooks that tear their lips, and no place to escape. Just like me.

AKIO: Where you from?

GOLDFISH: Faraway.

AKIO: Won't go home?

GOLDFISH: I can't say.

AKIO: What're you gonna do? Stay here forever?

GOLDFISH: I don't know.

AKIO: Doesn't make no difference what I ask, you dunno, eh?

GOLDFISH: Why did you save me?

AKIO: I couldn't just stand idly by and watch ya drown, could I.

GOLDFISH: I wasn't drowning. . . . Actually, I wanted to die. . . . *(She clutches* AKIO*'s shoulders, then beats on his chest.* AKIO *backs away.)* Why'd you save me? Why, why'd you save me?

AKIO: You wanta die again?

GOLDFISH: I wanted to die, but I ended up living after all. That day the little fish inside me was hooked on the line made of your saliva. That fish should've gone to sleep but it shouted instead, "I want to live, I want to have another chance at life!"

AKIO: And so you should. People have any number of chances at life. You never know. Your chance may be waiting for you here, or maybe someplace else. *(*GOLDFISH *does not reply.)* This is what I think—if only you get the chance, a real chance to discover who you really are, then you can change your life. If you can do that, you can find a way to go on living. . . . Me, you, any of us can find a way. . . .

GOLDFISH: It's out there somewhere for me to find?

AKIO: Absolutely. I'm sure you can. . . . What's your name?

GOLDFISH: Goldfish. . . . I'm the Goldfish caught on your line. The little red fish that first started to swim about in your bucket.

*(*GOLDFISH *bites* AKIO*'s finger, and from her mouth there extends a long*

red thread. Fadeout.)

ACT II

(Lights up on a noodle wagon being minded by AKIO *and* GOLDFISH. FATHER, MOTHER, YONG-HEE, HARUO, SHIKIO, KEWPIE, *and* STELLA *are eating ramen.* FUYUO *is playing some distance away.* USELESS EUSTACE *and* JENNY *are drinking saké.)*

AKIO: Eat up! Eat up, folks! To celebrate our opening, everything's half price.

GOLDFISH: Eat up, everybody!

MOTHER: We're family. You oughta make it free.

AKIO: Uh uh. Me and Goldfish got debts to pay off.

MOTHER: You mean to team up with this here girl?

AKIO: Uh huh. We plan to open a shop together.

MOTHER: You all right with that? You don't even know where she comes from!

AKIO: She's like one of the family, she is.

MOTHER: Well, I have to admit, it does me good just to see you working for a change. Ain't that right, hon'?

FATHER: Mmm!

MOTHER: What?

FATHER: This ramen's tasty!

MOTHER: What the hell are you talking about?

YONG-HEE: *(To* HARUO.*)* Have my ramen, will you? I feel like puking.

HARUO: Mind yer mouth.

YONG-HEE: I'm gonna die.

HARUO: Listen to ya. Practically packed away all the noodles too.

YONG-HEE: Folk get greedy knowing it's their last meal.

HARUO: Speak for yourself.

YONG-HEE: Hey, d'ya think there really is a heaven?

EUSTACE: There is if you believe in one.

YONG-HEE: There'd be no more pain if I went there?

EUSTACE: No pain at all.

YONG-HEE: In that case, I'll live a wee bit longer. Don't matter if I've got to suffer some more—I'll live a bit longer and fill me belly with some decent grub.

HARUO: You'll live longer than me, for crissake.

MARLENE: *(Entering.)* You still eating, Kewpie?

KEWPIE: I was hungry!

MARLENE: Ain't nothin' uglier than a stripper with her belly stuck out.

KEWPIE: But that's why I came to Seatown—so's I wouldn't go hungry.

MARLENE: *(To* AKIO.*)* How's business?

AKIO: Fine, thanks to the money you invested.

MARLENE: Hey, it's give and take, right? Besides, I'm charging interest.

JENNY: Aren't you free with your money, though. No way they're gonna pay you back.

MARLENE: Sure they will.

JENNY: Thieves, the lot of them.

MARLENE: You still holding a grudge, are you?

JENNY: Those were me life savings!

MARLENE: But you went to the bank and found out nobody took any of yer money. You even got yerself a new passbook. Right?

JENNY: So what?

MARLENE: You're drunk, ain't ya?

JENNY: So? What if they *had* taken the money?

MARLENE: All's well that ends well.

JENNY: Easy for you to say.

MARLENE: You're the one who's changed. Money, money, that's all you ever talk about now.

JENNY: Give us a break! We all got to work, don't we?

MARLENE: Not just for the money.

JENNY: What else for?

MARLENE: For the family.

JENNY: Rubbish.

MARLENE: What about you? Aren't you working to send money home? (JENNY *does not reply.*) We're all in the same boat here. Why, if it wasn't for that, Stella and Kewpie here wouldn't be out on the streets.

STELLA: I want to go home, I want to go home right now, to that green island I come from.

JENNY: Now, don't you start griping on us. If we went home empty-handed, a cold welcome we'd be getting, let me tell you. Folks chipped in to send us away.

BARON: *(Entering.)* Evening, all. What's with the long faces? Akio's opened his noodle wagon and Natsuo's got a bout to defend his title— that's plenty of cause for celebration today. So, I'll sing you a song.
(*Accompanied by* SETSUO *and a team of cheerleaders, he sings a torch song.*[4])

SETSUO: That stunk! Shit, Baron, you can't put torch songs and cheerleaders together.

BARON: It's you that's out of place. You mean you can't put a bleeding queen and cheerleaders together.

SETSUO: Whatever. Fact is, I'm Elizabeth Taylor.

BARON: Excuse me?

SETSUO: My natural born elegance, the "flower" of my talent. Ah, the eyes of the audience are all upon me. I'm dazzled.

BARON: Nobody's looking at you.

SETSUO: *(To the audience.)* You musn't, you know. You're falling in love with me.

BARON: Falling in trouble's more like it.

SETSUO: The audience is waiting for us. Come, Baron. Try and try again.

BARON: Ladies and gentlemen, I'm sorry to have kept you waiting so long. We've had our troubles, we've had our tears, we've toed the primrose path and weathered the storms to bring you the flower of our hearts, the Way of the Torch Song. I, the Baron, will be your balladeer this evening.

(A gong rings. Lights up on the bout between NATSUO *and* HAMMER HOSOI. NATSUO, *hit by* HAMMER HOSOI *with a counterpunch, falls to the mat, blood streaming from one eye. The referee begins to count to ten, but* NATSUO *does not rise. The spectators mill around the ring. Blackout as the count goes to "eight, nine, ten." The gong rings again. Lights up on the* POET *and the* OLD WOMAN.)

POET: That was Natsuo's first defeat in the ring. He seemed to crumple to the mat in slow motion. A pool of blood grew on that white mat. The crowd stood round, transfixed by shock and fear. You want to blame me for that too?

OLD WOMAN: People gathered in search of some kind of bond. . . . Gradually, their numbers grew, until they had created a little town, a town that was a stew of all sorts of feelings—joy, anger, sadness, pleasure. But people got sick and tired of eating the same stew day in, day out. They wanted something with a stronger, more exciting flavour. And that's when the bonds started to chafe.

POET: You telling me my stealing the music box started all this?

OLD WOMAN: Don't get so worked up about it. All I'm saying is it took just one little event to set things off.

POET: Why blame me?

OLD WOMAN: You blame yourself. No sense scratching and gnawing at your own heart like that, surely. The only blood you're going to let will be your own.

POET: . . . I'm sleepy.

OLD WOMAN: Sweet dreams, then.

POET: I don't want to sleep.

(Lights up on NATSUO *and* USELESS EUSTACE. *They are drinking. The* BARON *is reading some kind of textbook. Next to him sits* FUYUO. SETSUO *is making up his face;* FATHER *and* MOTHER *are silently working.* HARUO *is standing there vacantly.* YONG-HEE *is knitting.)*

NATSUO: I won't turn out like Jack Johnson, I tell ya. No way I'm gonna let myself just stand there and get slugged. I don't wanta be hurt. I don't wanta lose. Not even if they have to drag me dead out of the ring, I won't go down to defeat.

EUSTACE: I know already.

NATSUO: I'll let off fireworks in town, red rockets in the night sky, like

Carpentier.

EUSTACE: Carpentier's fireworks were blue.

NATSUO: You don't know what the fuck I'm talking about. Nobody understands.

JENNY: *(Entering.)* Ready to go, hon'?

NATSUO: Don't want to.

JENNY: What're you saying? I promised the manager at the cabaret we'd both be there.

NATSUO: I might wither and waste away, but once I was champ.

JENNY: Maybe so, but now you're just a Cyclops.

NATSUO: What the fuck—!

JENNY: Ya can gripe all ya like but it ain't gonna change nothing. Ya still gotta eat. Ya can't waste your life moping around all the time.

NATSUO: . . .

JENNY: As for meself, I've got no choice but to go home once my artist's visa expires. What'll ya do then? *(NATSUO does not reply.)* Cheer the fuck up.

NATSUO: I ain't going.

JENNY: Come on, surely it ain't wrong to make a bit of money. Don't make me the breadwinner all the time!

NATSUO: Money—that's all you ever talk about.

JENNY: That's what makes the world go round—money.

NATSUO: Show me a little kindness, why don't you.

JENNY: You've got a lotta nerve saying that! After all I done for you.

NATSUO: Kicking me when I'm down.

JENNY: Gimme a break already. I'd like a bit of kindness too. Don't think you're the only one who can pull a long face like some tragic hero. . . . Didn't I find that job as barker at the cabaret for you?

NATSUO: Yeah, thanks a million.

JENNY: If that's how ya feel, I'd have been better off hitching up with Akio. Seems he had a thing for me. Missed me chance.

(NATSUO hits her.)

JENNY: You're scum. *(Exits.)*

SETSUO: Love's a game, lover boy, so you'd better play it with a bit more style.

HARUO: Got another date?

SETSUO: That's right.

HARUO: With that "Horsy"?

SETSUO: This time with "Deery." Oh, I'm a sinful woman!

DEER: *(Entering.)* Setsu baby!

SETSUO: Call me "Queeny."

DEER: Queeny, I've come for you.

SETSUO: That's got a nice ring to it. Thank God I'm twisted!

HARUO: The whole world's gone mad.

SETSUO: I'm off. You dirty dog, you.

DEER: *(Happily.)* Yes, your Highness.

   (DEER and SETSUO exit.)

MOTHER: What ever did I do to deserve this! Tell me, what did I do?
Where did we go wrong? Didn't we teach him right? Honey!

FATHER: Leave him be.

BARON: Come home, ma! Come home! I beg you, PLEASE! Any better?
(Pause.)

FUYUO: Ah.

HARUO: *(To MOTHER.)* What's up with him?

MOTHER: The Baron's wife ran out on him and he's going on TV, on one
of them talk shows. He's taking lessons from Fuyuo on how to show
how sorry he's feeling.

BARON: I was wrong. I can't begin to tell ya just how bleeding sorry I
am! How's that?

FUYUO: Ah.

BARON: Thanks, Fuyuo. Shit, I hope this works and she comes home to
me.

MOTHER: Sure she will. Now, we got to figure out what you owe us.

BARON: You mean, you're charging me a fee for that?

MOTHER: Why, of course we is. Time is money, as the saying goes.
Didn't Fuyuo spend some of his valuable time to teach you all he
knows?

BARON: All hell's broken loose at the gym too, ya know. It's like I've
been hit with a double punch.

MOTHER: *(Punching the calculator.)* This is the figure.

BARON: What do you bleeding take me for? *(Hands her some money.)*

HARUO: Wish I could remember Shylock's line.

MOTHER: Forget it. It wouldn't do you no good anyway.

HARUO: Maybe not for you, ma. But for me, it would.

MOTHER: Quit dreaming, boy. You can't dine on dreams.

HARUO: I ain't like the rest of you. My organism's not poisoned with
alcohol.[5]

MOTHER: What the fuck are you on about?

FATHER: *(He is making stilts out of tin cans for FUYUO.)* Here ya go, tin
shoes to stand on.

FUYUO: Ah.

MOTHER: Pop, don't you think we oughta take this boy to hospital one of
these days?

FATHER: Don't talk rubbish. How could we dump our own flesh and
blood in a place like that?

FUYUO: Ah.

HARUO: *(To NATSUO.)* Natsuo, if you ain't gonna box no more, how 'bout
taking over the family business for me?

NATSUO: And what'll you do?

HARUO: I'll leave this town, start a new life.

YONG-HEE: If that's what you want, dear, why, I'll follow you anywheres. *(*HARUO *does not reply.* AKIO *enters with* GOLDFISH.*)*

AKIO: *(Handing an envelope to* MOTHER.*)* Here, ya go, ma.

MOTHER: Ta, Akio. You're a godsend. The only one I got.

AKIO: *(To* NATSUO.*)* Hey, Natsuo. You're not going to the cabaret with Jenny? Is that all right? *(*NATSUO *does not answer.)* And she's the one who got you that job in the first place.

NATSUO: You lecturing me?

AKIO: I ain't lecturing nobody.

NATSUO: Then what would you call it? Bullshitting?

AKIO: I'm just concerned about you.

NATSUO: Words can dress up anything. But what people think is another matter altogether. Can't trust anybody with a glib tongue. They'll talk you up and kiss yer ass, then suck you dry.

AKIO: You can't spend yer whole life stuck on boxing.

NATSUO: None of you know what the fuck I feel!

AKIO: Easy does it! *(Hands* NATSUO *some money.)*

NATSUO: Ten thousand yen? Is that all the champ's worth now?

MOTHER: Natsuo, that's a lot of money for Akio!

NATSUO: So that's what I've become, eh? A sponge! *(Exits.)*

MOTHER: What'll we do with that boy?

HARUO: I know just how he feels.

FATHER: Again and again, you have to drink bitter water. That's what life's all about. Water's clear and you don't know till you drink it if it's bitter or sweet. And if you're thirsty, then you got no choice but to drink it. No way a man can survive if he don't like to drink. I've been made to drink bitter water time and time again. Like it or not, ya gotta drink. Ya got no choice.

(Blackout. When the lights come up again, GOLDFISH *is dipping her legs into the water.* SHIKIO *watches her.* NATSUO *enters and* SHIKIO *hides himself.)*

NATSUO: Does that feel good? *(*GOLDFISH *nods.)* You sure is a lovely sight. It always does me heart good to see you. . . . What is it about this town? All anybody ever thinks about is money. Everybody, except for you, that is. *(He pours some water over* GOLDFISH's *legs.)* . . . I could swears I heard your voice someplace before. *(She does not respond.)* But I can't for the life of me remember where. *(She dries her legs with a towel.)* You can talk, can't ya. So how come ya never speak when I'm around. . . . Not like I ever tried to do anything wrong to you. *(She makes to leave, but he grabs her hand.)* All I wanta do is talk to you.

GOLDFISH: You lonely? *(*NATSUO *does not reply.)* Lonely people, I understand them. Deep in their eyes there's a fish asleep, a fish that's swallowed a hook. That fish would give anything for somebody to pull that hook out. *(*NATSUO *tries to speak, but she cuts him off.)* But I can't pull out the hook you've swallowed. . . .

NATSUO: I feel so bad. I just want somebody who can understand me. I've never felt this way before and don't know which way to turn. It's like there was this dark sea inside of me.

GOLDFISH: Go ahead and cry, cry your heart out. That's what I do. That dark sea inside of you will start to churn and shift a bit.

NATSUO: Goldfish, what I need is somebody who'll stand by me.

GOLDFISH: I can't help you. I've got Akio.

NATSUO: Akio can look after himself.

GOLDFISH: No he can't. He lacks what I have and has what I lack. But you, you lack for nothing.

NATSUO: But ever since I lost me eye I've been just like the rest of you.

GOLDFISH: That's not what I mean.

NATSUO: Nobody in this world has got everything.

GOLDFISH: You can fend for yourself. You don't have to force yourself to fit in. You'd only jam up the works if you did. . . . *(She exits.)*

NATSUO: Whose breast should I cry on? I wanted to cry on the breast of Mother Time. But Time don't need me no more. Time's pulled away from me like the tide. How should I live? I call out, but there's no answer. The dark sea says nothing, does nothing but churn and churn. *(He punches the surface of the water.)*

OLD WOMAN: Look carefully. Your second crime begins now.

SHIKIO: *(Approaching* NATSUO.*)* Don't fool yourself, brother. That girl's no mermaid.

NATSUO: Mermaid? Mermaids don't exist, never have.

SHIKIO: She got into trouble in the town down the way.

NATSUO: What kinda trouble?

SHIKIO: She used to chat up guys on the telephone.

NATSUO: . . . That voice.

SHIKIO: She fooled 'em all. Had 'em all for fools.

NATSUO: Who told you this?

SHIKIO: The guy who came to buy second-hand TVs.

NATSUO: You musn't tell anybody this. *(*SHIKIO *nods.)*

POET: That was the truth.

OLD WOMAN: Didn't you tell me you didn't like the truth?

POET: . . . It was so filthy, I couldn't. . . .

OLD WOMAN: Isn't it the poet's job to turn what's filthy into lovely words?

POET: I was still a kid.

OLD WOMAN: Yeah, a kid nurturing stinking bones to his breast. . . .

POET: Stop it!

OLD WOMAN: All you have to do is forgive. Forgive yourself.

POET: I can't! No way I can forgive myself!

(ONDINE rises out of the water, holding the music box in her hands.)

ONDINE: Shikio, why did you have to say that?

SHIKIO: It pissed me off.

ONDINE: What?

SHIKIO: My brother, being duped by that woman.

ONDINE: She didn't dupe anybody.

SHIKIO: How would you know?

ONDINE: You were the one who threw the music box into the water, right? You didn't break it, you just dropped it in the water. . . . You didn't want to see your brothers taken away, did you? *(SHIKIO does not respond.)* People change. You'll change too.

SHIKIO: How come they change? They change their personalities as easy as an overcoat.

ONDINE: That's just the way it is.

SHIKIO: It stinks!

ONDINE: They may laugh when they're changing, but they're hurting just the same. . . . Shikio, I won't come again, not even if you call me.

SHIKIO: Why?

ONDINE: I'll be gone. . . . You never know what you've got till it's gone. . . .
(She slips under the water.)

SHIKIO: Don't leave me here! Don't leave me alone!
(Blackout.)

POET: She was as good as her word. I never saw her again. No matter how many pebbles I threw into the river, all they ever stirred up were ripples. Then they buried the river.
(Blackout. When the lights come up, NATSUO is on the telephone. From the receiver come the sound of waves and the voice of GOLDFISH, singing.)

GOLDFISH: *(Singing.)* Shall we cast her away?
   The canary's forgotten her song.
   Cast her away with the kerria rose,
   The rose that bore no fruit,
   And the strawberry ice that melted,
   Cast them all away,
   On a moonless night, a starless night,
   Cast them all away, away?[6]

NATSUO: . . . I waited and waited, waited so long for you. . . .
(Blackout. When the lights come up GOLDFISH and AKIO are pulling their noodle cart.)

GOLDFISH: Look how beautiful the moon is tonight, dear.

AKIO: Ah, it's lovely.

GOLDFISH: We did a fair bit of business again tonight.

AKIO: Thanks to you.

GOLDFISH: It's 'cause our ramen's tasty.

AKIO: Each and every day's just like a dream. Life's so good to us. . . .
It's like we was sleeping on a ship, sailing out to sea in the springtime.

GOLDFISH: Hope we sell lots of ramen tomorrow too.

AKIO: We'll sell lots of ramen and sail off to the moon together, just the
two of us.

GOLDFISH: And what'll we do when we get there?

AKIO: Run a noodle cart.

GOLDFISH: Same old thing.

AKIO: That's right, same old thing. There we'd be, on the shining moon,
looking up at the blue, blue earth, making noodles together.

GOLDFISH: What'll we do for customers?

AKIO: Who needs customers? I'll make the noodles and you, you'll just
park yourself there and let the time go by. That's enough for us.
(NATSUO *approaches with* HORSE *and* DEER.)

AKIO: We're closed for the night, brother.

NATSUO: I ain't come for no noodles. I'm here to give you a bit of
advice.

AKIO: Advice?

NATSUO: Akio, have you any idea what kind of woman you've got here?
(AKIO *does not answer.*) She used to make a living picking up guys
over the phone. *(Still no response from* AKIO.*)* You'd call a number and
hear a recorded message with a woman's voice, a voice singing over
the sound of waves. You'd leave a message where you want to meet
her and she'd show up there. . . . She was notorious in the next town
over, called herself the Siren.

AKIO: Quit kidding around.

NATSUO: These two left her messages over the phone.

HORSE: Hey, Goldfish. It's me. Remember me?

DEER: No way you'd have forgotten me.

GOLDFISH: Never seen you in my life, either of you.

HORSE: Show us some heart.
(HORSE *and* DEER *sit down like they were old friends of hers.*)

AKIO: You leave her alone.

NATSUO: Akio, I'm only telling what's good for you. You'd be better off
without her.

AKIO: I couldn't give a damn what Goldfish might've done.

NATSUO: Might catch some kinda disease from her. And folks like her
noodles, eh?

AKIO: You gonna smear her, is that what you mean to do, Natsuo?

NATSUO: All I'm saying is, rumours are awful things. Right? (AKIO *does
not respond.*) Ya oughta leave her. Do it tomorrow. Nah, make it
tonight.

AKIO: Forget it.

NATSUO: Now, you don't have to go get smart with me.

AKIO: If it don't work out in this town, we'll just move on to the next.

NATSUO: Word has a way of getting around.

AKIO: In that case, we'll go to the moon.

NATSUO: *(Laughing.)* The moon?

AKIO: You're jealous.

NATSUO: What have I got to be jealous of you for?

AKIO: Your luck's run out and you're jealous 'cause your no-good little brother is making a decent living and doing just fine with Goldfish.

NATSUO: Say any more and you'll get it. Don't care if you are my little brother.

AKIO: Leave us alone.

NATSUO: It'll be interesting to see how many customers you get tomorrow.

AKIO: You smear me and I won't let you get away with it!

NATSUO: What can a stutterer do to me?

(AKIO lunges at NATSUO, but is held back by HORSE and DEER. NATSUO punches AKIO in the belly and drags GOLDFISH behind the noodle cart.)

GOLDFISH: Akio! Akio!

NATSUO: I'll show you what kind of woman she is!

GOLDFISH: Stop it! Help me, Akio!

AKIO: Goldfish! Goldfish!

(HORSE and DEER hold AKIO back. GOLDFISH screams. Presently, NATSUO emerges from behind the cart.)

AKIO: Why? Why'd you do it? . . . We're brothers, ain't we?

NATSUO: It's 'cause we're brothers that I couldn't let her get away with it.

(AKIO punches NATSUO, who strikes him back. The two brothers launch into a no-holds-barred fistfight. AKIO falls to the ground.)

NATSUO: I am the champ!

(NATSUO leaves with HORSE and DEER. GOLDFISH emerges, her clothing in disarray.)

GOLDFISH: Akio! Akio! *(AKIO does not respond.)* Say something, Akio. *(Still he does not reply.)* What should I do? *(Still no answer.)* What should I do?

AKIO: Let's go. . . .

GOLDFISH: I don't want to. . . . Help me, Akio. Help me.

AKIO: I want to be strong. . . .

(The silhouettes of several women are illuminated through the room's curtain.)

WOMEN: *(Singing.)* Sleep, my child,
My hungry, weeping child,
The blue bird of happiness

Will come to your dreams,
So feast on her feathers,
All's not what it seems.

Sleep, child, for tomorrow
Will bring more sorrow
More sorrow and more fear,
So sleep now, sleep, my dear.
(The POET *sleeps. Blackout.)*

INTERLUDE

*(*HARUO *enters.)*

HARUO: "Farewell to this world, and to the night farewell. We who walk
the road to death, to what should we be likened? To the frost on the
way to Adashigahara, a dream within a dream. Have pity upon us!"[7]
. . . Fuck it! Don't matter what I do, I make it all sound so, so
theatrical. And I still can't remember Shylock's speech. Shit, I love the
theatre. But I've had enough. This is the end. The time's come for me
to face death, there in the raging surf. Right, then! So, ta ta,
everybody! *(He throws himself into the river.)*
VOICE 1: Suicide!
VOICE 2: Who is it?
VOICE 1: The Kanemoto kid, Haruo!
(Enter FATHER, MOTHER, SETSUO, FUYUO, *and* YONG-HEE.*)*
ALL: Bloody hell!
(They desperately drag HARUO *out of the river.* FATHER *puts his ear to*
HARUO*'s chest.)*
MOTHER: Is he dead, pop?
FATHER: Still ticking.
YONG-HEE: Haruo!
HARUO: *(Waking.)* Am I still alive?
FATHER: Bloody right you is. Think you'd kill yerself jumping in where
it's shallow? Best you could expect was a knock on the head.
HARUO: A joke. Life's a bleeding joke.
(Blackout.)

ACT III

(Several boxers are lined in ranks, shadowboxing. AKIO *is among them. It
is the* BARON*'s gym.)*

BARON: Ya gotta be hungry. Ya gotta be tough if ya want to get ahead.
Fact is, the most important thing in boxing, more important than skill,
or power, or stamina, or any of them things, is the will to survive. But

that's not all. Boxing's now entered the age of Science.

MOTHER: *(Entering.)* Akio, I brought your lunch.

AKIO: Can't eat right now.

MOTHER: How come?

AKIO: I'm practising abstinence.

MOTHER: Abstinence. What's that?

AKIO: I can't eat.

BARON: I tell you, Mrs. Kanemoto, Akio's in absolutely top form. He's got a good shot at world champion.

MOTHER: I hate boxing. People are in it only to make money, beating each other's brains out.

BARON: It's not for the money.

MOTHER: I want my boy to get involved in something more respectable. What the hell's he doing if he can't eat?

BARON: It's for the dream. The dream all men have.

AKIO: Not me.

MOTHER: Why don't you come home? *(*AKIO *does not respond.)* Did something happen between you and Natsuo? *(Still he does not answer.)* How come you quit the noodle stand? *(Still no reply.)* Is it all 'cause of that woman?

AKIO: She didn't have nothing to do with it.

NATSUO: *(Entering.)* Hey!

BARON: Hey, Natsuo. How're ya doing?

NATSUO: Looks like things have picked up round here.

BARON: And about time too. It was hard to fill the hole you left, kiddo.

NATSUO: Hey, I'd be back in the ring in a flash if you asked me. . . . Former champ, one-eyed boxer makes astounding comeback. It'd get a lot of play.

BARON: Now that's what I call a circus act.

NATSUO: If I couldn't get in the ring, then I could be coach, or even just trainer.

BARON: We're doing fine right now.

NATSUO: I can't get the smell of pine resin out of me nostrils. When I rub the toes of me shoes they squeak. The sound makes me blood boil.

BARON: Natsuo, it hurts me to have to tell you this, but your days are over. An old-fashioned boxer like you, all he had to do was keep plugging away like a madman. But what we need nowadays is Science, Science and that hungry spirit. It's time for a guy like Akio.

NATSUO: I tell you, I still got it in me. What say I gave Akio a try in the ring?

BARON: You quit when you were ahead. These kids here got an image of you burned in their brains, like you was Apollo or something. That goes for me too. . . .

NATSUO: I'll beat the shit out of him!

AKIO: I'm ready for you!

BARON: Haven't I taught you boxing's a science, Akio?

MOTHER: Stoppit! Please, stoppit! What are you trying to prove, two brothers beating each other's brains out? I didn't give birth to yous just so you'd hate each other's guts.

NATSUO: Let's have it out, then! (AKIO *is reluctant to take up the challenge.*) All right, come on!

(AKIO *goes into a fighting position. Suddenly,* GOLDFISH *is heard singing, "Shall we cast her away?"* AKIO *and* NATSUO *falter.*)

GOLDFISH: *(Entering.)* Anyone for ramen? Bowl of hot noodles? Folks tell me, when I started out just on my own, they weren't as tasty as before, my tears made the soup too salty. But when word got around that I was still selling ramen, why, people wanted to see what all the fuss was about. I made money hand over fist. Others' hard luck makes for a sweet sauce. Word's got around my cooking's improved. That's why I came—tell me if there's something missing, or you can't figure out what that flavour is. Are the noodles al dente? Is the soup not too salty? How 'bout the slices of roast pork, not too thin, are they? Feel free to tell me what you think.

BARON: Akio's abstaining.

GOLDFISH: All I need you to tell me is if it tastes good or not. If you don't like my noodles, I'll slink out, tail between my legs. But if you tell me you like them, then I'll feel my life hasn't been in vain. *(Holds out a bowl of noodles.)*

NATSUO: Here, let me try 'em. (GOLDFISH *spills the noodles.*) Slut!

GOLDFISH: I'm no slut. When I heard those voices over the phone, each time I thought, maybe this time I can believe him, maybe now I can believe. Each time, those voices—men I'd never met before—sounded so sweet, so gentle. So I'd run out to meet them. But they'd betray me, betray me with a one-night stand. Words with no shape or form to them betrayed me. Still, I went on believing. Not what I heard over the phone, but what they told me to my face. . . . There's nothing I believe anymore.

(GOLDFISH *exits.* NATSUO *follows after her.*)

BARON: He's a goner. Ain't it a corker how fast folks can fall.

MOTHER: He ain't a goner yet. So long as we're still a family, he'll get back on his feet. I'm sure of it.

(Blackout. The OLD WOMAN *and the* POET.*)*

OLD WOMAN: All sorts of things sleep in the sea. Gather up all the submarines that humans have ever made, they'd still never reach the deepest depths of the sea. In the cold waters of the ocean's floor another kingdom exists, but still you can't get there. Humans are the same way. They hold inside of them a deep, deep sea. And there, you'll find a mermaid, a sleeping mermaid, just one, alone in a wide,

wide sea. She sleeps, waiting for someone who can wake her, somebody like a foghorn in the gloom. . . .

(Lights up on the ramen cart. GOLDFISH *pours a bucket of goldfish into the river, then gazes at its surface.* NATSUO *enters, leading a bevy of* WOMEN.*)*

NATSUO: It's on me, girls! Go ahead and order!

GOLDFISH: Tonight again? What're you after?

NATSUO: I'm a customer, ain't I.

GOLDFISH: I'm not in business to serve you.

NATSUO: But you is, to serve these here girls. (GOLDFISH *does not reply.*) Gimme some saké. Saké!

GOLDFISH: *(Slams down the bottle of saké.)* If you're here to wash away your sins, you're knocking on the wrong door.

NATSUO: Show me some heart, woman.

GOLDFISH: I'm not your woman!

NATSUO: I could smash your shitty little stall in a second if I wanted. *(*GOLDFISH *does not respond.)* Hurry up! Give us some ramen. These girls have worked up an appetite.

JENNY: *(Entering.)* Make sure you pay for the ramen yourself. (NATSUO *ignores her.)* Don't send me no bills. *(Still no response from* NATSUO.*)* You got a lot of nerve, out every night carousing. . . . You girls, get on home with ya. I'm sending yous off to the boondocks tomorrow.

(The WOMEN *slink out.)*

JENNY: So, you got the hots for the ramen girl, have ya.

NATSUO: Shut yer face.

JENNY: Open me wallet but not me mouth, eh? So, no respect for me neither. *(To* GOLDFISH.*)* He's all yours. I've had it with him. I can't take it no more.

NATSUO: You can leave anytime you likes.

JENNY: That's easy for you to say. . . . Do you remember, Natsuo? Your first match, you were just a rookie up against a three-time winner. I was still like them girls, didn't know left from right. The ticket you gave me was for a ringside seat and I thought it must be some mistake. But when I saw you in the corner, smiling so sweetly at me, I knew I was glad I came. The glaring spotlight, the dazzling, white ring. Then you, standing right in the centre. Your footwork was like you'd sprouted wings and was dancing lightly over the canvas, your jabbing punches never let up. And that night you said to me, "You're my Goddess of Victory." . . . Back home, nothing but trouble. And here too, nothing but trouble. But you was like a lighthouse way off in the distance, guiding me. . . . If I got you, I can put up with no end of trouble. . . . That's what I believed then, but not any more. (NATSUO *says nothing.)* My artist's visa expires soon. It's good for only sixty days. One thing's for sure. I ain't coming back here no more.

NATSUO: Jenny.

JENNY: I love you, my champion. You always was my champ. *(She exits.)*

NATSUO: Everybody leaves. Ever since I lost the title, nothing sticks around. . . . *(To* GOLDFISH.*)* The only thing I got left is your voice. I can still hear your voice on the phone, singing to me. That voice will forever stick like a burr to my brain.

*(*NATSUO *lies down and falls into a drunken stupor.* GOLDFISH *approaches him.* SETSUO *enters.)*

SETSUO: Look at that bum! Dead drunk, he is. *(*GOLDFISH *does not reply.)* But I should talk—so am I. Shit! Never in my wildest dreams did I ever think I'd be the one who got dumped. Ah, but I'm a flighty girl. *(Sings.)* "If you leave me, buster, there's plenty more like you." *(*GOLDFISH *remains silent.* SETSUO *takes some money from his wallet.)* My compliments. *(*GOLDFISH *attempts to give him change.)* That's all right, that's all right. I've got a big heart. Anyway, it's a big sister's job to cover for a kid brother in trouble. *(Hoists* NATSUO *over his shoulder.)* Oof!

*(*SETSUO *and* NATSUO *exit. As* GOLDFISH *starts scrubbing away at the dishes,* AKIO *enters, shadowboxing.)*

GOLDFISH: Hi there. *(*AKIO *ignores her.)* The moon's so pretty tonight. It's just like, like that other night. . . . Remember? *(Still no response from* AKIO.*)* The night you said we should run away to the moon with our noodle stand. . . . *(Laughs.)* Just a fairy tale, eh?

AKIO: Goldfish, What're you still doing in this town? . . . You oughta go back where you came from.

GOLDFISH: There's nothing there for me any longer.

AKIO: Still, you oughta go back home.

GOLDFISH: Home. It changes so fast you wouldn't recognize it. Just like us. . . . You know what folks are calling me now? *(*AKIO *says nothing. She picks up a toy goldfish.)* The Tin Goldfish. Drop it in water and it won't sink, just sits there floating on the surface. A tin goldfish painted in pretty reds and blues, but rub it and the metal shows through.

AKIO: If you can't go back home, go back to my big brother. . . . He needs you.

GOLDFISH: A goldfish made of tin, but my heart still frets. *(She thrashes in the water with the toy goldfish.)* The fish still flaps around in the dark sea inside me. I keep telling myself, forget about it, forget, but the fish still flaps around. Cut the line but it's swallowed the hook and it flaps around, twisting and writhing. And you can still say what you did? *(*AKIO *attempts to restrain her.)* If that's what you want, I just might do it. But in that case, buy me first. . . . You were the one who told me, that somewhere—maybe here, maybe not, but somewhere—

my real life is waiting for me. That if I find it, I can start all over. You gave me those words for free, but I want you to buy them back from me. I know it's too much to ask you to buy them when you gave them away to begin with, so take me too.

AKIO: I can't do that.

GOLDFISH: Then you can scrunch me up like an old tin toy and forget all about me. Forget that I never cost you anything in the first place. You can tell yourself you were a fool to waste your time looking after something that never cost you anything. Buy me, buy me!

AKIO: I can't bleeding well do that! *(He lets go of her and turns away.)*

GOLDFISH: Liar! *(*AKIO *does not respond.)* You're a liar! I try to wash them and wipe them away, but I can never get rid of your filthy lies. . . . *(*GOLDFISH *exits.* AKIO *continues to shadowbox. Lights up on the* POET *and the* OLD WOMAN.*)*

POET: What did him in was me.

OLD WOMAN: Nobody does anybody in. They do themselves in.

POET: I shouldn't have said what I did.

OLD WOMAN: No sense getting into a flap over words.

POET: What should I do?

OLD WOMAN: Look. Look straight at things the way they are.

POET: I've had enough of dreams.

OLD WOMAN: So long as your past lies coiled up inside you, you'll go on dreaming, again and again.

POET: . . . I feel sleepy.

OLD WOMAN: Everybody's waiting for something that won't come round again. Say you love somebody more than they love you—the time comes when, no matter how much you love her, you'll get a mind to destroy her, just so you aren't hurt any more.

(Blackout. In the darkness, wild cheers. As the lights come up, AKIO *is seated in a chair next to* SHIKIO. *It is a locker room before a bout. When* AKIO *speaks he hardly stutters at all now.)*

SHIKIO: Give it your best shot, brother.

AKIO: Fact is, I don't want to box.

SHIKIO: Then why do you do it?

AKIO: Hatred. . . . In the old days, I never ever felt that way. All I waited and wished for was that one day, someday, my real life would come looking for me. . . . But things are different now. I want to pound all that right into the canvas with me fists. . . . No tomorrow, no future. No glory, no victory. . . . The only thing waiting for me the yawning, dark sea. *(*SHIKIO *remains silent, listening.)* A dark, bottomless sea. You punch and punch away, but your fists meet no resistance. . . . I'm afraid, afraid of myself. Afraid that someday I'm gonna kill somebody in the ring.

(Lights up on GOLDFISH *and* NATSUO *washing bowls.)*

NATSUO: Goldfish, what say you and me leave this town and go off and live, just the two of us? I've been in love with you ever since I first heard your voice.

GOLDFISH: I don't believe in anything anymore.

NATSUO: I ain't got nobody but you, Goldfish.

GOLDFISH: I can fend for myself. . . .

AKIO: Hatred. Every day I'm filled up with more and more hatred.

GOLDFISH: Why don't you give up boxing too? Start again from scratch.

NATSUO: Let's do it. The both of us.

AKIO: I'd like to make a fresh start. Someplace else, where they don't even know what boxing is.

SHIKIO: But the whole town's hopes are pinned on you, brother.

GOLDFISH: Me, I gave up on hoping for anything.

AKIO: I look at the opponent's face and he looks like somebody else.

NATSUO: Goldfish.

AKIO: Sometimes it's my own face.

NATSUO: Goldfish, I got a favour to ask you. You're the only one who can save me.

AKIO: That's when this unspeakable hatred starts to well up inside of me.

GOLDFISH: You suffer 'cause you still have hope. But you can live just as well without it.

NATSUO: Is Akio so good to you? . . . I'm not gonna give you up to anybody.

GOLDFISH: I don't belong to anybody anymore. So get out! Clear out and don't show me your ugly face again!

(NATSUO *stabs* GOLDFISH.)

AKIO: I empty my mind of everything and just beat away at the other guy's face. Just keep pounding and pounding away at him.

(NATSUO *stabs* GOLDFISH *again and again.*)

GOLDFISH: Help! Somebody help me!

AKIO: Just beating the shit out of him.

SHIKIO: Don't be so hard on yourself. You're the champ, brother.

GOLDFISH: I-I don't want to die! . . . I don't care if I've got nothing, not even dreams, I just want to live!

SHIKIO: It's time.

GOLDFISH: Akio!

SHIKIO: What's the matter?

AKIO: It felt like somebody was calling me.

SHIKIO: C'mon, let's go. They're all waiting for you.

(*Cheers.* AKIO *and* NATSUO *stand up at the same time.*)

NATSUO: Stand up, Goldfish. It's time. The times are calling us.

(NATSUO *and* GOLDFISH *sink together into the river. Blackout.*)

POET: That morning, a dusting of light snow turned the town all white and the season turned toward winter. Natsuo lay sleeping by the riverside, curled up in a ball, arms hugging his knees. The Natsuo who'd escaped the jaws of death that day was no longer my brother, the one who'd shone for all the world as champ. My brother Natsuo, shoving his face into the corner of a white wall, was empty like a great big cavern. Everybody in town got together and they all dredged the river, but there was no sign of Goldfish. Maybe she drifted further downstream, or maybe she was never murdered after all, or maybe the woman called Goldfish never existed in the first place—all sorts of wild rumours about her flew around. Then people started calling our town Crazy Town and, one by one, folk started leaving, like rats off a shipwreck, till only one family was left behind.

(The stage lights are turned up, revealing FATHER, MOTHER, SHIKIO, HARUO, YONG-HEE, AKIO *and the* BARON, *busily packing for a journey.* SETSUO, FUYUO *and* USELESS EUSTACE *are seeing them off.)*

MOTHER: Setsuo, look after Natsuo for us. We're counting on you.

SETSUO: Not a problem. I work nights, so's I can visit him every day.

FATHER: Let's hope he gets better.

SETSUO: Sure he will.

MOTHER: Mind you, I feel awful leaving it all to you on your own to look after. . . .

SETSUO: What're you talking about? We're still family no matter how far you go. What with the way Natsuo turned out, so long as I can't have kids, it's like he was my own.

MOTHER: You plan to keep working the gay bars, do you?

SETSUO: Sure thing. Piggy is opening a place for me.

HARUO: You sure have a knack for going through the men.

SETSUO: Love's a watermelon that don't have seeds.

HARUO: You're a riddle, a bleeding riddle to me.

MOTHER: Fuyuo, you sure you don't want to come?

FUYUO: Ah.

MOTHER: You sure you'll be all right? You're the one I worry most about.

FUYUO: Ah.

MOTHER: Here you go—your savings account and seal. Your ma put every penny you made into savings.

FUYUO: Ah.

SHIKIO: Give the boxing your best shot, eh, brother?

AKIO: I'll write you while I'm on the road.

BARON: Don't you worry, everybody. I'll look after this kid like he was me own. Lost me wife, me house, the only thing they can hang on me anymore is the boxing.

FATHER: *(Bowing to the* BARON.*)* M-much obliged to you.

BARON: I'll look after Natsuo too.

MOTHER: And Akio, you know, if you ever get sick of boxing, you can always come live with us.

AKIO: I'll give it my best shot, for just a wee bit longer.

BARON: Don't you folks worry 'bout him. Ever since he made his debut, Akio's been like a bleeding hurricane, straight wins, no losses, all the way.

MOTHER: Got your towel?

AKIO: Uh huh.

MOTHER: Soap?

AKIO: Yup. Don't worry, wherever I go, I'll be thinking of you all.

YONG-HEE: *(To* HARUO.*)* We'd better make a move on, honey.

HARUO: Guess so. . . .

MOTHER: You all right there with the wheelchair?

YONG-HEE: I mean to have this man push me in my wheelchair to the end of the earth, if needs be. Ain't that right, honey?

HARUO: I got it. I remember Shylock's line.

YONG-HEE: How's it go?

HARUO: "It's what I've done. I, that did void my rheum upon my own beard."[8]

MOTHER: And now the whole family's scattered. All of us—including Ondine, who died—used to live together like two hands joined, like ten fingers entwined.

EUSTACE: *(To* SHIKIO.*)* Hey, kid. Make sure you remember this town and the folk who lived here. And don't forget about me, neither. *(*SHIKIO *nods.)* Ah, it warms me old heart just to think there's somebody still around who'll remember me.

(There is a gust of wind.)

SHIKIO: Hey, pop. The wind's up.

FATHER: Aye, just like the day we came to this town, eh?

SHIKIO: No matter which way the wind went then, it always comes back, don't it?

(They all look up at the sky.)

FATHER: Cast adrift, we're cast adrift, God knows where or for how long. . . . Since we put our hometown behind us, we've been turned away by every town. But still, we gotta live, don't we?

MOTHER: Cheer up, dear, everybody. Come on, let's make a move.

FATHER: Right you are, ma.

(A desolate sea appears. FATHER *and* MOTHER *drift away. The rest split up and go their separate ways.)*

SHIKIO: Farewell, Seatown. Farewell, dear memories. Farewell, my youth.

*(*SHIKIO *leaves. Blackout. When the lights come up, the* POET *and the* OLD WOMAN *are sitting on the bench.)*

POET: And then, the town vanished. Fact is, I loved that town, the town where people took care of each other, looked out for each other, helped each other. I loved the people in that town—we were all like driftwood thrown up on the beach, rubbing our shoulders against each other.

OLD WOMAN: But the town's gone now.

POET: I've no longer got any place I can go back to. So why is it I still keep dreaming of that town?

OLD WOMAN: It's because it's all still there, in your dreams.

(As in a revolving lantern, images from the past float up, then disappear.)

OLD WOMAN: Forget all those wounds from your dark past, they never did anything for you anyway. Everything goes back to the water, both what you can see and what you can't. . . . No way you can hear the music box that sunk to the river bottom.

POET: Old woman, you wouldn't happen to be Goldfish, would you? . . . Didn't you say all sorts of things sleep in the sea? That there's a kingdom lying in the depths of the cold, cold sea? If that's the case, the mermaids can't die, but drift here and there, eternally in the dark waters. Please don't laugh, hear me out. Ever since that day, I felt sure that Goldfish didn't die, but turned into a mermaid and returned to the sea.

OLD WOMAN: What would you do if I was Goldfish?

POET: There's something I want to say.

OLD WOMAN: One of those pointless statements half-baked poets make?

POET: No.

OLD WOMAN: I'm just an old woman, you know.

POET: Even if you are just an old woman, there's one thing—just one thing—I want you to say.

OLD WOMAN: Words again?

POET: Just three little words.

OLD WOMAN: So, what do you want me to say to you?

POET: "I forgive you."

OLD WOMAN: I'll say it if that'll make you feel any better. . . . I forgive you, I forgive you for everything. . . . That's all past and gone now, dreams . . . just dreams.

(The OLD WOMAN disappears.)

POET: I guess I'll have no more dreams. I won't dream anymore of that town. Not since I know that big ship, with its white sail billowing in the breeze, won't come for me. Not since I've been left without a compass and all I can see around me is the dark, dark sea. Still, I've got no choice but to pull on the oars and light out for God knows where. . . . Facing the dark, dark sea, I cough up a single, thin thread. I'm like a mermaid, waiting for someone to reel me in.

(The POET spits out a red thread and, holding out the line to the audience, he slips into the water and disappears. GOLDFISH emerges from the water. In her mouth she tightly grips the red thread. Then,

gazing at the audience, she too slips away. Fadeout.)

Notes

1. Maxim Gorky's 1902 play has been immensely popular in Japan ever since Osanai Kaoru's seminal shingeki production in 1908. Haruo recites the Actor's line to the Baron in Act I of the play.
2. A reference to the Tokyo bargirl who became the mistress of former Indonesian President Sukarno.
3. The First Clown's speech, in *Hamlet*, 5.1.15-20.
4. Enka ("torch songs") are highly romantic and nostalgic ballads, often about the broken-hearted.
5. Another reference to *The Lower Depths*, the Actor's line to Satin in Act I.
6. This song is loosely based on a popular children's rhyme written by Saijō Yaso (1892-1970) that was first published in the November 1918 (vol. 1, no. 5) issue of *Akai Tori* (Red bird) and later set to music by Narita Tomezō (1893-1945).
7. These lines are taken from the michiyuki in Scene 3 of Chikamatsu Monzaemon's 1703 puppet play, *Sonezaki Shinjū* (Love suicides at Sonezaki). This translation is based (with some changes) on Donald Keene's *Major Plays of Chikamatsu* (Colombia, 1961). Adashigahara (or Adashino) was a noted burial ground in Kyoto that became a synecdoche for cemeteries.
8. Haruo has actually misquoted a line (1.3.114) from *The Merchant of Venice*.

Thread Hell
Kishida Rio

TRANSLATED BY CAROL FISHER SORGENFREI and TONOOKA NAOMI

*

Introduction

Tanigawa Michiko
TRANSLATED BY CAROL FISHER SORGENFREI

This translation is based on the 1998 Sanichi Shobō publication of
Ito Jigoku in *Gendai Nihon Gikyoku Taikei*, Vol.13.

Kishida Rio

The Silk Reeling Women greet the Master of the Thread-and-Yarn Store. Center: Master of the Thread-and-Yarn Store. Atelier Fontaine, Tokyo 1984. (Courtesy Takei Isamu.)

Mayu's memory of her mother with her lover; both are manipulated with strings. From left: Mother and Lover. Atelier Fontaine, Tokyo 1984. (Courtesy Takei Isamu.)

Mayu finds her real mother and strangles
her with a silk thread. Atelier Fontaine,
Tokyo 1984. (Courtesy Takei Isamu.)

When Mayu cries out, "Blow wind!" the Silk Reeling Women themselves become the wind, and become frenzied. Atelier Fontaine, Tokyo 1984. (Courtesy Takei Isamu.)

The Woman who played Mayu's mother
appears and asks the way to the Thread-
and-Yarn Store just as Mayu had. On the
central platform: the new Woman;
below, the Silk Reeling Women. Atelier
Fontaine, Tokyo 1984. (Courtesy Takei
Isamu.)

Introduction

Tanigawa Michiko
TRANSLATED BY CAROL FISHER SORGENFREI

WHEN I THINK OF KISHIDA RIO (b. 1950), the associations that rise to the surface are Terayama Shūji in the 1970s, *Thread Hell* in the 1980s, and the Heiner Müller Project (HMP) and Asia in the 1990s. These three associations form a symbolic triangle that will remain forever engraved, not only on the theatrical persona of Kishida Rio, but on the historical development of postwar modern theater.

Key companies of the 1960s *angura* theater movement, such as Terayama Shūji's Peanut Gallery, Kara Jūrō's Red Tent, Satoh Makoto's Black Tent,[1] Suzuki Tadashi's Waseda Little Theater[2] and others, arrived on the scene waving aloft the banner of revolt against the entrenched Western theater import, *shingeki* realism. This revolt formed a great watershed in postwar theater history. The loaded question of why "modernization" should equal "Westernization" was once again addressed, this time in regard to theatrical themes and techniques. The international theater community had its first inkling of a response in 1969, when Terayama Shūji's Peanut Gallery toured abroad to such Western theater festivals as Experimenta 3, offering the world a taste of contemporary Japanese theater other than *nō* or *kabuki*.

Born in Nagano Prefecture, Kishida Rio graduated from the Law School of Chuo University, and while qualifying for the bar, she joined the Peanut Gallery's Theater Laboratory in 1974. There she began her theater career as Terayama Shūji's collaborator. During Kishida's final years with Terayama, collaborative works such as *Shintoku-maru: Poison Boy*,[3] *The Audience Seats*,[4] and *Lemmings*[5] were born; in these works, it is not clear how much of the writing is Terayama's and how much is Kishida's. Sharing Terayama's ability to devise striking alienation methods, she adopted a multi-dimensional, resilient pose. At the same time, beginning in the late 1970s, she commenced to work independently from but parallel to the Peanut Gallery. As Kishida put it, "I obtained Terayama's permission to write by saying I wanted to write about women." In 1978 she founded With the Help of My Big Brother Theater[6] and presented her own works such as *The Foundling's Tale*,[7] *December Chronicles*[8] and *The Floating Bridge of Dreams*.[9]

In 1981 she founded Kishida Company. By the time of Terayama Shūji's death in 1983, her company had merged with director Wada Yoshio's Optimists Troupe,[10] forming "Kishida Company + Optimists Troupe." The following year, 1984, saw great success for her and for their first production. *Thread Hell*, also known as *Woven Hell*, the play that would become the troupe's signature work, won the 29th Kishida Kunio Drama Award. New versions were produced in 1987 and 1990. In 1992 they were honored with an invitation to perform the piece at theater festivals in Perth and Adelaide, Australia. Thus *Thread Hell* symbolizes both the culmination of Kishida Rio's theatrical activities up to that time, and the transformation of Japanese theater in the mid-1980s.

Thread Hell

Thread Hell opens with a prologue. In the darkness, matches are struck and shills float up out of the darkness. The scene is Tokyo, 1939, at the storefront of the Kameido factory of the Tokyo Muslin and Silk Manufacturing Company. The spiel of the shills goes like this, "This great factory is devoted to reeling raw silk from cocoons, and to spinning both cotton and silk thread." "Many of your sisters and others from your village are already enjoying the benefits of working for the company. Why don't you join, too?" The singing of "A Sad Song of Mill Girls" symbolizes this place, which appears to be a thread spinning factory in front, but is actually a brothel in the rear. In the middle of this *ie*, the Japanese word for house/home, is the holy family. Modern Japan is caught up in these tricks and lies. The storefront is a metaphor for the beginnings of Japan's crippled modernity.

The girl Mayu (Cocoon) has come here from out of the sea. In Scene One, "Me," before she is trapped, she asks, "Where am I? Who am I? Where did I come from?" After that, what floats to the surface is an event = a story = history = *Geschichte*.

Mayu, the girl whose origin is unknown, searches for a "warm *ie*." The shills give her directions to the storefront, but she has a great deal of trouble finding her way. The girls at the shop, who lack family registers and therefore have no way of knowing their real ages, parents, or names, wear "a white kimono when [. . .] spinning silk. A red one when customers are here." She joins these girls who go by names derived from the seasonal beauty of nature, as found in the Japanese flower card game *hanafuda* and as depicted in *The Tale of Genji*.[11] They have names like Matsu (Pine), Ume (Japanese Apricot), Sakura (Cherry), Fuji (Wisteria), or Shōbu (Iris). Although these women are unconcerned about not having family registers, the Registrar tells them that for the good of Japan, they must create true Japanese family registers. The man says that based on the New Family Registry Law, he can aid people who don't have family registers to get one. In filling out the registry application, the

Registrar reverses time. We learn that the Master of the store has taught the girls lies to tell their customers, and that Mayu, seeking answers about her past, is searching for her mother and father. One by one, before being asked questions, the girls begin to spin the membranes of their personal histories, which are filled with persecution complexes, revenge, and abuse. Then little by little, over the male-centered family tree that Mayu's mother took from the back of the Buddhist altar when she left home, the shop girls layer images of mothers and aunts. Questioning, they whistle up the wind. The spinning wheels seem to move smoothly, but the result is madness. Finally the Master of the shop declares, "I gathered women who had no family registers, I created a realm called house and home, I made them sell thread and yarn, and I made them sell their favors." The girls' spun threads become entangled with the Master's ropes, and he topples into hell.

Threading, thread cutting, thread hell. As they look death in the face, the girls once more whistle up the winds of thread hell. In Scene Ten, the last scene, "Thread Hell," Mayu has become one of the thread girls. As they await the imminent arrival of another new woman, she says, "Now that each of us is her own master, let's not leave her out in the cold." In that way, without masters, they continue to turn the spinning wheels.

The names of the people appearing in the play give hints to their characters. For example, Mayu (Cocoon) is a silkworm larva that produces the raw silk for spinning. The girls' male customers all have the metaphoric name Blank Mask. If one asks the reason for the use of elements such as these names, *ie*, family registers, or family lineage, the answer can be found by looking beneath the lies on the surface of history into the profound darkness deep below. The veneer of lies becomes transparent by illuminating the darkness in the deep layers of history and in the connecting spaces. "I want to write about women." Kishida Rio consistently reflects that thought in dialogue which is often written in a fluent seven-five meter, evoking the beauty of nature from the flower cards. This style conveys a sense similar to *kabuki*-inspired puppetry. With few female predecessors other than Akimoto Matsuyo (1911-2001), the 1980s produced a succession of female playwrights such as Watanabe Eriko, Kisaragi Koharu, and Ichidō Rei.[12] In this context, *Thread Hell* is representative of a robust outpouring of creative work in the 1980s.

Although Kishida Rio's works cannot be called clarion calls for feminism, a concern with eternal female issues is evident in the questions posed by characters such as the girl Mayu, who asks, "Where am I? Who am I? Where have I come from and where am I going?" In her *The Last House, Temporary Home—The Biography of Kawashima Yoshiko*,[13] winner of the 1989 Kinokuniya Books Drama Award, Kishida wrote about both the vertical and horizontal history of women. In *Our*

Eves,[14] 1992, she offered profiles of women of the Taishō era such as Itō
Noe, Kamichika Ichiko and Hori Tamoko. In her trilogy *Love: Three
Plays*[15] (1985-87) she wrote about love before World War II, just after
World War II, and today. *Eternity: Parts I and II*[16] (2000-01) questions
the meaning of love by depicting a love affair with a thousand-year-old
vampire. Her other plays about women such as *Hide and Seek*,[17] *A Mid-
summer Night's . . . Dream?*[18] and *Cat and Canary*[19] adroitly portray
male-female relationships in contemporary Japan as games of "hide and
seek"—lovers, friends and neighbors who cling to their own dreams
without ever quite connecting to each other, like ships passing in the
night. Whatever the situation, her keen vision is able to penetrate
everyday reality by combining the perspectives of distance and depth.

A special issue of *Theater Arts*[20] edited by AICT Japan Center[21]
focused on "The Emperor System and Theater." It featured an article
based on a panel discussion entitled "What Is the Relation of Theater to
the 'Emperor System?'"[22] in which Kishida Rio had participated. One
comment made by Kishida, who was the only woman on the five-
member panel, was especially striking:

> Ever since Akimoto Matsuyo, female playwrights have expressed
> almost no interest in the Emperor System. I, myself, don't know
> why. The history of women's relationship to the Emperor System
> in Japan has been an open issue since the 1970s, so this gap is a
> mystery.[23]

Thread Hell certainly expresses criticism of patriarchal authority from
the female perspective. First, it critiques the view, prevalent since the
Meiji era (1868-1912), that the Emperor is the patriarchal father of the
national "*ie*," and that "*ie*" and nation are two sides of the same coin.
Secondly, it critiques the lame, shallow modernization of Japan. But then
she said this:

> In the 1980s, my personal way of denying the significance of the
> Emperor System was to persistently criticize it as a Japanese
> woman. But in the 1990s, I became keenly conscious of nations
> such as Korea and the various countries of Southeast Asia. This
> consciousness planted seeds of doubt in my mind, and I began
> struggling with the question, "Do the people of Japan bear
> responsibility for the war, or not?" And so I started to create
> works that would empower women to overthrow patriarchal
> authority. Why women? Because throughout Asia, in every
> country, there has been a long history of discrimination against
> women. Because being a woman myself, I felt that denying the
> Emperor System and patriarchal authority was, in a sense, a way

> for women to restore themselves to themselves. In order to do that, we must kill the system.[24]

In the final analysis, these comments reveal that Kishida Rio has changed course since writing *Thread Hell*.

In 1990, Kishida Rio joined forces with director Suzuki Tadashi to bring the HMP to theatrical life. The seeds for this project were planted by a core consisting of Heiner Müller, the dramatist from the former East Germany, theater critics Nishidō Kōjin and Uchino Tadashi, and myself, a scholar of East German Theater. Kishida Rio herself said, "People can't help but be infected and changed when they are bitten by the Heiner Müller bug."[25] Until that time, it was commonly assumed that Müller's pieces were utterly impossible to produce. Kishida enthusiastically participated in readings, translations, symposia on contemporary theater, tours, and so on. The project was part of her ongoing search for a way to crack open the domestic autism of Japanese theater in the 1980s.

Part of that search corresponded to what we might call the worldwide transition from (modern) melodrama to (post-modern) performance. Theater as a construct was undergoing a paradigm shift, in which pure theatrical performance was crossing swords with text-based dramatic theater. At the same time, her goal became to use visionary, issue-oriented theater practice to cross international borders; around 1990, she began to concentrate on directing her own works. She inaugurated the "Theater Across Borders" production series in 1992, the same year that *Thread Hell* was offered an opportunity for overseas performance. Kishida Rio had begun to make conscious efforts to open up and look outward. About that time, she also began working to create successful theater interactions between Asian nations. In order to set up exchanges with Korea, she began studying Korean language. She even used Hangul titles for the plays she presented in Korea, *Sewoli Chotta* (Happy Days) (1993) and *Sora Hanur Langit* (Sky, Sky, Langit) (2001). *Bird! Bird! Blue Bird!*[26] (1994) and *Lost Angels*[27] (1996) were performed using a mixture of Korean, sign language and Japanese. These plays attempted to share the pain of those who had been forcibly stripped of their native language under what was euphemistically termed "colonial policy."

In 1997, she collaborated with the Singaporean director Ong Keng Sen on *Lear*, a deconstruction of Shakespeare's *King Lear*. In this version, the king is killed by his eldest daughter, and a mother character who is not in the original text appears. Various performance genres were incorporated into this production, including *nō*, Beijing opera, contemporary theater, and dance, and various native languages flew about the stage as the multinational performers presented these diverse forms of theater. During the performance, Japanese supertitles were projected for all dialogue, including the *nō* dialogue spoken in Japanese. This production toured Tokyo, Osaka, Fukuoka (the Japanese tour was sponsored by The Japan Foundation), Hong Kong, Perth, and Berlin (invited to the World Theater Festival). As a follow-up, in 2000 she again collaborated with Ong Keng Sen on *Searching for a New Asia*. The second installment of their collaboration resulted in *Desdemona*, an even more highly altered reworking of *Othello*. It demanded a greater leap of the imagination, because Kishida—the only Japanese person involved— wrote the script based on live improvisations by all the performing artists and musicians. Therefore, the script had to be translated into the native languages of the performers, who came from India, Myanmar, Korea and elsewhere. In performance, these various languages interacted with Kishida's Japanese words on a video screen, and transformed the stage into a mysterious space-time. The play was performed in such places as Singapore and Adelaide, but unfortunately, the only performance in Japan was at Fukuoka City's Asian Art Museum. The production not only crossed international borders, but like Heiner Müller, Kishida herself resolutely attempted to play the role of the playwright intent upon "making the playwright extinct."

> Both Suzuki [Tadashi] and Ninagawa [Yukio]—though offering disparate theatrical styles—are following in the pioneering footsteps of Terayama, and are distinguishing themselves by letting [the world] know about Japanese theater. That said, I myself live in Asia now, and to me, Europe seems distant, America seems distant.[28]

By making these statements at the panel discussion mentioned earlier, Kishida took a strong stance, asserting that her themes are inherently Asian. In her own manner, she has assumed the mantle as Terayama's successor. A further indication of her plucky self-confidence may be seen in her outstanding success as the Acting Director of the Fourth Asian Women's Theater Conference, a position she took over in February 2001, after the sudden death of playwright Kisaragi Koharu. Might these events suggest a trend for "the Japanese theater of tomorrow"?

Notes

1. For more information refer to the Black Tent in "Radicalism in the Theater of the 1980s."
2. Waseda Shōgekijō.
3. Shintoku-maru.
4. Kankyaku-seki.

5. Remingu.

6. Ka-i Gekijō.

7. Sutego monogatari.

8. Rōgetsuki.

9. Yume no ukihashi.

10. Rakuten-dan.

11. Genji monogatari.

12. The pseudonym of the all-female Blue Bird Theater Company. The term is commonly used as a command to the cast to bow at the curtain call.

13. Tsui no sumika kari no yado—Kawashima Yoshiko-den.

14. Watakushi-tachi no ibu.

15. Koi sambu-saku.

16. Towa pāto I to II.

17. Kakurenbo.

18. Manatsu no yoru no . . . yume?

19. Neko to kanaria.

20. *Shiatā Ātsu*, No. 13, April 2001, pp.8-31.

21. International Association of Theater Critics.

22. *Shiatā Ātsu*.

23. Ibid.

24. Ibid.

25. "The Heiner Müller Virus" in the Heiner Müller Special Edition of *Eureka*, June 1986.

26. Tori yo tori yo aoi tori yo.

27. Maigo no tenshi.

28. *Shiatā Ātsu*.

Thread Hell

Kishida Rio

TRANSLATED BY CAROL FISHER SORGENFREI and TONOOKA NAOMI

CHARACTERS

GIRL (MAYU—COCOON)
SCHOOLGIRL (SILK REELING WOMAN SAKURA—CHERRY BLOSSOM)
MR. NAWA (MR. ROPE), THE MASTER OF A THREAD—AND—YARN STORE
SILK REELING WOMAN 1 (MATSU—PINE)
SILK REELING WOMAN 2 (UME—JAPANESE APRICOT)
SILK REELING WOMAN 3 (FUJI—WISTERIA)
SILK REELING WOMAN 4 (SHŌBU—IRIS)
SILK REELING WOMAN 5 (BOTAN—PEONY)
SILK REELING WOMAN 6 (HAGI—JAPANESE BUSH CLOVER)
SILK REELING WOMAN 7 (TSUKI—MOON)
SILK REELING WOMAN 8 (KIKU—CHRYSANTHEMUM)
SILK REELING WOMAN 9 (MOMIJI—MAPLE)
SILK REELING WOMAN 10 (AME—RAIN)
SILK REELING WOMAN 11 (KIRI—FOG)
RECRUITER (MR. WARA—MR. STRAW)
RECRUITER (MR. TEGUSU—MR. SILKWORM GUT)
RECRUITER / REGISTRAR (MR. HIMO—MR. STRING)
RECRUITER (MR. MIZUHIKI—MR. GIFT—TYING STRING)
BLANK MASK 1[1]
BLANK MASK 2
BLANK MASK 3
BLANK MASK 4
PUPPET MOTHER 1
PUPPET MOTHER 2
MAN 1
MAN 2
KUROKO 1[2]
KUROKO 2
KUROKO 3
KUROKO 4
FATHER 1
FATHER 2

FATHER 3
FATHER 4
MOTHER 1
MOTHER 2
MOTHER 3
MOTHER 4

Prologue

(A match is struck in the dark. In the dimly growing light, a man blows out the flame as he says:
>   *"Tonight, she'll be a happy whore,*
>   *A concubine at the rice seller's store."*

Then, another man strikes a match. A close look into the dark seems to reveal four to five men. They are RECRUITERS, *collectors who buy girls.)*

RECRUITER TEGUSU: *(Striking a match.)*
   You've gone and broke a silken thread?
   No need to worry your sweet little head. *(Blowing out the flame.)*
RECRUITER HIMO: *(Striking a match.)*
   You've nothing but cabbage and lettuce to eat
   Meal after meal, no rice and no meat. *(Blowing out the flame.)*
RECRUITER MIZUHIKI: *(Striking a match.)*
   Eating like that, you'll just waste away
   Too weak to reel silk, you'll never earn pay. *(Blowing out the flame.)*
RECRUITER WARA: *(Striking a match.)*
   Buying a child? Reel her right in!
   We'll tempt her with silk and teach her to spin. *(Blowing out the flame.)*
RECRUITER TEGUSU: *(Striking a match.)*
   Don't just give your daughter away,
   Sell us cocoons and you'll reel in the pay! *(Blowing out the flame.)*
RECRUITER HIMO: *(Striking a match.)*
   No, mother, no, don't send me there!
   Not to the silk mill, the silk mill is where. *(Blowing out the flame.)*
RECRUITER MIZUHIKI: *(Striking a match.)*
   Girls spend their lives reeling in thread,
   No husband, no children, that's what I dread. *(Blowing out the flame.)*
   (Abruptly, the men start speaking in soft coaxing voices.)
RECRUITER WARA: *(Striking a match in the audience area.)* The year is
   1939. The Kameido Silk Mill, a division of the Tokyo Muslin and Silk
   Thread Corporation, is located three blocks east of the Kameido
   Tenmangū Shrine, one of the showplaces of Tokyo. *(Blowing out the
   flame.)*
RECRUITER TEGUSU: *(Striking a match in the audience area.)* The

company has capital valued at fifteen million yen. This great factory is devoted to reeling raw silk from cocoons, and to spinning both cotton and silk thread. *(Blowing out the flame.)*

RECRUITER MIZUHIKI: *(Striking a match in the audience area.)* We provide a brand new boarding house, a school, and a hospital, all free of charge, right on the factory premises. *(Blowing out the flame.)*

RECRUITER HIMO: *(Striking a match in the audience area.)* The school, in addition to general education, offers careful instruction in sewing, flower arrangement, tea ceremony, etiquette, cooking and other skills. *(Blowing out the flame.)*

RECRUITER WARA: *(Striking a match in the audience area.)* Many of your sisters and others from your village are already enjoying the benefits of working for the company. Why don't you join, too? *(Blowing out the flame.)*

RECRUITER TEGUSU: *(Striking a match in the audience area.)* You can begin work anytime, but the sooner you come, the more you'll make. Lose no time. Come and join the company. *(Blowing out the flame.)*

RECRUITER HIMO: *(Striking a match in the audience area.)* Wages are paid in accordance with age. Your starting salary will be sixty to seventy sen[3] per day. *(Blowing out the flame.)*

RECRUITER MIZUHIKI: *(Striking a match in the audience area.)* In three months time, it will increase to more than thirty yen per month, in six months to more than fifty, even sixty yen. *(Blowing out the flame.)*

RECRUITER WARA: *(Striking a match in the audience area.)* After that, there's no limit to how much you can earn, depending on your ability. *(Blowing out the flame.)*

RECRUITER TEGUSU: *(Striking a match in the audience area.)* We provide tasty meals of white rice and side dishes at only twelve sen per day. *(Blowing out the flame.)*

RECRUITER MIZUHIKI: *(Striking a match in the audience area.)* For more details, please inquire at your nearest recruitment office or send a post card directly to the company.

RECRUITER TEGUSU: *(Striking a match in the audience area.)* A prompt reply is assured. *(Blowing out the flame.)*

RECRUITER WARA: *(Striking a match in the audience area.)* For the greatest profit, decide today! *(Blowing out the flame.)*

(The last flame is blown out, the darkness again. The melody of "A Sad Song of Mill Girls"[4] rolls forth.

Lyrics:
> *"Life in a mill dorm's a sad, hard tale,*
> *Like a bird in a cage, like a pris'ner in jail.")*

Scene One: Me

(Darkness. . . . A sound is heard. What sound? It is like the sound of water. Going and coming, coming and going . . . the waves. Yes, the waves. Then again, a sound. What sound? The sound is spinning fast. What is that sound? An incomprehensible sound. A sound that seems to clinch one's whole body. When the dim light comes up, there is a GIRL. The GIRL is surrounded by darkness, and she seems to be floating in the air.)

GIRL: Just now, I awoke to see that I am here. Where am I? *(Straining her ears.)* Won't someone tell me? Who am I? *(Straining her ears.)* Won't someone answer? *(Unintentionally looking at a knotted cord in her right hand.)* What's this?

(Abruptly an arrow of light strikes the GIRL. Somebody has shone a flashlight on her.)

GIRL: Ouch!

(A man's voice behind the light utters a soft cry, "A woman," and the light goes out. Then another flashlight strikes the GIRL from another place.)

GIRL: Ouch!

(Another man behind the light utters in surprise, "And she's drenched." He puts out the light. After a momentary pause, they both light their flashlights at the same time, throwing light on each other. They call each other's names, "Wara!" and "Tegusu!" and put out the lights.)

WARA: *(Lighting TEGUSU.)* Did you see? *(Putting out light.)*

TEGUSU: *(Lighting WARA.)* Yes, I saw! *(Putting out light.)*

WARA: *(Lighting himself.)* A girl who's drenched from head to toe, but it's not even raining. *(Putting out light.)*

TEGUSU: *(Lighting himself.)* All alone, in the dead of a moonless night.

WARA: *(Lighting the GIRL.)* Who are you?

GIRL: I don't know. *(WARA puts out light.)*

TEGUSU: *(Lighting the GIRL.)* Where are you going?

GIRL: I don't know. *(TEGUSU puts out light.)*

WARA: *(Lighting the GIRL.)* How old are you?

GIRL: I don't know.

WARA: *(Still shining light on her.)* Your parents?

GIRL: I don't know.

(WARA puts out his light.)

TEGUSU: *(Lighting the GIRL.)* Where are you from?

GIRL: *(As if by reflex.)* From the sea.

TEGUSU: *(Still shining the light on her.)* Your name?

GIRL: *(As if by reflex.)* Cocoon. *(Considering after having answered the question.)* I came from the sea. My name is Mayu. . . . It means Cocoon. I am Mayu, I am the cocoon, under the grass, under the gate, a thread and an insect.

*(*TEGUSU *puts out his light.)*

WARA: *(Lighting the* GIRL.*)* You came from the sea?

GIRL: Yes.

WARA: *(Still shining his light on her.)* And your name is Mayu?

GIRL: Yes. *(When* WARA *puts out his light.)* Turn the light on!

*(*WARA *turns his light back on in haste.)*

GIRL: Where am I?

WARA: *(Still shining his light on her.)* On a road. A straight road by the sea. *(He puts out the light.)*

GIRL: Turn the light on!

*(*TEGUSU *turns his light back on the* GIRL.*)*

GIRL: *(Asking in rapid succession.)* Who are you? Who are you and what are you doing? What are your names?

*(*TEGUSU *extinguishes his light for a moment, then shines it on himself and announces, "I am Tegusu." Then he puts out his light.)*

WARA: *(Lighting himself.)* I am Wara. *(He puts out his light.)*

TEGUSU: *(Lighting* WARA.*)* What we are doing is. . . . *(He puts out his light.)*

WARA: *(Lighting* TEGUSU.*)* Making the rounds, being on the lookout. We're the night watchmen. *(He puts out his light.)*

GIRL: Turn the light on!

*(*WARA *and* TEGUSU *turn the lights back on at the same time.)*

GIRL: I'm hungry, and I'm cold and sleepy.

(The men put out the lights. In the dark.)

GIRL: Tell me!

WARA: *(Lighting on the* GIRL.*)* Tell you what?

GIRL: I want to go.

WARA: *(Still shining the light on her.)* Go where?

GIRL: *(Impatiently.)* To the place where people go when they're hungry, cold and sleepy. To go there . . . understand?

*(*WARA *puts out his light. In the dark.)*

GIRL: There, where it's warm and bright, where it smells of food. And people are there, and sleeping mats. Do you see? Where is that place? What do you call it?

*(*WARA *lights the* GIRL *in silence.)*

GIRL: I can't remember.

*(*WARA *puts out his light.* TEGUSU *lights the* GIRL *in silence.)*

GIRL: I can't remember.

*(*TEGUSU *puts out his light. After a momentary pause, they turn the lights back on at the same time.)*

TEGUSU: The word is, "home."

GIRL: Yes, "h-o-m-e." Where is home?

(The men are twiddling the lighted flashlights.)

WARA: Go straight down and you'll find a house—a home—at the end of the road.

TEGUSU: There's a house, a home, called the Thread-and-Yarn Store.

WARA: Don't wander off. Go straight down.

TEGUSU: And don't take the wrong way.

(The men go away, turning their flashlights on and off as they recede from view. In the dark.)

GIRL: How can I get to the Thread-and-Yarn Store.

(From nowhere apparent, a woman's voice answers the question, "Go straight down." The GIRL asks the question again, and the voice answers again. Gradually the voices of women multiply.)

Scene Two: Spinning Wheels

(Sounds in the darkness. Spinning sounds. The sounds multiply and quicken, then there is light. The sounds are the sounds of spinning wheels. Simultaneously, all eleven SILK REELING WOMEN in white kimono are revolving various spinning wheels. Then.)

SILK REELING WOMAN 1: Oh!

(At her cry, the other ten SILK REELING WOMEN all together look at WOMAN 1.)

SILK REELING WOMAN 2: Oh!

(At her cry, the other ten SILK REELING WOMEN all together look at WOMAN 2.)

SILK REELING WOMAN 10: Oh!

(At her cry, the other ten SILK REELING WOMEN all together look at WOMAN 10.)

SILK REELING WOMAN 11: Oh!

(At her cry, the other ten SILK REELING WOMEN all together look at WOMAN 11.)

SILK REELING WOMAN 1: A length of thread has tangled.

SILK REELING WOMAN 2: Tangled into knots.

SILK REELING WOMAN 10: A tangled thread. . . .

SILK REELING WOMAN 11: Is an omen that someone is coming.

SILK REELING WOMAN 1: What a delight.

SILK REELING WOMAN 2: What a joy.

SILK REELING WOMAN 10: How lively it will be.

SILK REELING WOMAN 11: It's nice, isn't it?

SILK REELING WOMAN 1: *(To SILK REELING WOMAN 2.)* Have you untangled it?

SILK REELING WOMAN 2: Not yet.

SILK REELING WOMAN 10: *(To SILK REELING WOMAN 11.)* Have you untangled it?

SILK REELING WOMAN 11: No, not yet.

(SILK REELING WOMEN *make gestures of untangling thread. Unexpectedly the light goes on in a passage upstairs. The* GIRL, MAYU, *is at a loss.*)

MAYU: *(Looking at the Thread-and-Yarn Store downstairs.)* There it is, right there, but I can't get there. It's right under my eyes, but I can't reach it. If only I could get there, I'd gladly run all the way and I'd do anything just to avoid walking through life so totally alone.

(SCHOOLGIRL *in a sailor blouse appears. Addressing* MAYU, *"What are you doing here?"*)

SCHOOLGIRL: And just who might you be?

MAYU: I'm not anybody, yet. And you?

SCHOOLGIRL: I'm me.

MAYU: Your name?

SCHOOLGIRL: They'll give me a name soon enough.

MAYU: Where did you come from?

SCHOOLGIRL: From home.

MAYU: Where are you going?

SCHOOLGIRL: To the Thread-and-Yarn Store.

MAYU: Why?

SCHOOLGIRL: To look at the whores. I get a kick out of looking at them. And you, where're you from?

MAYU: From the sea.

SCHOOLGIRL: That's dumb! So, where're you going?

MAYU: Home. A house called the Thread-and-Yarn Store.

SCHOOLGIRL: Why?

MAYU: I'm hungry. . . .

SCHOOLGIRL: And?

MAYU: Cold,

SCHOOLGIRL: And?

MAYU: Sleepy.

SCHOOLGIRL: You really are stupid, aren't you? But I guess if a woman gets herself sold to that sort of place, it's gotta be for reasons like that.

MAYU: Sold?

SCHOOLGIRL: What are you, some kind of idiot? That's what they call a bawdy house. They sell thread and yarn out front, but in the back, it's their bodies they sell. I'm ditching school to take a peek at them. All the other girls in my homemaking course are in class busily sewing yukata[5] or doing some other dumb thing.

MAYU: I,

SCHOOLGIRL: What?

MAYU: I feel, it's as though I'm a sheet of paper. A sheet of white paper. When you speak. . . .

SCHOOLGIRL: What?

MAYU: I feel as if my body is being filled up with words I don't know, and in my body. . . .

SCHOOLGIRL: What?

MAYU: Letters that I don't know are heaping up. I. . . .

SCHOOLGIRL: What?

MAYU: Don't understand the words "bawdy house" and "whores."

SCHOOLGIRL: And?

MAYU: I don't understand "school," "homemaking course," and "in class." I think I understand yukata just a bit. I feel pangs of nostalgia when I hear that word.

SCHOOLGIRL: Let me get this straight.

MAYU: What?

SCHOOLGIRL: Making friends with a madwoman. . . .

MAYU: What?

SCHOOLGIRL: Or going to see the whores. . . . Which one is more fun?

MAYU: I . . . don't know.

(At this moment, a man appears in the Thread-and-Yarn Store downstairs. He is the MASTER OF THE THREAD-AND-YARN STORE, MR. NAWA.*)*

NAWA: Attention!

*(*SILK REELING WOMEN *straighten themselves.)*

NAWA: Matsu! Miss Pinetree!

SILK REELING WOMAN 1: Here.

NAWA: Ume! Miss Apricot!

SILK REELING WOMAN 2: Here.

NAWA: Sakura! Miss Cherry Blossom!

(There is no answer. NAWA *repeats, "Sakura!")*

MATSU: Please, sir,

NAWA: What?

UME: Sakura. . . .

SILK REELING WOMAN 10: Is dead.

SILK REELING WOMAN 11: By hanging herself.

SILK REELING WOMAN: She died!

SILK REELING WOMAN 3: Only the other day. . . .

SILK REELING WOMAN 4: It happened three days ago.

SILK REELING WOMAN 5: Sakura. . . .

SILK REELING WOMAN 6: Is in the depths of the sea.

SILK REELING WOMAN 7: No funeral was given.

SILK REELING WOMAN 8: No grave was dug.

MATSU: No posthumous Buddhist name, and no flowers.

UME: No chanting of the *"Namu amida butsu"*. . . .

SILK REELING WOMAN 10: The holy sutra.

SILK REELING WOMEN: *(In the tone of chanting the mock sutra "amida butsu.")* Nothing, nothing, Sakura had nothing. How miserable was Sakura, without Father, without Mother, without family register. And when she was dead, not even a home to return to. *(All together, they look at* NAWA.*)*

NAWA: It slipped my mind. *(Surveying* SILK REELING WOMEN.*)* And does that displease you?

MATSU: Her death doesn't distress us.

UME: But her absence makes us feel lonesome.

NAWA: I'll bring you a new Sakura soon, and all twelve of you women can play the *hanafuda* flower card game together. Cherry blossom and peony? *Sakura* and *botan*?

SILK REELING WOMAN 3: Four and six, that's *kabu*, a full house.

NAWA: Right, and?

SILK REELING WOMAN 4: Three and three, that's *roppō*, draw one without looking.

NAWA: Correct, and?

SILK REELING WOMAN 5: My cards add up to "a drink under the cherry blossoms."

NAWA: Yes, and?

SILK REELING WOMAN 6: Pinetree, Apricot, and Cherry Blossom, that's *akatan*—another winning combination.

NAWA: I'll soon bring you one more, and then you'll have all the players you need. Fuji! Miss Wisteria!

SILK REELING WOMAN 3: Here.

NAWA: Shōbu! Miss Iris!

SILK REELING WOMAN 4: Present.

NAWA: Botan! Miss Peony!

SILK REELING WOMAN 5: Here.

NAWA: Hagi! Miss Clover!

SILK REELING WOMAN 6: Yes.

NAWA: Tsuki! Miss Moon!

SILK REELING WOMAN 7: Present.

NAWA: Kiku! Miss Chrysanthemum.

SILK REELING WOMAN 8: Present.

NAWA: Momiji! Miss Maple.

SILK REELING WOMAN 9: Here.

NAWA: Ame! Miss Rain!

SILK REELING WOMAN 10: Here.

NAWA: Kiri! Miss Fog!

SILK REELING WOMAN 11: Present.

NAWA: *(Nodding.)* Now, about this morning. How did it go this morning?

MATSU: We didn't read the newspaper. And we didn't listen to the radio. And we didn't gossip, either.

SILK REELING WOMEN: It was a good morning.

FUJI: Then we cleaned the floor.

KIRI: Because the floor boards are reserved for valued gentlemen to walk on, we tucked up the hems of our kimono and with a loosened straw rope, we polished them all, from the alcove in the foyer to every nook and cranny in the hallways.

SILK REELING WOMEN: It was a good morning.

FUJI: Then we went to draw water. I waddled like a duck with a pail full of water.

SILK REELING WOMEN: We waddled and tottered, yo-ho! Yo-heave-ho! It was such a good morning.

NAWA: And then?

SHŌBU: Somehow I lost my footing, and from above, water splashed over me. The wooden floor was flooded. . . .

BOTAN: What shall I do?

HAGI: What shall I do?

TSUKI: What shall I do?

KIKU: What shall I do?

MOMIJI: What shall I do?

NAWA: What did you do?

MATSU: *(Half-heartedly.)* I got angry, in accordance with the rules.

NAWA: Show me.

MATSU: *(Murmuring.)* You fool.

NAWA: I can't hear you.

MATSU: *(In a normal voice.)* You fool.

NAWA: I have a feeling that I heard something.

MATSU: *(In a slightly louder voice.)* You fool!

NAWA: I think I'm beginning to hear something.

MATSU: *(In a loud voice with all her might.)* You fool!

NAWA: And then?

UME: You idiot!

AME: Imbecile!

KIRI: Old donkey!

MATSU: Stupid thing!

UME: Dumb ass!

AME: Jackass!

KIRI: You're ugly!

MATSU: You're a brat!

UME: Lewd!

AME: Homely!

KIRI: Slut!

SILK REELING WOMEN: It was a very good morning!

   (Abrupt darkness.)

Scene Three: Summer Wind

(When the light downstairs goes out, SCHOOLGIRL *upstairs says "Good-bye.")*

MAYU: Where are you going?

SCHOOLGIRL: To the Thread-and-Yarn Store. Sakura is dead. That means, they're one woman short. So I think I'll just give it a shot—being a whore. It ought to be fun. *(She heads toward the stairs.)*

MAYU: That place is both a house and a home. I have a feeling that a home is something precious. But what are you supposed to do at a house?

SCHOOLGIRL: A house is where everybody wears a smiley-face mask. A bawdy house is where everybody tells lies.

MAYU: Lies? What are they?

SCHOOLGIRL: They're living things. I'm good at lying. *(She descends the stairs.)*

MAYU: Wait! *(She starts after* SCHOOLGIRL.*)*

(Abruptly the light from downstairs strikes MAYU.*)*

MAYU: The light is so bright. . . . I can't see anything. I can't go down. *(Moving backward like a puppet.)* Don't pull me! Who's there, behind me? Somebody's pulling the string behind me. . . . I want to go down the stairs. Stop manipulating me! There's a house over there. I want to go down to the house.

(Still, MAYU *keeps moving backward, being manipulated by somebody. As the light fades out, a soprano voice of a boy flows in from nowhere apparent. "This Town and That Town"[6] by Noguchi Ujō is sung in the dark.*

Lyrics:
In this town and that town,
Light is falling, light is falling
Take this path that we have followed,
Let's make our way home, let's make our way home.

Step by step, home
Is receding, is receding.

Take this path that we have followed,
Let's make our way home, let's make our way home.

In the sky, evening
Stars are coming out, stars are coming out.

Take this path that we have followed,
Let's make our way home, let's make our way home.

The singing voice mingles with the sound of spinning wheels. When the light comes up downstairs, twelve SILK REELING WOMEN *are discovered. Eleven women are in black kimono, and one is in a sailor blouse. This one is the* SCHOOLGIRL. *In front of the* SILK REELING WOMEN *are* NAWA *and the* REGISTRAR, HIMO. *They are standing facing each other like mirror images.)*

HIMO: It looks like a funeral.

MATSU: When the world weighs heavy on us, we wear black kimono.

UME: When we receive our customers, we wear red kimono.

KIRI: When we reel thread, we wear white kimono.

AME: The funeral was over three days ago.

*(*SILK REELING WOMEN *make a bow together, as if they were leaves swaying in the wind. Only* SCHOOLGIRL *who has become* SAKURA *does not bow.)*

HIMO: In short, since you are receiving me in black kimono, it means I am not welcome.

MATSU: I don't like having strangers sniffing about.

UME: What's more, I don't like having the entire Japanese population of seventy million sniffing about.

HIMO: I am a certified registrar of Japan.

SAKURA: What's a registrar?

NAWA: That one's a newcomer.

HIMO: *(Matter-of-factly.)* He who adheres to the necessary legal formalities, as stipulated by the New Family Registration Act, in order to provide new family registers to whomsoever may lack said registers, that is who I am.

UME: Please, sir. . . .

HIMO: What is it?

MATSU: We. . . .

AME: Though lacking family registers. . . .

KIRI: Have no problems.

HIMO: But for Japan it is a problem. You're like kites whose strings have snapped. Don't you see, if we don't do something about it, you won't be able to bear children, or get married, or anything.

FUJI: Do family registers bear children?

SHŌBU: Isn't it women who bear children?

KIRI: You ignoramus!

AME: You idiot!

MATSU: It's dogs that bear children!

SHŌBU: I didn't know that.

AME: Dogs have as many as eight tits because they bear children.

UME: But a human has only two breasts, so she can't bear children.

KIRI: She just raises them, that's all. Now you understand?

(SHŌBU's head droops.)

HIMO: Who taught you such a thing?

SILK REELING WOMEN: Our MASTER!

NAWA: Well, I realize that these women don't have family registers. But what am I supposed do about it? You can't make something out of nothing.

HIMO: Well then, let me ask you a question. *(Pointing at FUJI.)* What if you fell in love with this woman, married her, and then found out that she was your little sister?

NAWA: All humans are brothers and sisters.

HIMO: What?

NAWA: Haven't you heard about the Jukes?

HIMO: The what?

NAWA: A family line of criminals, the Jukes. Among five hundred and forty members of the family, sixty were habitual thieves, fifty were prostitutes, and one hundred and eighty were shiftless, lazy bums who never did an honest day's work. After thirty years, someone did a survey showing that these Jukes had multiplied to something over two thousand members. Of these, one hundred and seventy-one were criminals, a little less than three hundred were prostitutes. And over two hundred were unemployed bums.

HIMO: Don't say such things. You'll just give them the creeps and they'll all clam up. *(In a coaxing voice.)* Look, I'm going to show you something nice. *(He takes a string out of his pocket. At the end of the string is a black ball.)* This black ball represents bygone days. Those bygone days that you talk about when you say "once upon a time." And this string is time. Now, time is beginning to spin in reverse. *(Beginning to swing the string.)* Once upon a time, there was. . . . Do you see anything? Do you see a clue to your family register?

(With this, SILK REELING WOMEN begin to sway their upper bodies. Only SAKURA is the exception—she is staring at the scene with unblinking eyes. The sound of time ticking away seconds. HIMO and NAWA exit, leaving SILK REELING WOMEN there. At this moment, the eleven women each take a string with a black ball out of their bosoms and begin to swing them. Eleven strings swing eleven kinds of bygone days in eleven tempos.)

MATSU: A wind

UME: A wind is

FUJI: A wind is blowing

SHŌBU: A wind is blowing over the sea

BOTAN: The sea where the wind is blowing

HAGI: By the sea where the wind is blowing

TSUKI: I am by the sea where the wind is blowing

KIKU: I am by the sea where the wind is blowing, eating

MOMIJI: I am by the sea where the wind is blowing, eating, drinking

AME: I am by the sea where the wind is blowing, eating, drinking, and tasting

KIRI: I am by the sea where the wind is blowing, eating, drinking, and tasting the wind.

(Eleven SILK REELING WOMEN *stick out their red tongues and taste the wind.)*

KIRI: The summer wind   the wind flickering

UME: Flickeringly, swayingly, the wind   the summer wind

AME: No, dozing   the sun

KIRI: My skin loosening

MATSU, UME, *and* AME: Flickeringly, dozingly, flicker-dozingly

UME: My bones   unravelling

AME: Yes, wrinkles melting

KIRI: The summer wind   the wind   summer   the summer wind

UME: It's warm   the wind

AME: Dreamingly quiet.

MATSU, UME, *and* AME: Yes   summer   the summer wind   quiet

KIRI: *(Putting her tongue out and tasting the wind.)* It's sweet, the taste of the wind is thick and sweet, and it smells, a faint scent of straw.

UME: *(Putting her tongue out and tasting the wind.)* It's like the taste of the shady spot where I doze off. The summer wind whooshes into my belly and makes me drowsy.

AME: *(Putting her tongue out and tasting the wind.)* Slightly moist. A shower the day before yesterday, the rain still lingering, still refreshingly cool.

MATSU, UME, *and* KIRI: No, dozing in my body.

MATSU: In this way, when the wind is soft,

UME, AME, *and* KIRI: Eh?

MATSU: It reminds me of bygone days.

UME, AME, *and* KIRI: Eh? Yes.

KIRI: What was summer like?

MATSU: Summer was filled with polka-dots.

UME: The summer wind snapping

AME: Popping open on my skin

MATSU: Polka dots.

KIRI: The wind, the dozing summer wind

UME: Summoning the heat

AME: Dropping

MATSU: Polka dots.

KIRI: The naked wind

UME: Whistlingly, it fans me

AME: On the sand I am

MATSU: Polka dots.

UME, AME, *and* KIRI: Ah! A sigh. The wind   summer the summer wind.

KIRI: Wafting a flood of summer sunlight.

UME: Oozing a heavy, sour, fruity scent.

AME: Ruffling my beating, beating heart.

MATSU, UME, *and* KIRI: Yes the wind, the ark, the summer wind.

KIRI: Will the ark arrive?

UME: Eventually.

AME: Yes, in the far west, beyond the horizon.

> (*Four* SILK REELING WOMEN *murmur, "The wind, the summer wind, the summer wind is blowing and quiet" and seem drowsy. The lower floor is shrouded in the hazy dusk. Abruptly,* MAYU *upstairs murmurs, "Lies."*)

MAYU: Yes, all lies. The creature named "Lie" is secreting transparent threads connecting the whores to me. The summer wind was not suffused with light. It was wafting the stink of rotting lies. The wind? The wind is rising. I . . . I . . . am remembering something. My body aches. The wind is a scissors cutting and snapping the lying threads that have sewn up my memory. My body aches with the cuts.

> (*An evening glow from bygone days shines into the upper floor.*)

MAYU: The evening glow. . . . In this glow, the truth can be seen. The truth is floating in the shape of a man's body. . . . Yes, it's coming back to me. You, there in the twilight, a pale glow like watery blood, the man is you. . . . Sweetheart, do you remember?

> (*The evening glow is gradually becoming deeper at an almost unnoticeable pace.*)

MAYU: You were in a forest, just standing there, and you looked like you were going to hang yourself. I was watching, afraid, so afraid. Hiding behind a tree, but then I ran out and screamed, "No, don't die!" Do you remember, dear?

You looked at me, startled. I said, "You mustn't hang yourself!" and you started to laugh, but you were still frowning, which made your face look really strange. Then you said, "I have a toothache." You said that you hadn't slept because of that decayed tooth, aching and aching all night long, and the next day, too. That's why your face had the look of a man who wanted to hang himself. Do you remember, dear?

I had some thread. I was on my way home from the thread-and-yarn shop in town where I'd bought red thread, and I had a lot of it. So I tied a single length of red thread to your decayed tooth, and. . . .

Darling, do you remember, dear?

You and I, we played tug of war with that long red thread. A single thread that stretched from your mouth to me.

I held the end of the thread, and tugged. With all my strength, I tugged, I tugged with all my strength.

. . . Then it came out! I fell on my backside. . . . Remember, sweetheart? You held me in your arms and lifted me to my feet, then you said, "Thank you." After that, we went home together without saying a word. When night fell, I became aware, it wasn't till night that I realized—I was still holding your tooth tight in my hand. . . . This is it, that tooth, your tooth, your decayed tooth. . . .

(Taking the man's tooth out of her pocket, MAYU *presses it to her breasts. A deep sigh. The evening glow is gradually turning into moonlight.)*

Scene Four: The Knotted Rope of Memory

*(*MAYU *is staring at the moon absentmindedly.* WARA *and* TEGUSU *appear with scissors in their hands.)*

WARA: She's still here.

TEGUSU: The girl, the one who came from the sea, soaking-wet on a moonless night, she's here.

WARA: I can barely make her out. Hey, you!

*(*MAYU *looks at* WARA.*)*

WARA: Weren't you going to the Thread-and-Yarn Store?

MAYU: I tried, but the road stretched on and on. . . .

TEGUSU: And you got lost on that straight road?

MAYU: I went straight ahead.

WARA: And?

MAYU: The road was strewn with pebbles, stretching endlessly.

TEGUSU: Then?

MAYU: Then I walked into an alley.

WARA: And then?

MAYU: Another alley, then a little further on, still another alley.

WARA: And you didn't ask anyone how to get to the Thread-and-Yarn Store?

MAYU: I did. But at every house, the answer was always the same. "Go straight down," a woman's voice would say. So I walked down only to find an alley, and the road kept twisting and turning, in and out, this way and that, like tangled rope.

TEGUSU: In short, she got lost.

WARA: In fact, she's been lost for seven days and nights.

TEGUSU: And she's still here,

WARA: Yes still here. Now what are you doing?

MAYU: I'm looking at that. *(Raising her eyes to look up at the sky.)*

WARA: That?

MAYU: Yes, that. What's the name of that thing?

TEGUSU: That? That's the sky.

MAYU: I know the sky. . . . That thing in the sky. The one that's floating in the sky, balancing itself with the weight of dreams.

TEGUSU: The moon. That's the moon.

MAYU: Yes, the moon. I'm looking at the moon. Now I remember.

WARA: This girl, her mind's like a sieve, all full of holes.

TEGUSU: Yes, and words keep dripping through the holes.

MAYU: Say. . . .

WARA: Well?

MAYU: There's one thing I do remember.

TEGUSU: Tell us.

MAYU: There was a man.

WARA: What kind of man? What was his age, his name, what did he look like?

MAYU: I can't remember his face. I just remember what happened. We played tug of war with a red thread. Then a decayed tooth came out. His decayed tooth. . . . Say, *(To* WARA.*)* are you him?

WARA: I'm Wara.

MAYU: *(To* TEGUSU.*)* Are you him?

TEGUSU: I'm Tegusu.

WARA: We're Wara and Tegusu, and we're making our appointed rounds as night watchmen, that's what we're doing. Ah-choo! *(He sneezes.* MAYU *springs up to pat* WARA *on each of his shoulders.)*

MAYU: Tokomanzai.

WARA: What?

MAYU: It's a charm against sneezing, tokomanzai. *(Realizing something after she said this.)* Something just came back to me.

TEGUSU: What?

MAYU: When you sneeze, your soul flies out of your body. So you have to knot some thread to keep your soul tied up in a knotted ball. Here, like this. *(She shows them a length of knotted rope.)*

WARA: That's disgusting! *(Shrinking back.)*

TEGUSU: It looks like a dead snake. Crippled, deformed, covered with lumps! *(Shrinking back.)*

MAYU: It's everything that's ever happened.

WARA: It's just a wad of thread!

TEGUSU: Since you have such a long piece of thread, why not just use it to let yourself down, hand over hand?

WARA: Why not just go straight down using those knotted balls as footholds?

TEGUSU: The Thread-and-Yarn Store is right before your eyes.

WARA: Yes, the house is right there.

(TEGUSU *and* WARA, *stepping backward, recede from view.* MAYU, *left alone, mutters to herself,* "Going down . . . with this thread?")

MAYU: If I go down, I'll come to the house. All I have to do is let the thread down and then use it to climb down. Can I do it? A bird has wings, but thread is wingless. Still, I could at least fall. I don't need wings to fall . . . so, fall!

(She drops the length of thread-rope. At the same time, the lower floor lights up. The Thread-and-Yarn Store is in richly colored night. All SILK REELING WOMEN *are in red kimono. Directly below the knotted thread are* SILK REELING WOMAN AME, *and a customer,* BLANK MASK.*)*

AME: It began to rain. *(Touching the knotted rope as if receiving rain with her hand.)* . . . The rain in June is cool to the hand, and soft on the cheek. . . . It feels good. *(Untying one of the knots of the knotted rope.)* . . . The rain unties time, opens me up, and reminds me of something.

BLANK MASK: What does it remind you of?

AME: The old days.

BLANK MASK: Some kind of hard-luck story, is it?

AME: Yes, it just popped into my mind.

BLANK MASK: What's it about?

AME: Something that happened.

BLANK MASK: I'm willing to listen to a whore's hard-luck story, if it's a good lie, cause a good lie is like a lullaby, but true stories are just plain boring.

AME: But it just came back to me, and I want to talk about it.

BLANK MASK: Must you?

AME: Yes, I must.

BLANK MASK: Then go ahead. I'll listen with both ears closed.

AME: It was raining. The kind of rain that invades the memory like a moist flower's cloying, sweet-sour scent.

BLANK MASK: Well?

AME: On a rainy day in June, a lovers' suicide.

BLANK MASK: Who were they?

AME: Me, and a man. . . .

BLANK MASK: When?

AME: At dawn. . . .

BLANK MASK: And it was raining, you say?

AME: Yes. . . . We had seen the evening stars, but when we awoke, it was raining. . . . We had to go, we. . . .

BLANK MASK: Go where?

AME: To die together. We awoke planning to go somewhere, but we sensed the rain falling, pouring.

BLANK MASK: The neighborhood was shrouded by the scent of rain. . . .

AME: And yet, we sensed the glimmer of what seemed to be serene blue sky high above, glimmering only for the two of us.

BLANK MASK: Serene blue sky. . . . *(Showing signs of a wry smile.)*

AME: Say. . . .

BLANK MASK: What?

AME: You look alike.

BLANK MASK: Eh?

AME: You, mister, you look like him.

BLANK MASK: Like who?

AME: Him. Me and my man, the two of us, we were walking on a footpath in a rice field. We held hands so tightly that my hand felt hot, as if a fire were spreading from him to me. We were walking fast. Hurrying along a railroad track.

BLANK MASK: Why were you hurrying?

AME: We were going to commit double suicide. Our plan would be ruined if somebody saw us.

BLANK MASK: Why?

AME: Eh?

BLANK MASK: Why did you want to commit suicide?

AME: We were poor.

BLANK MASK: That's easy to understand. And then?

AME: Dogs.

BLANK MASK: Eh?

AME: Dogs.

BLANK MASK: Dogs?

AME: Yes, dogs surrounded us. Before we were aware . . . in the morning . . . three dogs. . . .

BLANK MASK: . . . were storming around, barking, barking, and barking, jumping up and pawing at us. . . . *(Suddenly he puts his hands on the ground and gets on all four, becoming a dog.)*

AME: No! Dogs! Dogs, dogs. . . . Dogs! I cried out, and dropped his hand, his dear hand, I let go of his hand. . . . (BLANK MASK *still on all fours, leaves her.)* How long was I there *(without noticing that she is left alone),* how long. . . how long. . . . He wasn't with me, no, he wasn't with me. Deep water, engulfing me. A dark swamp, surrounding me. Torrents of rain, wicked flashes of lightning, raging wind, the water raging, writhing, surging, and I. . . was alone. What happened to him, I wonder? Was he swept off his feet, carried away. . . . I never saw him again. Fate rules our life, doesn't it? *(Becoming aware.)* Sir? Where have you gone?

(She leaves, looking for the customer. Replacing her, another SILK REELING WOMAN, KIRI, *comes out of the group of* SILK REELING WOMEN *behind. She murmurs, "Fog. . . ." Murmuring "Fog is setting in," she touches the knotted rope as if to feel the fog.)*

KIRI: The fog in autumn is cool to the hand, and soft on the cheek . . . it feels good. *(Untying a knot of the knotted rope.)* The fog unties time, opens me up . . . and reminds me of something.

(Abruptly, she straightens herself and bows low. Unnoticed, BLANK MASK *is back as* KIRI'S *"customer.")*

BLANK MASK: It looks like the sea. White fog is settling in, and just outside the door . . . the sea.

KIRI: That's exactly what I was thinking, how like the sea it is. And you know, I just remembered something.

BLANK MASK: What did you remember?

KIRI: The old days.

BLANK MASK: Your life story?

KIRI: Yes, I remembered my house. In the woods, there were three oleaster trees, and as you left the woods, there was a brook, and then you walked down a winding path at the side of the brook, and then you'd find a house, and that was my house.

BLANK MASK: I've already heard one life story tonight.

KIRI: But you have two ears. It just popped into my mind. I want to talk about it.

BLANK MASK: Must you?

KIRI: Yes, I must.

BLANK MASK: Then go ahead. I'll doze off as I listen.

KIRI: Hushabye, trav'ler, just rest and retire,

This inn that is me fills ev'ry desire.

Hushabye, sleepyhead, dream until dawn.

My heart will be saddened after you've gone.

(BLANK MASK *falls asleep.*)

KIRI: He's asleep. Fast asleep. Once . . . I killed a man who was asleep. (BLANK MASK *squeezes himself in.*) . . . Don't worry. I'll strangle you softly. Gently and softly, I'll do my best to cut your head off. I'll bury your body in a plowed field, and then I'll sow seeds over you. We'll play together just like we did in the old days. Know what? You look alike. You look just like the man I killed.

(*The lower floor fades out.* BLANK MASK *gets up in the fade-out. He goes to the stairs.*)

Scene Five: Autumn Wind

(MAYU, *lingering upstairs, murmurs, "The knotted ball is loosening."*)

MAYU: I have a feeling that I've been tied up by all sorts of things. My hair was tied with ribbons, my body was tied with sashes and cords, and when I hurt myself, I was bound up with bandages, and when I did something wrong, I was bound with ropes. And yes, after dark, I made knots in a long piece of thread. The thread became a rope, and when I asked, "What do I do with this?" somebody answered, "That rope is made of sacred lotus flowers. While you're alive, you make a rope to bind yourself, and when you're dead, you'll be bound tightly by it. That rope is meant to restrain the dead." I asked again, "Who ties up the dead?" and the same person answered, "The living do."

Then the same person told me, "When I am dead, bind me with my rope. When you are dead, I will bind you with your rope." . . . I can't remember . . . who the person was . . . I can't remember.

(BLANK MASK, *ascending the stairs during* MAYU*'s speech, takes off his mask. He is* NAWA.)

NAWA: Something's wrong. . . . Yes, there's something wrong. Two of my silk reeling ladies began to tell life stories that I never taught them. My stories were about things like taking shelter from the rain, or walking under the same umbrella, or about cheerful rain, but most definitely not about double-suicide in the rain. And the fog story—that was about playing hide-and-seek and tag in the fog, not about murder. Nevertheless, those two told stories that were new to me. . . . What the hell is this? Who put those stories in their heads?

(MAYU *murmurs upstairs,* "Who taught me the story?" NAWA, *at the stairs, murmurs,* "Who taught them the stories?")

MAYU: Who?

NAWA: Who?

MAYU: Who?

NAWA: Who?

MAYU: Who?

NAWA: Who?

(*Inquiring and inquiring, then* NAWA *abruptly cries out,* "Now I see!" *He stares fixedly at* MAYU.)

MAYU: Me?

NAWA: You there!

MAYU: Who is it?

NAWA: It is I.

MAYU: Do you know me? I don't know you.

NAWA: You are Mayu. You are truly Miss Cocoon, a silkworm that spins.

MAYU: Don't come near me. I'm scared of strangers. Don't come near me.

NAWA: I'll catch you.

(*Abruptly music flows in. Four* BLANK MASK MEN *appear. They pull strings. The strings are tied to* MAYU. MAYU *staggers, being pulled.*)

BLANK MASK 1: Paper, scissors, stone. I want that girl, alone. (*Pulling the string.*)

BLANK MASK 2: Paper, scissors, stone. That girl's to me unknown. (*Pulling the string.*)

BLANK MASK 3: Paper, scissors, stone. That homeless girl's to me unknown. (*Pulling the string.*)

BLANK MASK 4: Paper, scissors, stone. Her strings are cut, she's lost, an orphan girl, alone. (*Pulling the string.*)

MAYU: Stop tying me, stop binding me, stop manipulating me. Stop pulling me down to the hell made of thread.

*(*MAYU, *although trying hard, is unable to escape. She struggles and writhes. She flounces around like a fish caught in the net. The men keep pulling the string.) [Translators' note: The action is highly rhythmic.]*

BLANK MASK 1: Silk reeling, cat's cradle, true-lover's knot. *(Pulling the string.)*

BLANK MASK 2: Fishing line, blackened rope, girdle and belt. *(Pulling the string.)*

BLANK MASK 3: Woolen yarn, bandage, silkworm's gut, straw. *(Pulling the string.)*

BLANK MASK 4: Silken thread, tug of war, crimson-colored cord. *(Pulling the string.)*

MAYU: I haven't finished weaving the thread, but my whole body's already sewn up. Stop it! Be gone, you faceless, blank masks! Don't sew me up with invisible threads!

NAWA: I have something to ask you.

MAYU: Please, cut the thread. I'll answer your question.

NAWA: Why did you come here?

MAYU: I didn't come. I was here. I discovered that I happened to be here. I don't want to be here. I want to run away.

NAWA: A thousand threads are behind you.

MAYU: Just one would be enough to help me escape.

(Abruptly MAYU *runs to the stairs. A ray of light shines from downstairs aiming at* MAYU. *Yet* MAYU *keeps going down. When the light comes on downstairs,* SILK REELING WOMEN *in white* kimono *spin their spinning wheels in silence. The sound of spinning wheels reverberates. As if possessed, the* SILK REELING WOMEN *spin the wheels.)*

MATSU: Tick tock one minute.

UME: Tick tock two minutes.

SAKURA: Tick tock three minutes.

FUJI: Tick tock four minutes.

SHŌBU: Tick tock five minutes.

BOTAN: Tick tock six minutes.

HAGI: Tick tock seven minutes.

TSUKI: Tick tock eight minutes.

KIKU: Tick tock nine minutes.

MOMIJI: Tick tock ten minutes.

AME: We've made enough time pass.

KIRI: That's enough, now. She should be out of danger.

*(*SILK REELING WOMEN *give a sigh of relief. Slowly they spin the spinning wheels.)*

MATSU: Something inside me was pushing me on.

UME: My hands moved spontaneously,

SAKURA: To spin the spinning wheel.

FUJI: As if somebody were

SHŌBU: Ordering me to spin the wheel,

BOTAN: As if I heard

HAGI: A voice whispering to spin the wheel,

TSUKI: Without knowing why

KIKU: Without even thinking

MOMIJI: I was spinning the spinning wheel.

AME: I wonder why.

KIRI: It was probably just a passing whim.

> (MAYU *stands riveted in the middle of the stairs. She murmurs, "I can't go down.")*

MAYU: But I can't go up, either. Suspended in midair between here and there, between above and below. Somebody's pulling the string from above. Somebody's pulling the string from below.

Two fibers, both alike in forcefulness

Conspiring and tugging me here and there

Opposing filaments of equal stress

Pulling and binding, my soul's in despair.

> (*Abruptly* SILK REELING WOMAN MATSU *asks, "Eh?" to nobody particular.* SILK REELING WOMEN *look at* MATSU *together.*)

MATSU: Did somebody call me?

> (SILK REELING WOMEN *shake their heads "no" together, and spin the spinning wheels in silence. Then again abruptly* SILK REELING WOMAN UME *asks, "Eh?"* SILK REELING WOMEN *look at* UME *all at once.*)

UME: Did somebody call me?

> (SILK REELING WOMEN *shake their heads left and right together, and negating, spin the spinning wheels. Then the same happens to* SILK REELING WOMEN AME *and* KIRI.)

MATSU: I have a feeling that somebody called to me.

UME: I have a feeling that I've been called to by some dear name.

AME: By a word that tickles my nose like the scent of milk,

KIRI: I have a feeling that somebody has called to me.

> (*The four women exchange glances. At this moment,* MAYU *in the middle of the stairs murmurs, "Mother."*)

MATSU: Eh? (*The other three look at* MATSU.)

UME: Eh? (*The other three look at* UME.)

AME: Eh? (*The other three look at* AME.)

KIRI: Eh? (*The other three look at* KIRI.)

> (MAYU *on the stairs, in surprise.*)

MAYU: I, now, just now, I called out "Mother." And then, yes, I was reminded of something. At the place called home, there is Mother. Someone is at that house. Mother is there. Who is Mother? Someone is Mother. But Mother doesn't have a face yet.

(SILK REELING WOMAN MATSU *murmurs, "The wind is rising."* SILK REELING WOMAN UME *says, "The autumn wind," and* SILK REELING WOMAN AME *replies, "The wind of autumn," then* SILK REELING WOMAN KIRI *says, "The wind is blowing.")*

MATSU: When the autumn wind hints of frost,

UME: The wind of autumn puffs up my sleeves.

AME: The roar of the autumn wind is stronger than stone,

KIRI: And a whiff of autumn wind snuffs out a flame

ALL FOUR: Whoosh. *(A sigh.)*

MATSU: My breath mingles with the scent of autumn wind,

UME: And in that dead autumnal wind, whiffing and whistling,

AME: Whiffing and whistling,

KIRI: A whore dies.

MATSU: Whiffing and whistling,

UME: Whiffing and whistling,

AME: Whiffing and whistling,

KIRI: Whiffing and whistling,

MATSU: More amorous than the springtime wind,

UME: Even more amorous than the summer wind,

AME: Far more amorous than the winter wind,

KIRI: When I open my body to the autumn wind,

MATSU: More amorously than the springtime wind,

UME: Even more amorously than the summer wind,

AME: Far more amorously than the winter wind,

KIRI: The autumn wind runs through my body.

MATSU: Whiffing and whistling,

UME: Whiffing and whistling,

AME: Whiffing and whistling,

KIRI: Whiffing and whistling,

MATSU: A hundred men, scurrying like deserting soldiers,

UME, AME, *and* KIRI: Whistling, whistling,

UME: Run through my body.

MATSU, AME, *and* KIRI: Whistling, whistling,

AME: Although I hover in the corner of an alley, warming my body in a small patch of sunlight

MATSU, UME, *and* KIRI: Whistling, whistling,

KIRI: When the autumn wind whistles, my body grows cold.

MATSU: The cold wind,

UME: Whistling,

AME: The freezing wind,

KIRI: Whistling,

MATSU: An old woman's hair is tousled in the amorous wind,

UME: Tangled,

AME: Knotted,

KIRI: Swirled,
MATSU: Unraveled before she knows,
UME: Thinning out,
AME: Falling out,
KIRI: Gone.
MATSU: When you notice—gray hairs.
UME: When you touch—wrinkles.
AME: When you feel—bones.
KIRI: When you look—dust.
ALL FOUR: Whoosh. *(A heavy sigh.)*
   (The lower floor fades out.)

Scene Six: The Sacred Family

(A children's song is sung in the dark. "Cutting the Thread"[7] by Noguchi Ujō.

Lyrics:
Which thread shall we
Have the locust cut?
The thread is loosened,
Have it twisted and cut.

The locust
Has cut the red thread.

With its tiny mouth
It has snapped the red thread.

When the solo voice has thinned away in the wind, a light the color of smoke fades up as if throwing a light on MAYU*'s memory. On the upper floor,* MOTHER 1 *with a patch over her right eye—being manipulated by* KUROKO 1—*nestles up to* MAN 1 *dressed in student black—manipulated by* KUROKO 2.
On the lower floor, MOTHER 2 *with a patch over her left eye—being manipulated by* KUROKO 3—*is wooed by* MAN 2 *dressed in student black—manipulated by* KUROKO 4.
On the stairs is MAYU.*)*

MAYU: There weren't any locusts. Then I saw it. The day—like a void, windless—and then I saw something, like a mirage. The sliding paper door just slipped open, as though controlled by some mechanism, and I saw them. Mother and him.
   *(*MOTHER 1 *and* MOTHER 2 *are manipulated so that they each brandish a pair of scissors.)*

MOTHER 1: I'll cut it.

MOTHER 2: I'll cut it.

   (MAN 1 *is manipulated to draw back.* MAN 2 *is manipulated to draw close to* MOTHER 2.)

MAN 1: What are you going to cut?

MAN 2: What are you going to cut?

MOTHER 1: I will cut the bonds of love.

MOTHER 2: I will cut the bonds of love.

MAN 1: Can you do that?

MAN 2: Can you do that?

MOTHER 1: Of course I can.

MOTHER 2: Of course I can.

   (MOTHER 1 *is manipulated to move like a puppet.*)

MOTHER 1: The thread, if I can't tie you with the red thread of love, then I'd rather cut it and be done with it forever.

   (MOTHER 2 *is manipulated to move like a puppet.*)

MOTHER 2: The thread, if you try to tie me with the red thread of love, then I'd rather cut it and be done with it forever.

   (MOTHER 1 *and* MOTHER 2, *in the exactly same movement.*)

MOTHER 1: Becoming disgusted, she cuts her throat,

MOTHER 2: A lonely mother with tousled hair,

MOTHER 1: Killing the fires that burn her heart,

MOTHER 2: Slashing the air,

MOTHER 1 *and* MOTHER 2: Yes, I will die.

MAN 1: Don't frighten me.

MAN 2: Don't frighten me.

MOTHER 1: It's no joke. I wouldn't lie

MOTHER 2: About a thing like this.

MOTHER 1: I'm serious. *(She is manipulated to cut the ties of love.)*

MOTHER 2: I'm serious. *(She is manipulated to cut the ties of love.)*

   (MAYU *cries out, "Stop!"* MOTHER 1, MOTHER 2, MAN 1, *and* MAN 2 *are manipulated to come to a standstill.*)

MAYU: I tried to cry out "Don't," but the voice stuck in my throat. And my feet wouldn't move, either. From behind, someone pulled the string, sewing me to the ground. Even my voice was sewn up deep in my throat. In my whole body, only my eyes were free. I didn't care if they were open or closed. Then I saw it. I forced my eyes to stay open, and I saw it. Though I didn't want to look, I saw it.

   (MOTHER 1 *is manipulated to be near* MAN 1. MOTHER 2 *is manipulated to be separate from* MAN 2.)

MOTHER 1: What shall we do?

MOTHER 2: What shall we do?

MAN 1: We should hang ourselves.

MAN 2: We should hang ourselves.

MOTHER 1: Eeny, Meeny, Miney, Mo. I want to catch you by the toe. I want you.

MAN 1: I don't want you. I want the girl. Red Rover, Red Rover, send little girl over.

MAN 2: Eeny, Meeny, Miney, Mo. I want to catch you by the toe. I want you.

MOTHER 2: I don't want you. I want the girl. Red Rover, Red Rover, send little girl over.

MOTHER 1: I hate the girl.

MAN 1: I love the girl.

MAN 2: I hate the girl.

MOTHER 2: I love the girl.

MOTHER 1: That girl, who's child is she? My child.

MOTHER 2: I can't cut the ties because she's my child.

MOTHER 1 *and* MOTHER 2: I want to cut the ties because she's my child.

MAYU: Everybody said there was a lovers' suicide in the woods. But it wasn't a lovers' suicide. It was a murder. Mother and he went into the woods to commit double suicide, but only the man died. Mother killed him. . . . Now I remember why I came here.

(MAYU sits down holding her knees in her arms. She stares in the air. The lights upstairs and downstairs go out. Only the figure of MAYU can be seen clearly.)

MAYU: Here I am suspended in the middle of a sloping road. I can't go upstairs or downstairs. The sun's shining, but everything seems so dim. Like a scene engulfed in thick fog. The wind's died down, and the sound has died away. The silence—it's not a piercing silence, just as still as death. And it seems to be getting darker and darker, little by little, even though the sun's still shining.

(MAYU speaks in order to avoid facing the restored memory. Unexpectedly at the top of the stairs appears NAWA.)

NAWA: Have you remembered?

MAYU: Yes.

NAWA: When? Where? What happened?

MAYU: In the old days, at my house, Mother and he. . . .

NAWA: You saw it, right?

MAYU: Yes.

NAWA: How?

MAYU: With my own eyes.

NAWA: You say that with your own eyes, you saw what happened behind the closed sliding paper door?

MAYU: Eh?

NAWA: Your eyes may have been open, but the sliding paper door was closed.

MAYU: It was open! My eyes and the sliding paper door were both open.

NAWA: It was closed. That's why what happened always comes back in two kinds of scenes.

MAYU: Mother tried to seduce him, she tried to bind him with the threads of love, but she failed, and so she killed him.

NAWA: Mother was almost seduced by him, she was almost bound by the threads of love, but she became frightened, and so she killed him.

MAYU: I don't know . . . which was true . . . but. . . .

NAWA: But?

MAYU: She killed him. In the woods.

NAWA: Did you see it?

MAYU: I heard about it.

NAWA: Nothing happened. You're just a puppet, and all your movements are manipulated by a string called imagination.

MAYU: No, that's not true.

NAWA: You secrete threads of imagined hatred for Mother, you spin webs around yourself until you're tightly bound. Then you hang there suspended, unable to go either up or down. That's you.

MAYU: No. I finally remember why I came here, why I found the way.

NAWA: Tell me. Why?

MAYU: *(Murmurs.)* I came here to kill Mother. I came here to cut the thread. Mother is down there, spinning thread. I end up dancing because Mother spins the spinning wheel. I came here to cut that thread.

NAWA: There's a woman for every month of the year down there. Which one is your mother?

MAYU: Someone is Mother. The one whose life story is the story I know, that one is Mother. Someone who unties the knotted ball and lets me remember, that one is Mother!

(When MAYU cries out, the lower floor becomes bright.)

Scene Seven: Dog / Tattooed

(WOMEN are reeling silk off cocoons in the hazy daylight. MAYU on the stairs, asks.)

MAYU: You there, are you my mother?

MATSU: Somebody has been constantly asking that question for a couple of days now. Is she asking me? I'm not a mother.

MAYU: You there, are you my mother?

UME: There'a fly buzzing in my ear, constantly asking for Mother. Such a bother. I'm not a mother.

MAYU: You there, are you my mother?

SAKURA: Stupid.

MAYU: You there, are you my mother?

FUJI: Sippi-dee, dippi-dee, cricki-tee, bee!

Just beautiful faces we happy girls see.

MAYU: You there, are you my mother?

SHŌBU: Fiddle-dee, diddle-dee, piggle-dee, pen!

  Been sold to the butcher, poor chick's mother hen.

MAYU: You there, are you my mother?

BOTAN: Hoggle-dee, poggle-dee, ippi-tee, day!

  The weasel's at home while stepmother's away.

MAYU: You there, are you my mother?

HAGI: What's a mother?

MAYU: You there, are you my mother?

TSUKI: I'm a mother when I'm playing house.

MAYU: You there, are you my mother?

KIKU: Mother was somewhere.

MAYU: You there, are you my mother?

MOMIJI: You are my mother.

MAYU: You there, are you my mother?

AME: Don't bother me. It's a cloudy day and I feel uneasy, but there's a voice incessantly calling me mother, and it's really getting on my nerves. I'm a whore.

MAYU: You there, are you my mother?

KIRI: If you want a mother, look in the mirror. Your mother is trapped in the mirror, getting old at the same pace as you.

MAYU: They're lying. Someone's lying.

  (At this moment, BLANK MASK *appears. He is actually* NAWA.*)*

MAYU: Somebody, please unravel one of the knotted balls. Tell me your life story. . . . *(She throws the knotted rope downstairs.* SILK REELING WOMAN MATSU *takes the rope, and unties a knotted ball.* BLANK MASK *sits in front of* MATSU.*)*

MATSU: Sorry, hanky-panky's not permitted in daytime. We'll be dressed in white kimono as long as the sun is out.

NAWA: I didn't come for hanky-panky.

MATSU: Then you came to buy thread?

NAWA: I came to hear your life story.

MATSU: We don't sell such items here. We only sell thread and our favors.

NAWA: But I want to hear it.

MATSU: Whose life story do you want to hear?

NAWA: Yours.

MATSU: Really? . . . This knot, it's too tight, I just can't unravel it. . . . Ah! . . . Did you see it?

NAWA: What?

MATSU: A life story flew out.

NAWA: I didn't see a thing.

MATSU: That was my life story.

NAWA: Let me listen to it again. It went by so fast that I couldn't see or hear it.

MATSU: There was a dog. It was my dog. That dog. . . .

NAWA: What happened?

MATSU: It died.

NAWA: How did it die?

MATSU: My man came to the house. The dog was barking, and he said it was too noisy, so I cooped up the dog in a pickle barrel. . . . This was before we were married, so it was a secret meeting that nobody knew about.

NAWA: You're the one who cooped up the dog, right?

MATSU: Right. Because he said the barking annoyed him. So I cooped up the dog in the pickle barrel but I'd go to check on him every thirty minutes. I'd lift off the heavy stone weighing down the lid, and I'd lift up the lid, and I'd say, "I'll let you out soon."

NAWA: Then?

MATSU: Then time passed.

NAWA: Then?

MATSU: Then the man left.

NAWA: And?

MATSU: And I was there. I was there, entranced, having given myself for the first time.

NAWA: Then?

MATSU: Then the clock. Tick-tock one minute, tick-tock two minutes. Everybody's coming home. I have to change before they get home . . . the house will be full of people. I have to make everything seem innocent before they get home.

NAWA: Then?

MATSU: Then I remember the dog. I have to take the dog out of the pickle barrel. So I ran out to the yard. . . . It was hotter than usual. But the dog couldn't wait. His one chance in thirty minutes to breathe deeply was delayed by an hour, then two hours, and the dog couldn't wait any longer. It was a small dog, so it couldn't breathe in any more air, and it died. . . . Yes, that's how I killed the dog.

(BLANK MASK *glances at* MAYU. MAYU *shakes her head "no." She murmurs, "She is not my mother." Then* BLANK MASK *takes the knotted rope away from* MATSU*'s hand, and gives it to* SILK REELING WOMAN UME. UME *unties a knot.*)

UME: Ouch! (*A soft cry of pain.*)

NAWA: What's the matter?

UME: It's such a tight knot that I can't unravel it. In fact, it almost tore my nail off. (*Taking a knot in her mouth, she unties it using her teeth.*) Ouch!

NAWA: Did you almost break your tooth, this time?

UME: The thread-rope turned into a needle, and it pricked me. It pricked me into remembering.

NAWA: Tell me. I want to hear your life story.

UME: I had a man. And ume blossoms—apricot blossoms—were just beginning to emerge. Red ume blossoms, yes red . . . budding ume flowers . . . half out, in full bloom, then a petal fluttering down . . . falling by ones and twos, threes and fours, falling petals, yes falling by fives and sixes, and I was sorry, so sorry, then. . . .

NAWA: Then the man said, "Keep them." . . . "You can keep them," isn't that what he said?

UME: *(She nods. Two time periods are simultaneously present.)* Where? Where d'ya want me to keep 'em, big boy?

NAWA: On your skin, on your full blooming skin, you can keep the blossoms in all their glory.

*(*NAWA *as* BLANK MASK *begins to take* UME's *kimono off.* UME *lets him have his way.)*

UME: On my skin, I thought about it, then I decided. I want a single ume flower right under the left breast, a single, slender, flower blooming in the sun, swaying in the wind, just below my left breast.

*(*NAWA *as* BLANK MASK *gazes at* UME's *naked upper body.)*

NAWA: Are you sure? The man asked. Are you sure?

UME: I'm sure, I answered. Go ahead. *(She writhes abruptly and cries out.)* Oh! That hurts! Oh! . . . The first needle prick hurts the most . . . the second prick . . . the third prick, then gradually the flesh swells out with blood inside, beads of blood rising and bursting open. Snapping open and pricking, a needle pricking and a bead of blood snapping open. . . .

NAWA: We're pouring poison into your body. No wonder you cry out in pain, groan and shriek in pain.

UME: *(Abruptly she becomes entranced, and speaks sweetly.)* Oh. . . . It hurts, it hurts, it hurts. . . . It hurts. . . . The pain's beyond belief, I'm swooning with pain, I can barely stand it, but then. . . .

NAWA: Then it begins to change.

UME: Yes. It's a kind of intoxication, it wells up from my innermost self, deep down in the center of my body, it's rising and lapping, rising and lapping,

NAWA: Little waves of intoxication,

UME: Then it becomes a storm.

NAWA: The waves of pain

UME: The waves of intoxication

NAWA: Surging and ebbing,

UME: Surging and ebbing. . . . Out of the blue, I became connected to the pain. It was as though I was fastened to the pain by an invisible thread. *(She puts on her kimono again still showing some signs of intoxication.* BLANK MASK *looks at* MAYU.*)*

MAYU: No! Mother didn't kill a dog, and she never got tattooed. She didn't strangle a man in the fog, and she never went out in the rain. Someone's lying. Who is Mother? Someone is Mother! All of you, tell me your life stories, let me listen to them all!

(NAWA *as* BLANK MASK *gets up. He tears his mask off.*)

NAWA: It's time to change into red kimono. Hurry up!

(Blackout.)

Scene Eight: The Winter Wind

(The melody of "A Sad Song of Mill Girls" is heard in the dark. It rises and suddenly is cut off. At the same moment, the light comes in like a slap.

Eight SILK REELING WOMEN *in red kimono are found standing on the upper floor and the lower floor, in the roles of girl prostitutes. When* WARA *pulls the string in his right hand saying, "You are a cute little girl,"* FUJI *smiles. When he pulls the string in his left hand saying, "You are pretty,"* SHŌBU *bows. When* TEGUSU *lifts up the string in his right hand saying, "You are a darling,"* BOTAN *nods. When he raises the string in his left hand saying, "You are so gentle,"* HAGI *closes her eyes. When* HIMO *lowers down the string in his right hand saying, "You are meek,"* TSUKI *raises her right hand and beckons. When he lowers down the string in his left hand saying, "You are innocent,"* KIKU *coyly puts out her tongue. When* MIZUHIKI *waves his right hand saying, "You are pure in heart,"* MOMIJI *holds her bosom in her arms. When he thrusts out his left hand saying, "You are a good girl,"* SAKURA *casts a sharp glance at him and does nothing. Seeing this,* WARA *speaks up.)*

WARA: What's the point in loosening the string?

TEGUSU: You greenhorn!

HIMO: You stupid ass!

WARA: Pull the string. Like this, look! *(He shows* MIZUHIKI *how to do it, pulling the string. Upon this* FUJI *speaks.)*

FUJI: Welcome, sir.

TEGUSU: Or like this, look! *(He raises the string to demonstrate for* MIZUHIKI. *Upon this* HAGI *speaks.)*

HAGI: Shall I sing? Or shall I dance?

HIMO: Here's another example. Look! *(He lowers the string down. Upon this* TSUKI *speaks.)*

TSUKI: I cost three yen and fifty sen.

WARA: Give it a try.

TEGUSU: Yo-ho!

(With this call, WARA, TEGUSU, HIMO *and* MIZUHIKI *strain the strings in their right hands all at once, and the* SILK REELING WOMEN *who are manipulated by them turn on their heels together.* MIZUHIKI's *left hand*

remains thrust out in the air, and SAKURA *gives him a sharp glance.)*

SAKURA: Clumsy oaf!

MIZUHIKI: I'm sorry.

SAKURA: Bungler!

MIZUHIKI: I'll do my best.

(WARA, *leaving them alone, manipulates the strings so that* FUJI *and* SHŌBU *turn around on their heels.)*

WARA: This is a red kimono night.

FUJI: Yes, sir.

WARA: I've taught you what to do at night, right?

SHŌBU: Yes, sir.

(TEGUSU *manipulates the strings so that* BOTAN *and* HAGI *turn around on their heels.)*

TEGUSU: I've taught you etiquette, right?

BOTAN: Yes, sir.

TEGUSU: If you make a mistake, you'll have no supper.

HAGI: Yes, sir.

(HIMO *manipulates the strings so that* TSUKI *and* KIKU *turn around on their heels.)*

HIMO: The customer always wants to listen to your life story.

TSUKI: Yes, sir.

HIMO: And you each have one ready, right?

(*To this question,* FUJI, SHŌBU, BOTAN, HAGI, TSUKI, *and* KIKU *answer "Yes, sir" all at once.)*

SAKURA: This is so stupid.

MIZUHIKI: I'm doing the best I can.

SAKURA: I already have my life story prepared.

MIZUHIKI: OK.

TEGUSU: Let's just leave them alone.

HIMO: You pair of greenhorns, go over there and practice by yourselves.

WARA: Let's take this one. (*He pulls the string lightly two or three times, and* FUJI *makes gestures as though playing hopscotch.)* OK, time for life stories. Tell us one.

(FUJI *nods, and begins to tell her story.)*

FUJI: One night, me and my man went out looking for a good time, but when I got home the next morning, I came down with a fever. Then my father scolded me.

WARA: You're playing with fire, you sinful child!

That's why you're burning with fever so wild.

Your father's words now cast a spell:

Be tortured by fever and cast into hell.

FUJI: Hating my father, fearing the fever,

Invoking a curse as sharp as a cleaver:

Death to my father, a thousand times die

Die you old monster, old fool, curse and die!

And then. . . .

WARA: He died?

FUJI: When he died, snakes surrounded the house. And my man said it's really creepy, you smell just like a snake. . . . And everybody said. . . .

WARA: *(As if calling in spectators.)* Come one, come all! See the snake girl as she passes by. Tomorrow we'll present a funeral. Our prize attraction: that girl, the one and only, the snake girl. See her glistening scales! So pure! So lovely!

FUJI: But I didn't become a snake. Instead. . . .

WARA: Instead? What happened?

FUJI: Whoever makes love with me will become a snake. A tail, there, and then scales all over. . . .

(WARA, letting go of the string, calls out, "Stop it." FUJI *crumples to the ground.)*

WARA: Just you wait, I'll give you a lesson you'll never forget. *(Pulling the string in his left hand.)* It's your turn. Tell me your tale.

SHŌBU: It was a moment of madness. We were on a fishing boat, fishing for squid. The sea glittered with a phosphorescent light, as night bugs began to swarm around. And the moon was out. The full moon that pierced into the depths of the sea. Just as I drew a breath deep into my lungs, yes, a deep breath permeating my lungs, just at that moment, that's when it happened. Oh! A squid pulled the fishing line. Look out! I let go of the line, and saw a fish. Not a squid. A huge fish, a huge fish with silver scales glistening. I didn't know what to do, I was totally confused. He, yes, he looked at me silently. And I returned his look. The fish, with its lidless fish eyes, stared at us.

WARA: Then?

SHŌBU: I. . . .

WARA: What did you do?

SHŌBU: I pushed him. I pushed him off the boat. I made him into a feast for the hungry fish. This is how I did it . . . like this. . . . *(She approaches* WARA.*)*

WARA: Stop it!

(He lets go of the string. SHŌBU *crumples to the ground.)*

TEGUSU: These life stories, I've never heard them before. . . . It's no joke.

WARA: Something's wrong.

HIMO: Something's wrong somewhere.

WARA: These life stories sound like the stories we've taught them, but if you listen carefully, they're completely different. What's more . . . .

TEGUSU: Yes? What else is wrong?

WARA: Even I got caught up in their life stories. Look over here!

HIMO: What?

WARA: Look behind me, will you? Is there anybody right behind me?

TEGUSU: *(Looking behind* WARA.*)* No, nobody's there. It's just your shadow.

WARA: *(Incessantly nervous about what's behind him.)* You sure nobody's there?

HIMO: No, nobody's there.

WARA: So, nobody's turning me into a puppet, right?

TEGUSU: Sure, you're fine. It's your imagination.

WARA: I hope so.

TEGUSU: This time, I'll give it a try. You there, tell me your life story.

BOTAN: I was twelve years old. I was playing in a sandbox. Then that person came. It was a big person, and. . . .

TEGUSU: And?

BOTAN: It was a man. The man asked. . . .

TEGUSU: "Do you know how to fight?"

BOTAN: Sure I do.

TEGUSU: The man asked again, "How many ways do you know how to fight?"

BOTAN: Lots of ways, I said. Then. . . .

TEGUSU: For instance? The man asked.

BOTAN: What if I strangled someone, what would happen? I asked. Would he die? Then he said.

TEGUSU: "Try it."

BOTAN: All right, I answered. Then. . . .

TEGUSU: Then?

BOTAN: I strangled him. His face went all purple, but he was smiling. And yes, he said, "It feels good." Those were his last words. . . . *(Abruptly lascivious.)* Say, you wanna try? How about letting me make you feel real good? *(Drawing near.)*

TEGUSU: Stop it, that's disgusting!

(He lets go of the string. BOTAN *crumples to the ground.)*

TEGUSU: What's going on here? You there! Tell your story.

HAGI: He was a liar. He promised to take me to a festival, so I asked him, what do I get if you break your promise? What do I get?

TEGUSU: "Well, it's my tongue that tells the lies. *(Sticking out his tongue.)* This is the guilty party. So. . . ."

HAGI: So?

TEGUSU: "You can cut out my tongue."

HAGI: With scissors?

TEGUSU: "Yes, with a pair of scissors. If I lie, cut out my tongue with a pair of scissors. Just cut it off."

HAGI: Well, he'd promised to take me to the festival, but he didn't. So that meant he'd lied. Mother had a pair of scissors in her workbox. So I took out the scissors and polished the blades to give them a good shine. Because if the edges were rusty, it would hurt his tongue, so I polished and sharpened them till they flashed, and. . . .

TEGUSU: And?

HAGI: I cut it off. He's still mute. . . .

TEGUSU: What are you saying?

(He lets go of the string. HAGI *crumples to the ground.)*

TEGUSU: *(Seized with a strange dread.)* What'll we do?

WARA: I don't know.

HIMO: Shall we give it one more try?

TEGUSU: What if the next one recites another life story that we've never heard?

WARA: If that happens, then. . . .

HIMO: What'll we do?

WARA: Disinfection. We'll disinfect them. We'll spray them with insecticide and let them dry in the sun. They're bug-ridden. Or infected with germs. *(To* HIMO.*)* What do you think, shall we give it just one more try?

HIMO: All right. . . . I call on the holy name of Buddha—*Namu amida butsu.* . . . You there! Tell me your life story.

TSUKI: He closed the window. I said, don't close the window, it disrupts my view of the moon, but he closed the window. I said, keep the window open, and please take me on board, take me with you, I said. When he closed the window, the room turned all smelly and stuffy, and I started to sweat all over. I, I wanted to see the moon. I really, honestly wanted to see the moon. So. . . .

HIMO: So?

TSUKI: I killed him and opened the window.

HIMO: This one, too!

(He lets go of the string he holds. TSUKI *crumples to the ground.)*

WARA: That settles it.

TEGUSU: Disinfection.

(The MEN *exchange glances.)*

SAKURA: I haven't told you my life story.

WARA: We haven't taught you one yet.

SAKURA: What?

TEGUSU: A life story.

HIMO: You can't possibly tell one when we haven't taught you one.

SAKURA: You dunce.

HIMO: Eh?

SAKURA: I have six thousand two hundred and five life stories.

WARA: Six thousand two hundred and five stories?

TEGUSU: Where did you get that number?

SAKURA: Well, a year is three hundred and sixty five days. Let's suppose that one life story is created every day, since I'm seventeen now, if you multiply seventeen years by three hundred and sixty five days. you get six thousand two hundred and five stories. That's how many life stories I have, Uncle.

WARA: *(To* MIZUHIKI.*)* You there, shut her up!

MIZUHIKI: Yes sir! *(Although he answers yes, the string gets tangled.)*

SAKURA: You blunderer.

MIZUHIKI: I'm sorry.

SAKURA: I'll tell you my life story while you untangle the string.

MIZUHIKI: What kind of life story is it?

SAKURA: There was this old guy, a stranger. He was a cop, and he was just hanging around, not doing anything. And I was having a fine old time just wasting time, too. So. . . .

MIZUHIKI: So, what did you do?

SAKURA: I said to the stranger, hey Uncle, wanna have a drink of saké? Here, saké.

*(*MIZUHIKI *becomes the "uncle" and shakes his head no.)*

SAKURA: Why don't you have a drink? Here! Bottoms up! *(Handing a cup to the uncle.)* Uncle drinks one, then I drink one, then Uncle drinks another one, then I drink another one, Uncle and I, exchanging cups of saké like a couple exchanging nuptial cups at their wedding, so let's drink . . . Uncle.

MIZUHIKI: Well, here's luck! *(He drinks.)*

SAKURA: Ha, ha, ha. . . . *(Laughing frantically.)* Uncle drank saké.
That dirty old Uncle the cop
He drank and drank and wouldn't stop, *(*MIZUHIKI *writhes in agony.)*
Drank poisoned saké until he dropped. *(*MIZUHIKI *falls on his breast.)*
A cup of poisoned wine
To kill the bloody swine. . . . Ha, ha, ha . . . ha, ha, ha. . . .
My wedding gown's so creamy white
But look, it's smeared with blood tonight
Tomorrow will be clear and bright.
A cup of poisoned wine
To kill the bloody swine. . . . Ha, ha, ha . . . ha, ha, ha. . . .
A feast of dolls, this wedding fine
Drink poisoned saké, oh Uncle mine. . . .
(She abruptly stops laughing, and as if giving a challenge speaks.)
That's my life story.
*(*WARA *kicks* MIZUHIKI, *who doubles over in pain.)*

WARA: You better do something about this.

MIZUHIKI: Yes, sir!

TEGUSU: Let go of the string!

MIZUHIKI: Yes, sir!
*(*MIZUHIKI *lets go of the string in a flurry.* SAKURA *darts a glance at him and collapses.)*

WARA: I told you so. I objected right from the start.

TEGUSU: What are you getting at?

WARA: This one *(Kicking* SAKURA.*)* has a family register.

HIMO: Without a doubt, she has one. She's registered as the seventh daughter, Moyo, of Nakamura Ushitarō at 5 Ōaza Kameido, Azuma-chō, Tokyo. On top of that, we even know her date of birth. The first of January, 1922, the eleventh year of Taishō. As it is now 1939, the fourteenth year of Shōwa, she is precisely seventeen years old.

WARA: We never should have admitted a girl with a family register. That's what messed up the life stories.

TEGUSU: But. . . .

WARA: What?

TEGUSU: This girl cried in front of the Thread-and-Yarn Store for three days and nights, begging us to let her become the new Sakura.

HIMO: For safe keeping, she even gave the register of her entire family to me. To me, a lawfully appointed registrar of Japan.

WARA: If she's not the cause, how did these life stories creep in?

TEGUSU: There may have been another way.

HIMO: Eh?

TEGUSU: That girl. . . . In the moonless evening, from the sea, drenched. . . .

WARA: The girl who seems to drop words as though through the holes in a sieve.

(The MEN *become silent. After a while.)*

WARA: Disinfection! *(He cries out.)*

(The music "A Shallow River"[8] abruptly flows in. The SILK REELING WOMEN, *who were heaped on the ground, spring to their feet and begin to dance. The men cheer, beating time, "When the river is shallow, just tuck up the very bottom of your kimono." The* SILK REELING WOMEN *tuck up the bottoms of their red kimono. When the men cheer, "When the river is deep, tuck up your kimono all the way to your knees," the* WOMEN *dance with their kimono tucked up to their knees.*

The abrupt blast of a whirlwind. It hurtles through the electric wires. The SILK REELING WOMEN *come to a standstill. Sudden darkness. When the light is out, leaving only an after-image in the dark, candles are lit. Four* WOMEN *wearing masks on which the Japanese character for "Mother" is written, put the candles in their paper lanterns. The lanterns are also inscribed with the word "Mother," and that single Japanese character stands out clearly in the dark. Other candles are lit. There are four* MEN *wearing masks on which the Japanese character for "Father" is written. They are holding paper lanterns with the Japanese character for "Father.")*

MOTHER 1: Hello! My lost child!

FATHER 1: Hello! My child!

(They call out sorrowfully, searching for their "daughter" among the SILK REELING WOMEN, *who have turned into child prostitute dolls.)*

MOTHER 2: Hello! My missing daughter!

FATHER 2: Hello! My child—she was spirited away!

MOTHER 3: Hello! My runaway daughter!

FATHER 3: Hello! My child—the one who disappeared!

MOTHER 4: Hello! My dear child!

FATHER 4: Hello! My own child!

> (*They throw a light on each* SILK REELING WOMAN *but cannot find their own daughters. The* SILK REELING WOMEN *leave one by one, as each is revealed not to be any of their daughters. Only the four* MOTHERS *remain, huddled together. Above the four women, a light is turned on. The four* MOTHERS *tear off their masks under the cheerless house light. They are the* SILK REELING WOMEN MATSU, UME, AME, *and* KIRI.)

MATSU: We were

UME: Mothers, once.

AME: In our memories, we were mothers, once.

KIRI: When the wind blows, the memories come back.

MATSU: The wind,

UME, AME, *and* KIRI: (*Looking at* MATSU.) Yes,

MATSU: The winter wind.

UME, AME *and* KIRI: Yes the winter wind, the wind of winter.

MATSU: It blows for a while,

UME: Then everything returns to dust. The wind

AME: No, it's dancing and wafting,

KIRI: The alluring wind, the winter wind.

MATSU: The winter wind resembles the sea.

UME: There's a deep part,

AME: And a shallow part.

KIRI: A current rushes through the winter wind.

MATSU: Sometimes, there's an ebb tide,

UME: When memory foams, hollowly,

AME: At other times, there's a full tide,

KIRI: When joy surges in, lapping the shore.

FOUR WOMEN: Wind, don't blow, winter wind, don't blow, oh wind of winter.

MATSU: The wind blows, it's cold.

UME: The wind blows, it's cold.

AME: The wind of winter blows, it's cold.

KIRI: The winter wind blows, it's cold.

MATSU: The winter wind curls up in my stomach,

UME: The winter wind clings to the place beneath my skin,

AME: The winter wind pierces my heart,

KIRI: And the winter wind lingers, twisting my spine.

MATSU: Merely insects, we're tossed helplessly between heaven and earth,

UME, AME, *and* KIRI: The winter wind blows, the wind blows,

UME: Commanding us to remember.

MATSU, UME, *and* KIRI: The winter wind blows, the wind blows,

AME: Blowing through, yes, the wind, the winter wind

KIRI: Yes, blowing through, the old days, once,

MATSU: I, once, was a mother.

UME: I was a mother, once, too.

AME: We were once mothers.

KIRI: The wind of winter gave us seeds,

FOUR WOMEN: Once, we were mothers. We have memories—being pregnant with the wind. We have memories—giving birth to the wind.

MATSU: The wind of winter,

UME: Yes the winter wind,

AME: Is rising.

KIRI: A rattling wind, the winter wind.

(A dissolve. In the darkness, MAYU*'s voice, "Mother! You are the one!" resounds, tearing apart the blackness.)*

Scene Nine: Pulling the String, Cutting the String

(In the blackness, a clock is ticking away the seconds. As the light comes up along with the sound of ticking, AME *and* MAYU *are found downstairs, and* NAWA, *wearing the mask of* BLANK MASK, *is found on the stairs.*

AME—*in reality,* MAYU*'s* MOTHER—*and* MAYU *are sitting facing each other, each holding the end of a red thread. During the dialogue, the two women pull the thread, getting nearer to each other at a very slow pace that is almost unnoticeable.* MAYU *and* MOTHER *begin to speak and keep speaking without looking away from one another even for a moment.)*

MOTHER: Here, we have all the time we need . . . because there are no clocks. We sleep as deeply as if we were encased in a tightly closed shell, although the faint light of dawn creeps into the house from the place outside that is called the world. And before we're aware, noon has passed, and today is but a sequel of yesterday, and the only thing that changes is the sunlight. By the time our sleep is finally broken, evening is slowly sliding into another night. . . . This is a snug place to live in.

MAYU: Mother.

MOTHER: Yes, I'm your mother.

MAYU: I'm your daughter.

MOTHER: Have you tried peeking into the depths of our family's Buddhist altar?

MAYU: Nothing was there.

MOTHER: That's right, nothing should be there. Because behind the countless ancestral tablets standing together like a forest, there was once a family tree that was eating into it. So I took it and ran away.

MAYU: From house and home?

MOTHER: Yes, I left house and home.

MAYU: Why?

MOTHER: I wanted to be the last person to keep that worthless family tree alive.

MAYU: And what about me?

MOTHER: You're a cipher. Just a zero.

MAYU: You ran off and took the family tree with you, leaving me with nothing but ashes, although I searched for traces of the old days. Ashes, ashes were falling all around, and there was nothing but darkness, even with my eyes open. I. . . .

MOTHER: What?

MAYU: I asked for the wind. . . . The wind blew. The wind blew open a line in the ashes. I saw a thread over the wind. I left my house, my home, pulled by the wind. Walking along a pathway of thread, I came here. I came here with a bag full of wind, swollen with spite and hatred.

MOTHER: I thought I'd sewn up all the bags.

MAYU: Tightly closed bags are bound to break.

MOTHER: You stupid girl. And I went to all the trouble of conceiving you twice, and of giving birth to you twice.

MAYU: Twice?

MOTHER: The first time, I conceived you in my woman's belly and gave birth to you at home, in our house, and the second time I conceived our home, our house in my belly and gave birth to you in the world outside.

MAYU: I don't need two selves.

MOTHER: You are always one self. . . . How did you find me? Was it because you heard my life story?

MAYU: Words don't remind me of anything.

MOTHER: Then how?

MAYU: By smell.

MOTHER: Eh?

MAYU: By smell, Mother. There was a thick smell crouching down at the bottom of the wind, and as soon as I smelled it, my mind was filled with memories, like smoke rising, of the old days and of Mother.

MOTHER: You're like a helpless puppy.

MAYU: I learned something from that smell. You betrayed me twice. The first time was just a sham betrayal, but the second time was a real betrayal.

MOTHER: The sham betrayal?

MAYU: When you gave me birth,

MOTHER: The real betrayal?

MAYU: When you abandoned me.

MOTHER: Things happen. . . . Look at this thread. This is a thread of things that have happened.

MAYU: Yes, I can see them, Mother. *(Tracing the thread with her finger.)* Here, this is a cherry blossom viewing, and this is the Star Festival.

MOTHER: Nothing but sweet nostalgia, rising and trembling.

MAYU: *(Staring at* MOTHER.*)* And here. . . .

MOTHER: There?

MAYU: That's a betrayal.

> *(Unnoticed, the two have come nearer inch by inch, and are now so close that their faces almost seem to touch one another. They exchange steady looks, then* MOTHER *gets up, throwing away her end of the thread.* MAYU *remains seated, still holding the other end of the thread.)*

MOTHER: Why have you come?

MAYU: To kill you.

MOTHER: Why?

MAYU: There was a woman.

MOTHER: What woman?

MAYU: You, Mother. . . . He was my man. You took my man away, killed him, and abandoned me.

MOTHER: *(She picks up the end of thread, and looks at it.)* I abandoned you, like this.

> *(At the same moment that* MOTHER *throws the thread away,* MAYU *suddenly gets up and pulls the thread.* MOTHER *staggers.)*

MAYU: We're tied! *(Crying out.)* The only way for me to cut the bonds of love, was to tie them.

Knotting, binding, twisting, the threads of fate I weave

Discarded like her child, this rope she cannot leave

This lotus rope of fate, that binds my mother tight

Woven ropes will bind her beyond her dying night.

> *(The two women pull the thread against each other.)*

MAYU: Look at this, Mother. This thread-rope is your life. The threads have been chafed by time, the rope is shredded and worn out. This thread-rope that's covered with warts, the events of an ugly past, will strangle you to death, Mother.

MOTHER: A woman's body is her sole inheritance. I inherited mine from my mother but I used it all up by making a knotted ball, which is you. I gave you my body. There are no more mementos left to give.

MAYU: What about giving me a family register?   When you ran away, you took the family tree with you.

MOTHER: When you draw a family tree, you inscribe it only with mothers. My mother's mother's mother's mother's . . . no matter how many generations you trace back, you see only mothers' faces. Mothers don't have family registers.

MAYU: You don't have one, either?

MOTHER: No. Nothing but a long, worn-out thread of blood connecting you to generations upon generations. And behind the blood, there's always a faceless father. Look right behind you!

(MAYU looks behind instinctively. She is facing BLANK MASK.)

MAYU: Who are you?

NAWA: An event without a face. Now, continue with what you were about to do! Kill her. Kill your mother with spite.

(He pulls the string. MAYU spins around. The Prajñâ-paramitâ Sutra,[9] surges in like a torrent. Men appear and begin to manipulate MAYU. Being manipulated, MAYU "kills" MOTHER. The music is sharply cut off. MAYU approaches MOTHER who is lying on the ground like a bundle of waste thread.)

MAYU: *(In blank surprise.)* The thread is cut. . . . She's nothing but a bundle of waste thread. . . . *(She raises MOTHER in her arms.)*

MOTHER: You can kill me, but the blood won't die out. It'll just start all over again.

MAYU: Why?

MOTHER: You haven't found out yet?

MAYU: What?

MOTHER: You're already with child.

MAYU: *(Stiffening herself.)* No! *(She throws MOTHER's body away on the floor.)*

(MAYU gets up and staggers backward to the stairs. MATSU, UME, and KIRI appear.)

MAYU: Deep in Mother's shining black eyes, a bottomless swamp was spreading. In that swamp, I saw the faces of mothers. Dead faces, like melting waxworks, were floating in whiteness, smiling tenderly. I saw my mother's face, and my own face. That place was a hell of threads. . . . The dead faces of women were spinning threads, twining threads around faceless men, being entwined by threads. And tied to the thread that I was spinning, I saw small dead faces breathing stealthily and quietly. Am I with child? Yes, I am.

(MAYU has climbed up the stairs backward, and stands transfixed in the middle of the stairway. There, she calls out, "Mother." The three SILK REELING WOMEN gather around the body of MOTHER.)

MAYU: There's a scent of Mother, still. The wind is wafting the scent to me.

(The three SILK REELING WOMEN murmur, "The spring wind. . . .")

MATSU: Spring awakens. March, the month of springtime and the Festival of Dolls.

UME: Spring, when our sins float lightly in cups of wine.

KIRI: Shall we sing? Spring, when flowers have no name.

MATSU: When flowers are named cherry blossoms.

UME: Sorrow not, though blossoms fade, though cherry blossoms fade away.

KIRI: We'll put an end to time, we'll raise a joyous song, beneath the cherry blossoms.

MATSU: We'll share a cup of white saké. *(A gesture of pouring saké into a cup.)*

UME: But it's still so early. *(A gesture of receiving saké.)*

KIRI: Just a sip. *(A gesture of drinking saké.)*

(The three women drink up the cup. Giving a sigh.)

MATSU: A scented wind, the wind of spring, the spring wind.

UME: Enchanting, the wind, the wind of spring, the spring wind.

KIRI: The wind smells like breath, the wind of spring, the spring wind.

MATSU: When the spring wind rises from beneath my kimono,

UME: It gathers warmth from the place between my body and my kimono.

KIRI: Passing between my breasts,

MATSU: And rising from my bosom,

UME: It emerges with a slightly moist scent.

KIRI: It emerges with a faintly fleshy scent.

MATSU: Won't you have another cup of white saké? *(Pouring saké.)*

UME: Just a little. *(Receiving one.)*

KIRI: Yes, only a tiny, little sip. *(Drinking.)*

MATSU: Feeling tipsy, when I drink thick white saké,

UME: The smell of white saké, lascivious,

KIRI: Like the remnant of a man's scent,

MATSU: And my stomach stirs strangely,

UME: The soles of my feet, ha-ha, they're tickling.

KIRI: Don't be silly. Down there, that's what's trembling.

MATSU: There,

UME: There,

KIRI: Yes there.

MATSU: How many times have I lied?

UME: The number of lies, piled as high as a mountain, as deep as the sea,

KIRI: Piling one upon another, in a calendar full of women,

THREE WOMEN: The number of lies in our life stories.

(A dissolve downstairs. MAYU is left alone on the stairs. Behind her is NAWA.)

MAYU: On a straight, sun-baked road, there's a line of women. I am there, and my mother. Behind Mother is Mother's mother, and further behind her is Mother's mother's mother . . . mothers followed by more mothers, interminably. The mothers' bodies are all tied in a row, linked by a single thread. The mothers tell me to cut the thread. Right behind us all, further behind, still further behind, someone else is there. *(Turning around.)* It's you, the faceless one. *(She takes out a*

pair of scissors and holds it high.) I have a pair of scissors that I've kept hidden in my bosom, and it's never even been exposed to a rough wind. So I thought, even if it's able to do its work, the only thing it could pierce would be my body. But the Mothers order me. They tell me to cut the thread. To blind the faceless one who is right behind me manipulating the string.
(Blackout.)

Scene Ten: Thread Hell
(Upstairs, MAYU is found. Downstairs, NAWA is found.)

NAWA: Yes, I've been manipulating the strings. I gathered women who had no family registers, I created a realm called house and home, I made them sell thread and yarn, and I made them sell their favors.

MAYU: Why? What for?

NAWA: So that the creature that is myself can be reborn over and over again. I did it in order to live. I did it in order to overthrow the guidepost called the family register. I am Nawa, Master of the Thread-and-Yarn Store, who stretches my strings in all directions, manipulating them, until eternal night falls and time ends. Another kingdom may be hurtling to its death, but my Thread-and-Yarn Store overflows with the stink of flesh. I hammer down my stakes, and stretch out my strings. That's how I expand. How I increase. I entrap them all in my strings. This town belongs to me.

MAYU: Where is this town of yours? Where's your kingdom? Transformed to a murky, subterranean realm. And you—you're nothing but a blind man who's stumbled in by accident. The Thread-and-Yarn Store that you created has vanished.

NAWA: What have you done to my eyes?

MAYU: I sewed them up. Your eyelids have turned inside out. The man without a face who was always hovering somewhere in the background, just behind the women. It was you, the man who controlled the women. The father of women. A hundred strings are now entwining you, who once manipulated them. You'll hang in hell forever, suspended, with every limb of your body cross-stitched by thread.
(The SILK REELING WOMEN come out and manipulate NAWA. WARA, TEGUSU, HIMO and MIZUHIKI appear, and writhe as the SILK REELING WOMEN pull the strings around them. Music surges in. MAYU looks down at the strings pulling against one another.)

MAYU: You're suspended now by your own strings, falling like that for all eternity. You'll be lost among strangers. Now learn this. We're all, every one of us, the puppeteers of strangers. And even though you may imagine that you're the manipulator, you're actually being

manipulated. The spinning wheel is nothing but a fool's trick.
The spool is turning round and round
I reel you in, you're tightly bound.
But I ascend, my soul will rise,
I float to heaven, to paradise

(As soon as she finishes the speech, she leaps off the stairs holding a single string. In the same instant, NAWA *is suspended in the air.* MAYU *stands straight among the women. She cries out, "Blow, wind!"*
A wind blows in. The light comes on and off like the wind. The women themselves become the wind, and they become frenzied.)

MAYU: Blow, oh wind, blow. Blow, blow, blow, oh wind! I need neither permission, nor hesitation, nor bewilderment, nor sympathy, nor tenderness, so blow, oh wind. Blow, blow, blow, oh wind!
Blow it away, oh wind.
Blow it away,
Blow it away.
Without knowing darkness, without knowing grief, I've cut the bonds of love. I no longer need anything. I don't even need life, I want the wind.
Across the bridge of dreams,
I vanish in the winds of May.
A golden ball that softly gleams,
And gaily bouncing, springs away.

(Blackout. When the lights come up again, the Thread-and-Yarn Store is revealed. MAYU *is in the center, surrounded by the* SILK REELING WOMEN. *The spinning wheels turn.* MATSU *casually breaks the silence.)*

MATSU: I've lived, without meaning to. Quite inadvertently, I've lived. Merely insects, we're tossed unawares between heaven and earth, yet somehow my life happened, I've aged: my face seamed with wrinkles, my black hair streaked with white, how pathetic to grow old, I know it. . . .

(She breathes a sigh. Then UME *begins to speak.)*

UME: And yet, I'm still alive, still drawing breath.

(She gives a sigh. Then MATSU *begins to speak.)*

MATSU: When. . . . Yes . . . . When, blow, does the wind, when does the wind blow, the wind, when, blow. . . . *(A sigh.)*

UME: Yes, always thinking, days passing, days piling upon days, and now. . . . *(A sigh.)*

KIRI: And now . . . it blows, the wind, the wind blows. The wind, the wind blows in my. . . . *(A sigh.)*

MATSU: Body, deep down in the center . . . the wind. *(A sigh.)*

(MAYU spins the spinning wheel at her ease.)

MAYU: Perhaps you, too, can hear it? It's the wind. When I gather the residue of the wind, yes, the wind, in my body, it expands inside me, and now and then I let out a sigh, and I let the wind go. Then, my body, I, ever so slightly, it becomes lighter.

Like this, whoosh. . . . *(She breathes out the wind, and the* SILK REELING WOMEN *breathe out the wind together.)*

Or like this, whoosh. *(She breathes out the wind, and the* SILK REELING WOMEN *breathe out the wind together.)*

Little by little, bit by tiny bit, I breathe out, freeing the wind. I, a woman, who is dying more slowly than others.

(The SILK REELING WOMEN *keep breathing out the wind, whoosh, whoosh. Then* MATSU *cries out, "Oh!" All the other* SILK REELING WOMEN *together look at* MATSU.*)*

UME: Oh! *(She cries out, and all the other* SILK REELING WOMEN *look at her at the same time.)*

KIRI: Oh! *(She cries out, and all the other* SILK REELING WOMEN *look at her at the same time.)*

MAYU: Oh! *(She cries out, and all the other* SILK REELING WOMEN *look at her at the same time.)*

MATSU: A length of thread has tangled.

UME: Tangled into knots.

KIRI: A tangled thread

MAYU: Is an omen that someone is coming.

MATSU: What a delight.

UME: What a joy.

KIRI: How lively it will be.

MAYU: Now that each of us is her own master, let's not leave her out in the cold.

(She smiles quietly. The smile spreads among the SILK REELING WOMEN *like rippling waves. Then the light comes on upstairs. A* WOMAN, *played by the same actress who plays the* SILK REELING WOMAN AME, *is discovered.)*

WOMAN: Just now, I awoke, only to see that I am here. Where am I? *(Looking down at the lower floor.)* There's a house, a home. It reads Thread-and-Yarn Store. . . . How can I get to the Thread-and-Yarn Store?

MAYU: Go straight down.

WOMAN: How can I get to the Thread-and-Yarn Store?

MATSU: Go straight down.

WOMAN: How can I get to the Thread-and-Yarn Store?

UME: Go straight down.

WOMAN: How can I get to the Thread-and-Yarn Store?

KIRI: Go straight down.

(While they are questioning and answering, the light fades out.)

THE END

Notes

1. The mask is an egg-like face without a nose or a mouth; a blank face without features.
2. Stage hand dressed in black, used in traditional Japanese theater, conventionally invisible.
3. One sen equals 1/100 yen.
4. "Jokō aika."
5. A robe of soft, lightweight cotton.
6. "Ano machi, kono machi."
7. "Ito kiri."
8. According to Kishida, the title of the music is also the title of a game favored by lower-class geisha in the Taishō and the early Shōwa eras. They played "janken" (paper-scissors-stone) with their customers and tucked up the hem of their kimono every time they lost in the janken.
9. Hannya shingyō.

The Red Demon Akaoni
Noda Hideki

TRANSLATED BY ROGER PULVERS

*

Introduction

Hasebe Hiroshi
TRANSLATED BY ROGER PULVERS

This translation is based on the 1998 Shinchō-sha publication of
Akaoni in *Kaisan-go Zen-gekisaku*.

Noda Hideki (Courtesy Noda Map.)

After the storm, Tombi, played by Noda Hideki, finds a glass bottle washed ashore. Kintetsu Art Hall, Osaka, and Space Part 3, Tokyo 1996. (Courtesy Noda Map.)

On hearing Tombi's story about meeting Akaoni, Mizugane puts on an act of bravado. From left: Tombi and Mizugane. Kintetsu Art Hall, Osaka, and Space Part 3, Tokyo 1996. (Courtesy Noda Map.)

Spotting a flock of birds, a promise of a good catch of fish, the four express surprise in their various ways. From left: The Woman, Tombi, Akaoni, and Mizugane. Kintetsu Art Hall, Osaka, and Space Part 3, Tokyo 1996. (Courtesy Noda Map.)

The villagers lock Akaoni and The Woman in a cave by the sea on suspicion of their being accomplices to a foreign invasion. From left: The Woman and Akaoni. Kintetsu Art Hall, Osaka, and Space Part 3, Tokyo 1996. (Courtesy Noda Map.)

Introduction

Hasebe Hiroshi
TRANSLATED BY ROGER PULVERS

IT WOULD HAVE TO BE KARA JŪRŌ who occupies the throne in the pantheon of theater. Kara's theater is striking in three primary features: first, the freedom with which, in its structure, it plies between the present and the past; second, the nature of its dialogue, being based as it is on everyday conversation and yet brimming with poetic metaphor; and third, its thematic emphasis on the textures of original sin. Add to this the very real acrobatics of the actors and the tongue-twisting speed of their lyrical lines.

The theater of Noda Hideki established its original style on the foundation of these three elements under the influence of Kara Jūrō. Even from the time of the formation of his troupe, the Dream Wanderers, in April 1976, Noda—playwright, director, actor—was hailed in the media as the new genius of Japanese theater. By 1981, when *The Prisoner of Zenda Castle*,[1] a major work of his early period, was first performed at the Komaba Little Theater on the Komaba campus of the University of Tokyo, Noda had set his style: hark back thematically to the past, weave the narrative with mythical threads and, before the eyes of the audience, unravel a cloth that holds together the ancient, the medieval, the modern and the contemporary. In 1981 Noda mounted a production of *Young Boy Hunting—Groping in the Pitch Dark*[2] at the Kinokuniya Hall in Shinjuku, Tokyo, following this up with productions at the Honda Theater in Shimo-kitazawa, Tokyo, thus bringing his work to venues with a capacity of 600 seats. It was an attempt to break out of the mold of the small, limited theater space that had characterized the *angura* theater movement up to that time. Within this attempt are notable productions subsequent to those, productions which marked themselves as symbolically important events in Japanese theater, mounted in 1986 at the National Yoyogi Sports Stadium No. 1 Gym, namely the *Seven Variations on Stonehenge*[3] trilogy: *White Night Valkyrie*,[4] *Comet Siegfried*[5] and *Valhalla Up In Smoke*.[6] In one day he drew some 26,000 people to what had been the venue of the Tokyo Olympic Games.

This trilogy was significant not only as an event but also for presenting what became major works in his theater. Based on *The*

Nibelungenlied, portraying archetypes and their various confrontations, it told a grand spectacle of a tale from the birth of man to his soaring through the skies. It was from this time that Noda Hideki established himself as Japanese theater's front runner, as someone destined to take the lead in the drama of our time.

1987 saw him taking part in the Edinburgh Festival in Scotland; and the next year, mounting a production in New York. Around this time he could expect audiences of 50,000 for each production, and became a pioneer in gaining corporate sponsorship for his work, notably from Japan Railways Tokai and Mitsubishi Motors.

Today Noda still distinguishes himself amongst his peers for "the body that won't stand still." As before, he physicalizes his text, translating it into a whirl of action. Each line is demonstrated, with swift and differentiated physical movements or gestures that overlay the dialogue, making *shingeki*, the theater inspired by the West, pale in its established static approach to text. The rapid-fire delivery of a Kara Jūrō character had been infused with and rounded off by Noda's body movements. This was a theater of unfailing speed.

The audience watching the plays of the Dream Wanderers were exposed to a dizzying experience. Needless to say, this sort of theater called for actors who were up to its physical demands. In the eyes of the theater world at the time, this presentational style looked rather bizarre. But this style had such persuasive power that even famous actors began to use it in their work. Along with his work in the Dream Wanderers, Noda began to write and direct productions produced by Tōhō and the Ginza Saison Theater. He was welcomed onto the big stages as someone who might revitalize contemporary Japanese theater.

The Dream Wanderers disbanded in 1992. After spending a year in London as part of the Agency of Cultural Affairs' Artist Overseas Study Program, Noda returned to Japan in 1993 to found Noda Map. Since then, without his own set troupe, he has put on plays varying his cast and staff with each production. His first production under this system was *Kiru* in 1994, after which he went on to take up one social theme after another. While earlier the social themes of his plays had been secondary to their broad and colorful entertainment aspects, now Noda was turning to concrete subject matter for the core of his work: in *Kiru,* cultural imperialism; in *Crime and Punishment: The Parody*[7] (1995) and in *Kanon* (2000), terrorism; in *Taboo* (1996) and *Pandora's Bell*[8] (1999), the imperial system in Japan. Noda established himself as the leading theatrical figure in Japan, the only one who combined a very high artistic standard with a broad public base.

The theme of the 1996 play *The Red Demon Akaoni*, included in this anthology, is discrimination and communicating with people from outside Japanese culture. It takes up the subject of cultural interaction, and is a provocative treatment of people who act as if unpleasant and confusing friction between cultures does not occur. It depicts people who live on the periphery of a village and are the objects of discrimination. The only people who attempt to communicate with the Akaoni, which means red demon, a person from the West who has come to their shores, are Tombi and his sister, The Woman, and Mizukane, a shady character who has been excluded from the circle of people in the village. The people in the village react to the foreign presence with a strong sense of antipathetic rejection. This contrasts to the attitude of the sister who constantly endeavors, though discouraged by the difficulty of the task, to reach a state of mutual understanding with the outsider.

Akaoni becomes a kind of carnival freak for the villagers, who treat this foreign intruder, whose gestures and words are so different from theirs, as nothing more than a demon, a red devil. Not only do they refuse to communicate with him as a human being, they take the foreign vessel anchored in the harbor to be a spy ship intent on invading the village. Tombi, his sister, Mizukane and Akaoni get into a small boat to head for the ship. But the ship has by this time given up on Akaoni and has sailed off. Akaoni dies. Tombi, his sister and Mizukane, drifting aimlessly on the open sea, tortured by hunger, eat the flesh of the dead Akaoni. When the play was done by Noda Map as one of its special productions, the main parts were taken by Kaita Yasunori, Tomita Yasuko, Noda and Angus Barnett. They played the shady Mizukane, the sister and brother and, on occasion, even the people in the village who persecute them. The quick changes of character and costume that went off with lightning speed without using blackouts seemed perfectly natural. Akaoni was played by Barnett, who, though the play was performed in Japanese, spoke Irish, making it virtually impossible for the audience to follow his words, where English would have made them accessible. This was Noda's clear intention. In addition, for the first time Noda traded in the proscenium arch for a space in the round—a white curved playing area devoid, at the start of the play, of props. The first scene, of the four people perilously at sea, at the mercy of a storm, was done through physical action without a word of dialogue. The play was done with a minimum of scenery and props. Yet thanks to the artistic direction of Hibino Katsuhiko, a highly abstract atmosphere was created on stage, with, for instance, two duralumin poles on a small tire base fulfilling a number of functions, such as defining a window in the house that Tombi and his sister live in, through which Akaoni peeks in on them. Four poles became a cell that the villagers throw their captives, the sister and Akaoni, into. We see in this not a staged reality created by set and props, but a mode of presentation that in its clear-vision variations stimulates the imagination of the audience. *The Red Demon Akaoni* like the above-mentioned *Kiru* and the main productions since, does not present its grand theme and its story of the eternal in lyrical poetic terms. It attempts to establish theater that tells a universal tale unfettered by time and place. Though there is one scene which satirizes the closed society of the Japanese, it aims to reveal a story that can happen at any time anywhere in the world. Noda's work up to then, which had been based on dialogue with double meanings, alliteration and word associations, now becomes simple and straightforward. As such, this play may be seen as his first tactic in his world strategy.

In 1997 *The Red Demon Akaoni* received a second production, this time as a Japanese-Thai co-production. Jointly directed by Noda and Nimit Pipitkul, it was performed at the Setagaya Public Theater mainly in Thai with a cast that included a British actor. This production had 19 performances in Thailand the following year at the Saeng-Arun Arts Center in Bangkok, running from 19 May to 7 June. Opening night was attended by Her Royal Highness Princess Galyani Vadhana of Thailand. This production differed in tenor and effect from the earlier one, using as it did 15 actors instead of four and being infused with conventions from the traditional Thai theater, giving it a unique flexibility and sensitivity in which the various situations on stage were expressed through combinations of body movements. The three parts played by Japanese in the original production were taken over by Thai actors. Consequently, when Angus Barnett came on the scene, he did so as a European, thus giving the play a new thrust, that of Asia vs. Europe.

When the play was done again in Japan in 1999 the part of Akaoni was taken up by Noda himself, with all of the other parts being played by 13 Thai actors, transforming the theme into one of Asian vs. Asian. The play took on a whole new meaning, with the suggestion of Japanese aggression into Thailand during World War II and, more recently, the invasion of Japanese companies into Thailand after the war.

In 2000 and 2001 Noda conducted workshops of the play in London using British actors; and the play is scheduled for production in the U.K. in the not too distant future. Whatever the casting, the theme will probably be Asia vs. Europe, perhaps in the reverse sense of earlier productions. It is intriguing to speculate on how audiences in the U.K. will respond to what they see.

We don't have to look farther than the pamphlet for the 1998 Bangkok production of *The Red Demon Akaoni* to see how Noda Hideki feels today about international theater exchange. He wrote in that pamphlet:

> The text for this play is as thick as a graduation album, thanks to the three languages—Japanese, Thai and English—that it is written in, as if we were preparing to do simultaneous interpretation. We've got to turn the page every time an actor says about five words. Blink once and you've lost your place. And if

that isn't enough, Akaoni's dialogue is totally incomprehensible, because that's the way it was conceived. So we have no one to blame but ourselves. If we panicked we found ourselves in a muddle, hopelessly flummoxed.

The weight of the text was increased by the gravity of cultural difference. The thing that caused the muddle was the very preciousness of cultural difference itself. That's it! When differing cultures come into contact with each other, people readily find themselves dislocated and disoriented. But there's great pleasure to be had from that state, the kind of excitement that cannot be savored in everyday life. Exaltation. Cultural exchange is not mutual understanding. It is the relishing of cultural differences. To me, that's the thing to be savored.

Notes

1. Zenda-jō no toriko.
2. Shōnen-gari: sue wa ayame mo shirenu yami.
3. Sutōn henji nanahenge.
4. Byakuya no warukyūre.
5. Suisei jiifuriito.
6. Waruhara jōhatsu.
7. Gansaku: tsumi to batsu.
8. Pandora no kane.

The Red Demon Akaoni

Noda Hideki

TRANSLATED BY ROGER PULVERS

CHARACTERS
MAN 1
MAN 2
WOMAN 1
THE WOMAN
HAG
TOMBI
MAN 3
WOMAN 2
MAN 4
WOMAN 3
WOMAN 4
WOMAN 5
AKAONI
MIZUKANE
MAN 5
WOMAN 6
FATHER
MOTHER
ELDER
HEAD ELDER
TOURISTS 1, 2, 3, 4, 5, 6
OLD MAN
OLD WOMAN
JUDGE

There are four principal characters in this play—TOMBI, THE WOMAN, MIZUKANE, and AKAONI. The actors who play the first three roles also play all the other characters. The one playing TOMBI also plays MAN 2, MAN 4, WOMAN 5, MOTHER, HEAD ELDER, TOURIST 1, TOURIST 4, OLD WOMAN, and the JUDGE. The one playing THE WOMAN also plays WOMAN 1, WOMAN 2, WOMAN 3, WOMAN 6, ELDER, TOURIST 2, and TOURIST 5. The one playing MIZUKANE also plays MAN 1, HAG, MAN 3, WOMAN 4, MAN 5, FATHER,

TOURIST 3, TOURIST 6, and OLD MAN.

Scene 1

(Four people are adrift in a rough sea. One of them is carried away by a wave. The other three are washed up on shore. The person set adrift floats away some distance from the shore, bobbing up and down like a coconut on the waves. The three, now on shore, bolt up, transformed into three rescuers.)

MAN 1: They're still breathing.

MAN 2: Quick, get them to safety. Make it snappy!

MAN 1: We gotta keep them warm.

WOMAN 1: Are there any more of them?

MAN 1: Only these three.

MAN 2: Look, it's them. They're alive. They made it back in one piece.

MAN 1: Look, The Woman's here too.

WOMAN 1: That's all I needed! She's not worth saving. Let's just fling her back into the sea.

MAN 2: What do you think you're doing? She's alive. Just leave her where she is, will ya?

(WOMAN 1 is transformed into THE WOMAN by being wrapped in a blanket. At the same instant MAN 1 becomes HAG. HAG brings THE WOMAN a bowl of soup.)

THE WOMAN: Thank you. It tastes so good.

HAG: Uh huh, it's shark's fin soup. I don't give this to just everybody, you know. You're getting it 'cause you managed to survive.

THE WOMAN: What was that?

HAG: I said, not everybody gets this.

THE WOMAN: No, I mean the soup. What kind did you say it was?

HAG: Shark's fin. The fin . . . of the shark?

THE WOMAN: This isn't what shark fin tastes like.

HAG: You've had shark fin before?

THE WOMAN: Of course I have, every day out at sea.

(MAN 2 becomes TOMBI, THE WOMAN's elder brother, while at the same time, THE WOMAN becomes WOMAN 1 and HAG becomes MAN 1.)

TOMBI: My little sister died two days after eating shark's fin soup. After she had so narrowly escaped from the jaws of death, she went and threw herself off a cliff right back into the sea.

MAN 1: And after all the trouble we went to to save her in the first place.

WOMAN 1: An ungrateful bitch till the end, no two ways about it.

MAN 1: You mean she just picked herself up and smashed herself to pieces on the rocks after we had brought her back to life?

WOMAN 1: Don't look at me. That's the kind of woman she was.

TOMBI: No one can . . . fathom the reason why my little sister died.

Except me. I've got an idea why. I mean, I may be as thick as two planks, oh, not that I myself think I'm thick as two planks but everybody and his dog always says that I'm thick as two planks, if not three planks, so sometimes I start thinking that I might be and that's why I don't feel like telling you why my little sister really died because you'll just be furious with me if I tell you, that's why.

MAN 1: We won't be furious.

TOMBI: No, I know it from long experience.

WOMAN 1: Come on, tell us. We won't get mad at you.

TOMBI: Cross your heart?

WOMAN 1: *(Crossing her heart.)* And hope to die.

TOMBI: My little sister, I mean, died because she drank up that shark fin soup.

WOMAN 1: *(Angrily.)* Who in the hell do you take us for, eh?!

MAN 1: Cut the crap, will ya?

WOMAN 1: You telling us she was poisoned by the very soup that we took such pains to make for her, eh?

MAN 1: Geezus, you're ungrateful, just like your goddamn sister. Too bad you didn't drown along with her.

TOMBI: See, I knew you'd be furious with me. I should have kept my mouth shut like I wanted to. When people like me who have something missing upstairs tell stories, the stories always have something missing too. That's why you have to bear with me and hear me out, okay? I'll speak as slowly and plainly as I can. "The story of my little sister who was killed by a bowl of shark's fin soup." Okay? It begins on a day like the day she lost her life, on a beach in the evening, a beach swept clean by a fierce storm. . . .

MAN 3: I've had it. Sea's too rough tonight and the pickings are slim.

TOMBI: Not mine.

WOMAN 2: How many did you pick off?

TOMBI: One, two, a whole lot.

WOMAN 2: Three comes after two, not a whole lot.

MAN 3: Just a lousy bunch of bottles.

TOMBI: But I really got a whole lot.

WOMAN 2: That's what I asked you. How many?

TOMBI: One, two, a whole lot.

MAN 3: Toss 'em back. What good are a few lousy bottles that get washed up on shore? All you get out of them is the roar of a storm echoing when you put them up to your ear.

WOMAN 2: We took in some pretty good stuff after last year's storm, didn't we.

MAN 3: Yeah, you got that Buddha statue with the huge nose.

WOMAN 2: That was the so-called Karola Buddha, for your information. Nothing to be sneezed at.

MAN 3: That piece of driftwood?

WOMAN 2: Fetched a pretty penny.

MAN 3: I take it back.

TOMBI: Everything that drifts our way from out there is worth a hell of a lot of money, you know.

MAN 3: Ridiculous, not everything. What about those rotten gourds and that dolphin who was half dead?

WOMAN 2: You forget, you yourself bashed that dolphin to death and cleaned up on its skin.

MAN 3: Who'd buy a half-dead dolphin? By making a killing out of a dolphin's skin I was demonstrating the dolphin's real worth in life.

WOMAN 2: Remember that bear that came riding on the iceberg?

MAN 3: Poor thing looked so washed up I couldn't bear watching it.

WOMAN 2: Where do all those things come from anyway?

MAN 3: There's a waterfall beyond the open sea, they say, and ships just sail right off it.

TOMBI: Hey, what's this thing here?

MAN 3: It's a coconut, what do you think it is? We get 'em drifting in here all the time.

TOMBI: Your coconut just stood up, you know.

MAN 3: Numskull, of course coconuts sometimes . . . stand up?

(The three are floored to see the man, who appears in their eyes as a most bizarre creature, stand up. They rush about making comments about him. When they have calmed down somewhat, MAN 3 *speaks to* MAN 4, *played by the actor who played* TOMBI.)

MAN 3: *(Confused and flustered.)* Wa . . ter, somebody, please, wa . . ter.

MAN 4: What's come over you?

MAN 3: I saw it. It was out of this world. Simply not to be believed.

MAN 4: Exactly what did you see?

MAN 3: A beast. It's not human, I tell you.

MAN 4: Neither are you, so what's the big deal?

MAN 3: You don't believe me? I'm telling you . . . with my own two eyes.

MAN 4: No, you're telling me with your mouth.

MAN 3: Whatever, it was monstrously large with a face all covered in fuzz and it was soaked to the bone and it had . . . wa . . ter . . . blisters.

MAN 4: Huh? What'd you say?

MAN 3: Wa . . ter . . . blisters.

MAN 4: Monstrously large, you say, with a fuzzy face and soaked to the bone . . . and water blisters? What in the hell is that?

MAN 3: Search me.

MAN 4: *(To* WOMAN 3, *the former* WOMAN 2.) Beats me, too. Haven't a clue, even though I must admit, it's truly incredible.

WOMAN 3: Incredible? In what way?

MAN 4: Just plain incredible, that's what. Everyone who's seen it says so.

WOMAN 3: And have you seen it yourself?

MAN 4: Who, me?

WOMAN 3: Oh, ho, ho, so you haven't actually seen it, have you.

MAN 4: Have too. Right under my nose. Front row seat, I had.

WOMAN 3: So what kind of a monster was it, then, huh?

MAN 4: Well, its face was a bright red, and not only its face. When it opened its mouth you could see what looked like burning lava inside. And the minute it set eyes on me it charged at me like a bull at a bullfight. Behind me the sheer drop of a cliff, before me the beast approaching, horns down. . . .

WOMAN 3: Huh? You mean it had horns?

MAN 4: You bet it did. And what's more, yeah, it had water blisters.

WOMAN 3: Huh? What?

MAN 4: Water . . . blisters.

WOMAN 3: Yeah, sure, it has horns and goes "snappety-crack." What do you mean?

MAN 4: Beats me.

(WOMAN 3 *speaks to* WOMAN 4, *the former* MAN 3, *and to* WOMAN 5, *the former* MAN 4.)

WOMAN 3, WOMAN 4, *and* WOMAN 5: Did you hear that?!

WOMAN 3: My husband didn't merely hear it, he saw it himself.

WOMAN 4: Really? Well, so did mine.

WOMAN 5: So what. My husband was bitten alive.

WOMAN 3: He's lucky he didn't get himself gobbled up in the process.

WOMAN 4: So the monster eats humans after all.

WOMAN 3: And other things besides.

WOMAN 5: What do you mean, "other things"?

WOMAN 3: You remember, that cow was eaten up last year, don't you?

WOMAN 4: What? You yourself claimed it was Judy Garland who came back as a ghost and ate that cow. Come clean.

WOMAN 3: It didn't make sense, though. I mean, you wouldn't expect Judy Garland to do something like that, would you.

WOMAN 5: You're right. Besides, only half of the cow was eaten. The other half is still alive and kicking.

WOMAN 4: I get it. The monster must've come to finish off the other half.

WOMAN 5: You talk about it as if you knew what it was. What in the devil is it, anyway?

WOMAN 3: It's got horns and, what's more, that's right! It goes "snappety-crack" before it takes a big bite out of you.

WOMAN 4: Snappety-crack? What do you mean?

WOMAN 3: It's demon language for "twist your neck off."

WOMAN 5: What? What did you say just now?

WOMAN 4: A demon? Is that what it is? You said demon, didn't you. Admit it.

WOMAN 3: Don't tell me you didn't know. It's a demon all right, with a red face. Akaoni, a red demon.

WOMAN 5: What's a red demon doing here?

WOMAN 3: It's got to be because of you-know-who.

WOMAN 4: Can you please explain yourself?

WOMAN 3: You know, The Woman.

WOMAN 4: Right. I'd forgotten. The Woman summoned a red demon here.

WOMAN 4 *and* WOMAN 5: It's The Woman who's behind all this.

Scene 2

*(*WOMAN 3 *becomes* THE WOMAN. WOMAN 5 *becomes* TOMBI, *who rushes in. He quickly puts up a wall to enclose them.* THE WOMAN *and* TOMBI *disappear from sight, but can be glimpsed in spots through holes in the wall.)*

THE WOMAN: What's happening? It's so oppressive in here I can hardly breathe. Open a window, will you? What are you shivering in the corner like that for? Tombi?

TOMBI: You really don't know?

THE WOMAN: Oh, the red demon.

TOMBI: Huh?

THE WOMAN: You mean about a red demon coming here, is that it?

TOMBI: Did you know or didn't you?

THE WOMAN: Total nonsense. And to make matters worse, everyone's going around saying that I sent for it or something.

TOMBI: Yeah, that's right. Did you, Sis?

THE WOMAN: Did I what?

TOMBI: I mean, send for . . . a red demon.

THE WOMAN: Who you talking about?

TOMBI: You've been known to send for some pretty weird things on the odd occasion.

THE WOMAN: What have I sent for, eh? Name one thing.

TOMBI: Well, these storms, you know, and King Kong and when Elton John landed on the beach, that was your doing too, people say.

THE WOMAN: They blame me for all the bizarre things that happen here.

TOMBI: Might be because you're so gorgeous, I'd say.

THE WOMAN: Do you have any idea what gorgeous means?

TOMBI: Yeah. It means a woman who a man wants to pounce on.

THE WOMAN: Did you think that up all by yourself?

TOMBI: No, I heard it from Mizukane. He said that all women fall into two categories: the ones you want to pounce on and the ones you gotta pounce on.

THE WOMAN: Doesn't leave us much choice.

TOMBI: I'd say.

THE WOMAN: When it comes to men, there's only one category: the ones who want to pounce on a woman when they just see a morning glory vine coiled around itself. No other category.

TOMBI: You've got an attitude problem, you know that? All Mizukane wanted was to get on your good side.

THE WOMAN: All he wants is to get on top of me, that's what he wants. He doesn't even know my name.

TOMBI: Not so. He's always asking me about my little sister.

THE WOMAN: Little sister isn't a name.

TOMBI: Yeah, sorry.

THE WOMAN: Oh well, doesn't matter. The women around here all call me "The Woman," and you call me "Sis," and the men just stare at me in silence with that look in their eyes, so who needs a name?

(AKAONI peers in the window. TOMBI sees it over his sister's shoulder.)

TOMBI: Ah!

THE WOMAN: What's the matter now?

TOMBI: I just remembered something really important.

THE WOMAN: What is it?

TOMBI: I saw a red demon.

THE WOMAN: When?

TOMBI: On the beach, just then . . . the bottles . . . when I was picking one up, I . . . but maybe we shouldn't be so relaxed here . . . I mean . . . it's . . . behind you.

THE WOMAN: You know, Tombi, with each passing day you with your big ideas are turning more and more totally bananas.

(Trembling with fear, TOMBI goes around his sister to change places with her. It is the most ingenious method of showing her AKAONI that he can come up with. But, for better or worse, by then AKAONI is gone.)

TOMBI: I tell you it was there. Right behind you.

THE WOMAN: Look, nothing astonishes me anymore, not demons behind me, snakes behind me, nothing. The tree of astonishment is dead, killed by the weight of too many surprises. I don't have an iota of hope left in me.

TOMBI: Who did this to you, Sis?

THE WOMAN: People. It's not ghosts who astonish you. It's other people.

TOMBI: I was really taken by my little sister's dialogue that day. But when she came face-to-face with Akaoni the day after that, she may have felt like eating those words.

Scene 3

(TOMBI exits. THE WOMAN steps into a boat. It is the next day. She is

getting herself ready for a dive, alone. AKAONI *is already there,
underwater. He approaches the boat—the actor slides and glides across
the floor on his back in the manner of a shark. There is an atmosphere of
terror here.* AKAONI, *still in the sea, blows water from its mouth then
stands and climbs in the boat.* THE WOMAN *freezes in fear. She screams.
She starts to jump into the sea but, as luck would have it, gets herself
tangled up in ropes.* AKAONI *becomes scared when it hears the scream.
The two stare at each other in fear. A silence.)*

THE WOMAN: *(Mumbling out of fear.)* They say it's an old wives' tale that
when you come upon a bear you should play dead. Instead you should
look it straight in the eye and get away by stepping slowly backwards,
telling it, "I'm not going to hurt you now." *(She steps backwards but
hits the edge of the boat.)* I've been told that much, but no one told me
what you do when you can't go backwards anymore.

AKAONI: @@@@@@. (Water.)

THE WOMAN: Oh my God. I don't taste good. Awful, really.

AKAONI: @@@@@@@@@@@@@@@@. (I've been out at sea for
ages and have had nothing to drink. Give me some water, please.)

*(AKAONI attempts to explain himself through gestures, but these
gestures are unclear even to the audience. For instance, he does not
gesture "to drink water" with his hand but rather by getting on his
back on the floor and sticking out his tongue. The audience has no
way of comprehending his gestures or the kind of life he leads.)*

AKAONI: @@@@@@@@. (That water, there.)

(AKAONI reaches out toward THE WOMAN.)

THE WOMAN: Human beings aren't all that good to eat, I'll have you
know. They're 90% water.

AKAONI: @@@@@@@@@@@@@@@@. (Don't be afraid. All I
want is water.)

THE WOMAN: Please lower your hand. I'll give you whatever you want.

AKAONI: @@@@@@. (I want water.)

(AKAONI once again lies on the floor and sticks out his tongue.)

THE WOMAN: Are you trying to tell me you want water? Is that what you
want, water?

AKAONI: @@@@@@. (I want water.)

THE WOMAN: In that case, what I told you a moment ago was not actually
the whole truth. You see, humans are not made of water at all.
Theories like that just don't hold their water. That's probably a bit lost
on you. Human beings are not made of water. We're made up of rancid
blood and unchewable meat.

AKAONI: @@! (Water!)

THE WOMAN: Look, here's your water.

(She nervously pours some water from a water bottle into a cup and

holds it above AKAONI's *head.*)

AKAONI: *(Still on its back.)* @! @@@. (No! You feed it to me.)

(All red demons believe that water drunk from one's own hand is dirty.)

THE WOMAN: What is it? What do you want?

AKAONI: @@@@! (Feed it to me!)

THE WOMAN: Huh? What's he on about now? I can't cope with this.

AKAONI: @@@@@@@@@@@@@@@@@@@@@@@@@? (What kind of a country is this, anyway, where they don't even know how to give somebody a drink?)

THE WOMAN: What do you want me to do?!

AKAONI: @@@@. (She scares me.)

THE WOMAN: Huh? I get it. You want me to feed you some water? You can't use your hands, is that right?

AKAONI: @@@@. (Feed me some water.)

THE WOMAN: Okay, but just don't eat me. Oh, I get it. This is the way fish are caught, the way I'm being caught now. Okay, but once you've had your fill, you'll get the hell out of here, right, never show your face here again?

*(*THE WOMAN *feeds* AKAONI *water for a moment.* AKAONI *calms down a bit, as does* THE WOMAN *as well.*)*

AKAONI: *(With a circling gesture.)* @@@@@@! (Thank you. You've saved me!)

THE WOMAN: This is how you repay me?

AKAONI: @@@@. (Thank you.)

THE WOMAN: Now, easy does it . . . what can I expect next? What usually comes after drinking water? If it was me, let's see . . . I suppose I would be looking for something to eat.

*(*AKAONI *licks his chops. This is a gesture of affection.*)*

THE WOMAN: Tell me, is it true that demons eat human beings?

AKAONI: @@@@@? (You are a genuine lady, you know that?)

THE WOMAN: Please stop licking your chops like that, okay? Do you eat humans? You going to eat me? Cut all the kidding. If I'm going to be eaten I want to say a few words first. It hasn't exactly been easy for me to get to this stage of life, you know. So, if you're planning on making me your next meal after all I've been through in my life, then you're a real monster. People only call you demons because you eat humans. Demons wouldn't be demons if they didn't eat humans in the first place.

*(*AKAONI *opens his arms, embraces her. This gesture corresponds to a human gesture.* THE WOMAN *is convinced that she is about to be devoured. Blackout.*)*

Scene 4

*(*AKAONI *is gone.* TOMBI *and* MIZUKANE *enter on* THE WOMAN, *who seems oblivious to what transpired earlier.)*

MIZUKANE: *(To* THE WOMAN.*)* There's nobody who cares for you like I do, if I do say so myself. Ain't that right, Tombi?

TOMBI: Huh? Say something?

MIZUKANE: A mouthful, that's what. Now let her hear it from you. She's your sister, after all.

TOMBI: *(To* THE WOMAN.*)* Hey, okay, so just grit your teeth and let Mizukane slip it into you.

MIZUKANE: That's not what I wanted you to say.

TOMBI: What is it, then? Don't you want to give her one?

MIZUKANE: All I want is for your sister to open up a little bit to me.

TOMBI: What, her mind or her legs?

MIZUKANE: Look, I'm really quite an open-minded sort of guy, if I do say so myself. You know what they call your little sister around here?

TOMBI: The Woman. Right?

MIZUKANE: You knew, then. The Woman. The Woman. Any name that's got a "the" in front of it that's pronounced "thee" is mud. Thee wife. Thee store. Thee play. And as for you, Thee Woman, ever hear about the Akaoni who wept? Here, on this very beach, it's you who's the red demon despised by everybody. And I'm your own blue demon, if I do say so myself, the open-minded blue demon who's sacrificing himself so that you can get along and live with the human beings on this beach.

THE WOMAN: The real Akaoni would be in stitches if it could hear you now. Where're you going, Tombi?

TOMBI: He told me to beat it when he started talking about the blue demon.

MIZUKANE: Who said that? All I did was tell you to get some bottles off the beach.

TOMBI: Sure, you told me to get lots and lots of them all night, so many that I wouldn't come back.

MIZUKANE: Look, who buys those worthless bottles off you anyway, who pays through the nose for them, eh? Who?

TOMBI: You do, Mizukane.

MIZUKANE: You yourself know that nobody in his right mind would even look at that stuff. But I'm kind enough to take it off your hands.

TOMBI: Thank you.

MIZUKANE: Me, buddy, me.

THE WOMAN: Yeah, and you've probably got some ulterior motive for that, too.

MIZUKANE: Look here, I'm a new man now, you know, reborn, if I do say so myself. The people around here are the kind who bash dolphins to death for money after a storm, but not yours truly. They wouldn't touch the most valuable things that are washed up with a ten-foot pole, I mean, the bottles. Know what's inside them, eh?

TOMBI: I do.

THE WOMAN: Couldn't care less.

MIZUKANE: That which is beyond the sea . . . that's what's inside.

THE WOMAN: Well, I'll be. We've got a regular poet here on our hands.

MIZUKANE: A poet is somebody who calls the wind "God's chariot," ain't that right?

TOMBI: So whose chariots are the waves, then?

MIZUKANE: No wonder you can't make a living.

TOMBI: Yeah, I don't wonder either.

MIZUKANE: Look, nobody'll buy a poem.

THE WOMAN: So, why did you just say "that which is beyond the sea is inside the bottles on the beach" then?

MIZUKANE: What you find beyond the sea is not the dreams of a poet. It really exists. This coastline where we live is the closest thing there is to that place beyond the sea. The fishermen here catch fish. They're idiots. I fish for what's inside the bottles. You have to treat each and every bottle with kid gloves. Take a look inside, Tombi.

TOMBI: Ah, it's there all right.

MIZUKANE: Let's have a look.

TOMBI: What does it say?

MIZUKANE: Ha. Just another stupid SOS.

TOMBI: That's all I ever get. I guess people beyond the sea are really in trouble a lot of the time.

MIZUKANE: You wait. The time will come when what's inside this bottle will fetch more than all the fish in the sea.

THE WOMAN: I'm going to dive for shellfish.

TOMBI: You're behind the times, Sis. Open your mind and your legs. Open up every last orifice in your body . . . and turn them to what's beyond the sea.

MIZUKANE: Hey, man, pretty good. You're getting the hang of it.

TOMBI: Aw, shucks.

THE WOMAN: Tombi. You should take whatever Mizukane says with a grain of salt.

MIZUKANE: Yeah, my middle name is Fib.

TOMBI: Fib.

MIZUKANE: You know why? It stands for "Formations in Brine." They're UFOs. Unidentified floating objects. Someday the UFOs that wash up on this shore are going to make us all rich.

TOMBI: Is Akaoni one of those, too?

MIZUKANE: Huh?

TOMBI: The Akaoni that I saw. Maybe it's one of those UFOs, too.

   (A rattling noise is heard.)

MIZUKANE: Someone's there.

TOMBI: What is it, someone?

MIZUKANE: What's wrong? You look like you've seen a demon.

THE WOMAN: What demon! I don't know anything about any demons.

   (A pause after her all-too-vehement denial.)

TOMBI: It's true, you know. I was the one who met the demon. Not once, but twice, too.

MIZUKANE: There is no such thing as an Akaoni.

TOMBI: Is too.

MIZUKANE: It's just a rumor they always spread around this beach.

TOMBI: You wouldn't be talking like that if you saw it.

MIZUKANE: I'd say it especially if I saw it. Fine, let's suppose that your Akaoni really does exist. I'd walk right up to it and shake its hand. I'd even give it a big kiss. I'm open to everybody.

AKAONI: *(Entering.)* Rrrrrrgh!

MIZUKANE: Whooooooah! Tombi! What's this Akaoni doing here?!

TOMBI: Beats me.

MIZUKANE: Quick, get me a hatchet! I'll hack it to pieces.

THE WOMAN: What are you getting all worked up about?

MIZUKANE: Keep your distance from it. It'll eat you alive.

THE WOMAN: I thought you were going to shake hands with it, give it a big slobbery kiss.

MIZUKANE: You've been keeping this thing in your house like a pet just to show me up, haven't you. Since when have you been . . . ?

THE WOMAN: Since lunchtime. I gave it some water and it's been hot on my heels since.

MIZUKANE: It's not like a stray dog, you know.

AKAONI: @ @ @ @ @ @ @. (I'm starving to death.)

   *(*AKAONI*'s gesture for being hungry looks like sniffing cocaine.)*

TOMBI: Wow, the demon spoke.

MIZUKANE: Demons can't talk, bird-brain.

TOMBI: They can't?

MIZUKANE: Do horses talk? Do dogs talk? No, they just growl.

AKAONI: @ @ @ @ @ @ @ @ @ @ @ @ @ @ @ @? (I'm not asking for much, just food and water, please. And a bit of shut-eye. I'll do whatever you like once I'm back on my feet. I'm begging you. Isn't there one human being who understands what I'm saying?)

TOMBI: That's one hell of a long growl.

THE WOMAN: I think it's trying to tell us something.

MIZUKANE: Even monkeys can appear to be talking, you know.

AKAONI: @ @ @ @ @ @ @ @ @. (Okay. Just some food, that's all.)

THE WOMAN: I think it's trying to tell us that it's hungry.

MIZUKANE: You call that a gesture for being hungry?

THE WOMAN: But, look, this is thirsty.

> (THE WOMAN *imitates the gesture for thirst.*)

MIZUKANE: That?

THE WOMAN: Yep.

> (THE WOMAN *gives* AKAONI *water; he drinks in the same way as before.*)

THE WOMAN: See? So it must be hungry now, I guess.

MIZUKANE: Tombi, listen to me.

TOMBI: I'm all ears.

MIZUKANE: Go up to it and see if it eats you.

TOMBI: Me?

MIZUKANE: Don't you respect me, buddy?

TOMBI: I do.

MIZUKANE: Then get your ass over there.

TOMBI: All right.

> (TOMBI *stands before* AKAONI.)

TOMBI: It's not eating me. Look, I can wiggle my behind and it's not even touching it.

MIZUKANE: It must be full. Even a tiger would walk past a rabbit on a full stomach.

THE WOMAN: I think it doesn't eat people, maybe.

MIZUKANE: Doesn't eat people? It's a demon. A demon wouldn't be able to show its face if it didn't eat people. In a minute it'll be hungry again and attack you, you'll see.

THE WOMAN: You said that you'd shake Akaoni's hand if it came here. Why don't you, eh?

MIZUKANE: What do you take me for, eh?

TOMBI: I'd shake its hand.

MIZUKANE: What?

TOMBI: I will shake its hand.

> (TOMBI *reluctantly shakes hands with* AKAONI. *This gesture, however, is interpreted by the latter as a belligerent one.*)

AKAONI: @@@@@@@! (Get that hand away from me. Withdraw your hand!)

MIZUKANE: Christ, watch out, let's get outta here!

THE WOMAN: It won't do anything if we don't.

MIZUKANE: This ain't no wasp or something. One bite outta this one and you're a goner.

THE WOMAN: That's what I thought, too, when it hugged me.

MIZUKANE: It hugged you?

THE WOMAN: Uh huh.

MIZUKANE: And did it, uh, have its way with you, too?

THE WOMAN: No, just squeezed me real tight.

MIZUKANE: And then?

THE WOMAN: Nothing.

MIZUKANE: Come off it. A man's a man. It's not gonna stop with just a hug.

THE WOMAN: That's only humans you're talking about.

MIZUKANE: A demon's a man, whether you like it or not.

TOMBI: Who says it's a man. It looks sort of rough and tough because it's a demon, but, you never know, it could just as well be a woman.

THE WOMAN: No, it's gotta be a man.

TOMBI: Why?

THE WOMAN: I can tell by the way it looks at me.

(AKAONI *looks at the three of them.*)

MIZUKANE: You were wrong, see?

TOMBI: Yeah.

THE WOMAN: Trust me on this one. All males look at females in a particular way, irrespective of the species.

AKAONI: @.@.@.@.@.@.@. (Can't you see, I'm s-t-a-r-v-i-n-g.)

(AKAONI, *in doing the hungry gesture, lets down his guard.*)

MIZUKANE: Tombi, now's our chance, throw the net!

TOMBI: Wharggggh!

THE WOMAN: Give me a break, will ya? It's just asking for food.

TOMBI: Well, why don't we feed it, then?

THE WOMAN: I don't know what it eats. Can't you see that?

MIZUKANE: Humans. They all do.

THE WOMAN: It turns its nose up at anything I give it. It wouldn't eat fish or rats or anything.

MIZUKANE: What do you think, eh? It's only got an eye for human beings, I'm telling you.

AKAONI: @ @ @ @ @ @ @ @? (Are you getting the point about my being hungry?)

THE WOMAN: *(To* AKAONI.*)* You're trying to tell us that you want to eat, right?

AKAONI: @ @ @ @? (You follow me?)

THE WOMAN: I follow.

TOMBI: She's getting through to it!

MIZUKANE: Mind what you say to it. It might be asking if it can eat you.

AKAONI: @ @ @ @ @ @ @? (Am I getting through to you?)

TOMBI: *(As an interpreter.)* Can . . . I . . . please . . . eat you?

THE WOMAN: Sure.

MIZUKANE: Don't give in! *(*AKAONI *approaches them.)* You're going to be eaten by it.

(AKAONI *puts its arms around* THE WOMAN. TOMBI *holds flowers over her shoulder.* AKAONI *jumps on* TOMBI, *snatching the flowers from him and eating them with relish.)*

MIZUKANE: What'd you give it, eh?

TOMBI: Just some flowers.

THE WOMAN: So that's what it eats, flowers.

MIZUKANE: How did you figure out that it ate flowers?

TOMBI: A hunch.

THE WOMAN: Good going, Tombi. Bring some more flowers now.

MIZUKANE: Why are you doing this for a demon?

THE WOMAN: What's your problem, Mizukane?

MIZUKANE: Tombi, go and tell all the people on the beach, tell them that a demon is about to gobble up your sister.

THE WOMAN: Just go and get some flowers, okay?

MIZUKANE: Tell them she's going to be eaten alive.

THE WOMAN: Flowers, Tombi.

MIZUKANE: Your sister.

TOMBI: Right. *(Running out.)*

MIZUKANE: What does he mean "right." Probably doesn't know himself.

TOMBI: After that I ran up and down the beach at twilight grabbing all the flowers I could and hollering, "My sister's going to get gobbled up!"

(TOMBI runs about grabbing flowers and yelling, "My sister's going to get gobbled up!")

Scene 5

(THE WOMAN becomes WOMAN 6; MIZUKANE, MAN 5.)

MAN 5: Akaoni's here!

WOMAN 6: Where?

MAN 5: Staying at The Woman's house.

WOMAN 6: In that case, let it stay there.

MAN 5: But red demons get huger and huger when they eat human beings.

WOMAN 6: Now's the time to exterminate it.

MAN 5: We'd have the devil of a time doing it at night. I say we do it before the sun goes down.

TOMBI: The big problem was that while they were contemplating the best way to get rid of Akaoni, the sun went down. Akaoni had already made its escape by the time I got to my sister's. That night, faithful to its name and reputation, it demonized people all over the place.

(AKAONI appears in various spots among the audience, as people on the shore follow it, yelling, "There it is!" or "This way!" At one point a woman holding a baby, played by TOMBI, bumps into AKAONI. The woman puts the baby down in terror and flees. The baby cries. AKAONI stares at the baby then picks it up to mollify it, rushing off with it in its arms. MAN 5 becomes the baby's FATHER.)

FATHER: Our baby's been kidnapped!

MOTHER: Somebody, please save Hidematsu.

FATHER: It's your fault, you bitch. You let him out of your sight.

MOTHER: I'm sorry, darling.

FATHER: You're not fit to be a mother, dammit.

MOTHER: But the kidnapper grabbed Hidematsu right out of my arms. Hidematsu was having a little nap on the veranda and he jumped right up and said, "Hand over the little tyke."

FATHER: Red demons eat red-blooded babies. That's why they're red.

MOTHER: And blue demons eat blue-blooded babies.

FATHER: Everybody, listen! Don't let your babies out of the house!

(A meeting of elders, with village ELDER *played by* WOMAN 6. *The sound of crying babies is heard. The* ELDER *is speaking but his words are inaudible due to the noise.)*

ELDER: Someone shut them up! Why have babies been brought to such an important gathering as this?

FATHER: Please understand our position, sir. If we leave our babies at home they'll be devoured by Akaoni. We're all desperate, sir.

MOTHER: It's all The Woman's fault. Hidematsu was eaten instead of her.

ELDER: We do not know for sure whether he has been eaten or not.

MOTHER: We do. My baby is all alone with Akaoni. Do you think Hidematsu would eat Akaoni?

ELDER: Well, not exactly. . . .

MOTHER: I told you so. It means that Hidematsu's the one who's going to get eaten.

ELDER: Why don't we drop the question of who's going to eat who?

MOTHER: That's all a beast thinks about morning, noon and night. Why do you think it's called a beast, otherwise?

FATHER: My old mother's like that. All she thinks about is food.

ELDER: A baby brought up by a wolf turns into a wolf, they say. Not that I've known any wolves in my day.

FATHER: Does that mean that a baby brought up by a red demon will . . . ?

MOTHER: We've gotta save Hidematsu right away!

(Hysterical, she turns into TOMBI.*)*

TOMBI: Duh. . . .

ELDER: What're you doing here, Tombi? You don't belong at a gathering like this.

FATHER: Get your sister here right now! She should be the one who's eaten up, not my child.

TOMBI: Akaoni wouldn't eat any baby, I don't think.

FATHER: What'd you say?

TOMBI: Akaoni doesn't eat humans. It eats flowers. I saw it eat flowers.

FATHER: What's eating you, eh? All this nonsense about flowers.

TOMBI: A demon by any other name, perhaps.

FATHER: You're dead from the neck up, you know that?

ELDER: If this Akaoni does eat flowers as you say, then we can lure it to a sea cave using flowers from the beach as bait and drive it in.

MOTHER: Sweetie-pie?

FATHER: Yeah.

MOTHER: Tombi's definitely as thick as two toilet seats, but I think we ought to follow his advice.

ELDER: Everyone, start scattering flowers.

(Flowers are scattered. AKAONI *enters, holding the baby. The three of them observe* AKAONI *from afar.* AKAONI *munches on the flowers.)*

FATHER: Look, it's eating them. It's eating the flowers.

ELDER: It's a demon, all right.

FATHER: Shush. It's looking our way.

MOTHER: He's got Hidematsu. He's alive.

FATHER: Akaoni is trying to feed flowers to Hidematsu.

ELDER: It must believe that humans eat flowers, too.

FATHER: Do they?

MOTHER: You bet they do.

FATHER: They do?

MOTHER: Hidematsu's eaten a flower. And he's smiling, too.

ELDER: This is awful. Hidematsu is already turning into a red demon.

FATHER: He does look a little redder, come to think of it.

MOTHER: We've got to hurry. I beg of you.

ELDER: It's off guard, eating the flowers.

FATHER: Now's our time!

(They use the audience to surround AKAONI, *closing in on it. Finally they trap it in the cave, from which it can be glimpsed from time to time.)*

ELDER: We've got it where we want it now.

FATHER: Don't celebrate so quickly. Hidematsu's trapped with it.

ELDER: It's not going to get away from us, at any rate.

MOTHER: That means Hidematsu's finished.

ELDER: Akaoni eats flowers.

MOTHER: Just because it eats flowers, it doesn't mean that it couldn't eat a human as well.

ELDER: Huh?

MOTHER: We eat vegetables, but we eat meat, too. *(*ELDER *is silent.)* Don't we?

ELDER: I wasn't quite thinking along those lines.

MOTHER: Your wisdom's useless now, that's why.

ELDER: Be that as it may, Mizukane, we elders have come here to you because we understand you're knowledgeable about things beyond the sea.

MIZUKANE: That's news, your asking advice from someone who's too lazy to even catch a single fish.

HEAD ELDER: Has Akaoni come here from beyond the sea?

MIZUKANE: You village elders are much wiser than me, aren't you? You know all about life and stuff.

HEAD ELDER: Wisdom about life does not extend to beyond the sea.

MIZUKANE: Is that so? So you admit that there is a beyond, eh? I thought that ships just sailed on and on and then fell off the edge.

HEAD ELDER: That is what I still believe to be true.

MIZUKANE: You know what's beyond the sea? The same thing that is in the bottles. Nothing.

HEAD ELDER: You know, don't you. You know all about Akaoni.

MIZUKANE: You catch fish with a net. You also gather information in a net. Is that why it's called "The Net"?

HEAD ELDER: Well, then, you go rescue the baby from Akaoni.

MIZUKANE: Easier said than done.

HEAD ELDER: I won't put up with this. I can't stand young people like this who just turn on clever words whenever they want to.

MIZUKANE: Turn on? I'm not a faucet, you know.

HEAD ELDER: See, that's what I mean, dammit.

MIZUKANE: Oh boy, I'm getting it today. Sir. When asking a favor from somebody, it is customary to bow one's head.

ELDER: What?

MIZUKANE: Bow . . . one's . . . head.

HEAD ELDER: Not me. Never.

ELDER: Sir, I think we ought to act like palms and bend with the wind.
(The two elders bow reluctantly.)

MIZUKANE: Well, well, at last the time has come that Mohammed has rushed to the mountain. Call me Mt. Rushmore. No longer is Fib a fibber. That's right, Tombi.
(When ELDER *and* HEAD ELDER *bring their heads up they are* THE WOMAN *and* TOMBI.*)*

Scene 6

TOMBI: Phew.

MIZUKANE: You know, I'm a new man, if I do say so myself. I've never been able to refuse a man who's bowed down in front of me.

THE WOMAN: There's nothing new about that.

MIZUKANE: We ought to strike now, Tombi. I bet that Akaoni would trust your sister.

THE WOMAN: You go and talk to it. See if it buys that phony business about the bottles.

MIZUKANE: There was no information about Akaoni in the bottles.

THE WOMAN: So?

MIZUKANE: Go and rescue the baby. You'll be hailed as the heroine of the beach.

THE WOMAN: And what are you, a hero?

TOMBI: What am I?

MIZUKANE: You're the nitwit brother of the heroine.

TOMBI: Nitwit brother. Has a nice ring to it.

THE WOMAN: I don't buy it. They'd just conclude that I was one of the demons if they saw me communicating with Akaoni.

MIZUKANE: Say something, Tombi.

TOMBI: You shouldn't lose heart, Sis.

THE WOMAN: The trouble with you, Tombi, is that you've lost your marbles.

TOMBI: Maybe. But I've never lost my sense of hope, like you.

THE WOMAN: Both you and I, Tombi, are pretty hopeless.

TOMBI: Phew.

THE WOMAN: It's never occurred to you that you might be despised by people, has it.

TOMBI: Huh? Me, despised?

THE WOMAN: You're unaware of it, aren't you. Well, people loathe you.

TOMBI: Is that true, Mizukane?

MIZUKANE: Well, maybe not actually loathe . . . you're just sort of ignored by everybody. Except at festival time. At festival time you're definitely loathed.

TOMBI: I never realized.

THE WOMAN: Shocked?

TOMBI: Not particularly. 'Cause there's no real reason why people should hate me.

THE WOMAN: Yes there is.

TOMBI: Isn't.

THE WOMAN: Is. People hate people who come from the outside. That's all they need. Our relatives were all like that too, you know.

MIZUKANE: But the people who live by this beach will accept people who are hated by others.

THE WOMAN: Thanks but no thanks.

MIZUKANE: Don't you feel sorry for little Hidematsu?

THE WOMAN: Nope.

MIZUKANE: Then you do have no heart.

TOMBI: But you yourself said that you really got your rocks off on heartless women like her, didn't you? Isn't that what you said, Mizukane, that they really turn you on?

MIZUKANE: You think I'm a sexed-up lecher, don't you.

TOMBI: You said yourself there are men like that in this world and you're one of them.

MIZUKANE: Look, I have your best interests at heart, believe me, and I've been dreaming of the day when you would be accepted by the people who live by the beach, when there are no more secrets and there is nothing to hide.

THE WOMAN: Is that why you grab hatchets when you see demons, eh?

MIZUKANE: Don't you see, it's a monster.

THE WOMAN: And once you've rescued the baby, you're all planning on beating the monster to death, right?

MIZUKANE: We wouldn't do that.

THE WOMAN: It's what you've been doing up till now.

MIZUKANE: But Akaoni is a monster who devours beautiful flowers one after another.

THE WOMAN: You eat plants too, don't you. *(Pause.)* Mizukane.

MIZUKANE: What now?

THE WOMAN: Make a deal with the beach people, okay? After Akaoni hands over Hidematsu, you won't touch it for three days, no make that seven, ten.

MIZUKANE: But it's too dangerous to leave Akaoni on the loose.

ELDER: *(After an instantaneous change.)* Got it.

MIZUKANE: Huh?

ELDER: We'll go along with what The Woman says and not do a thing for seven days. But, in exchange, we want her to rescue Hidematsu from the sea cave right away. Tell that to The Woman, Mizukane.

TOMBI: I wonder what was going through my sister's mind while she made her way to the cave. She no longer uttered the word "hopeless" after that. I still can't fathom the meaning of that word. I've never encountered anything hopeless before. Please, somebody, where can I find something hopeless?

Scene 7

*(*THE WOMAN *approaches* AKAONI *in the sea cave.)*

AKAONI: MAMA.

THE WOMAN: Huh?

AKAONI: MAMA.

THE WOMAN: You looking for your mama?

AKAONI: MAMA.

THE WOMAN: You referring to me? Am I Mama?

AKAONI: @ @ @ @ @ @ @ @? (Mama is you?)

THE WOMAN: It's true, then, you do speak a language.

AKAONI: @ @ @ @ @ @ @ @ @.

THE WOMAN: It takes everything out of me when you act like this. I'm not sure, but you're not a demon at all, are you. You're a person.

AKAONI: @ @ @ @ @ @ @ @ @.

THE WOMAN: If you think you're going to get through like that, forget it.

Look, this is for your benefit. The first thing you gotta do is learn our language. It would set us at ease, you know. Do you follow me? Follow me? Me . . . you . . . teach . . . langu-age. I sound like goddamn Tarzan. Uh . . . you, you de-mon. Um . . . demon, demon, demon. Not getting through. Tombi, could you come here for a moment, please?

TOMBI: *(To* AKAONI.*)* Uh, hi.

THE WOMAN: You, demon. Him, moron. So, friends.

TOMBI: Huh, am I its friend?

THE WOMAN: Shut up, will ya? My name is Fu-ku.

TOMBI: Was that your name? Amazing.

THE WOMAN: Fuku. It's Fu-ku. What's yours? *(*AKAONI *does not speak.)* Fuku. Me, Fuku.

AKAONI: Fu-ku. Fuck you.

THE WOMAN: Fuck me? Well, it's progress. MAMA, Fuck. You? Your name? *(*AKAONI *is silent.)* Okay? *(Pointing to herself, then* TOMBI*, then* AKAONI.*)* Mama, Fuck. Tombi, moron. Demon. Now it's your turn.

AKAONI: Fuck Tombi. . . .

TOMBI: He's gotta have a name. Even a stray dog you take in's got a name.

THE WOMAN: But if he can just say his own name then we'll know he's a human being.

TOMBI: Is that the kind of creatures humans are?

THE WOMAN: That's right. Humans are animals that can pronounce their own names.

TOMBI: Then, what about mutes?

THE WOMAN: Let's discuss that some other time.

AKAONI: Angus.

THE WOMAN: What'd you say?

AKAONI: @@@@@@@@. (My name? It's Angus.)

THE WOMAN: Angus. Then, you're Angus.

AKAONI: Angus. Fuck. Moron.

(They communicate with each other for a little while using only their names, TOMBI *calling himself "Tombi," and finally* AKAONI *doing the same.)*

TOMBI: Gee, feels like we've known each other for years just calling each other's names.

THE WOMAN: Angus, give back the baby. Baby. Follow? Tombi, act like a baby.

TOMBI: Huh?

THE WOMAN: A baby.

TOMBI: Yeah.

*(*TOMBI *does an impression of a baby, very badly.)*

MIZUKANE: Hopeless. I'll do it.

*(*MIZUKANE *does a very skillful baby.)*

AKAONI: @@@@@@! (Oh, the baby!)

THE WOMAN: I think he got it.

TOMBI: He got it!

(The three are terribly pleased with themselves, until they notice MIZUKANE.*)*

THE WOMAN: What? Have you been hiding here, Mizukane?

MIZUKANE: I'm noting everything down, about Akaoni. Akaoni, real name Angus. @@@@@@, baby.

THE WOMAN: Angus, give ba-by back to Mama Fuck. Act out handing something over.

TOMBI: Hand over? That's really hard.

*(*MIZUKANE *and* TOMBI *do the gestures for handing over.)*

MIZUKANE: Do you think it got through to it?

AKAONI: @@@@@@@@@? (By hand over do you mean @@@@@@?)

THE WOMAN: You say @@@@@, do you?

AKAONI: @@@.

THE WOMAN: Okay. Angus @@@ baby to Mama Fuck.

*(*AKAONI *hands over the baby immediately.)*

THE WOMAN: He got it.

TOMBI: He returned the baby.

MIZUKANE: So @@@ is hand over. Tombi, go and tell all the people of the beach that Hidematsu is safe.

Scene 8

*(*TOMBI *snatches the baby immediately and becomes* MOTHER.*)*

MOTHER: Hidematsu!

FATHER: Murder Akaoni!

THE WOMAN: Hold your horses. You promised, remember? You said you'd wait seven days.

MOTHER: Are you kidding? Do you have any idea what I've been through with my baby snatched away from me? I'm wasting my breath on a woman like you who screws every man she sees and has never had a baby to boot. How could you understand a mother's pain?

FATHER: Exactly. If you're going to stand between Akaoni and us, we'll just have to burn both of you alive.

THE WOMAN: But the village elder agreed. Where is he?

MOTHER: What would you do if we let Akaoni go free and another baby is taken away from its mother, eh?

THE WOMAN: He's not a demon, you know. A person. He's a human being.

MOTHER: Ha, she's calling the demon a human.

FATHER: For all we know you're one of them.

THE WOMAN: Just like I said, a rotten bunch of people. But I won't lose heart, Tombi. I've still got seven days grace to drum it into the skulls of these people that Akaoni is a person. If I fail, I can always give up hope after that. All right, if you've a mind to set fire to this cave, no one's going to stop you. But remember, with that fire you will be showing your own sins for all the world to see. The more wicked the sin, the higher the flame will climb. Go on. I'll be watching you, to see just how wicked to the core you really are.

MOTHER: It's you who will burn in hell.

FATHER: Burn the cave!

TOMBI: After that the beach people armed themselves to the teeth and forced their way into the cave with torches in their hands. How many miracles can we expect in life? It's beyond me. But this one time, I can say for certain that a miracle did happen. The people who held torches in their hands froze where they stood, holding their breath, with eyes wide open.

THE WOMAN: There were the greenest trees under the sun, golden birds, lapis lazuli butterflies, fruits of scarlet and crystal streams. And there were those coconuts that we sometimes saw washing up on the beach.

(They look and sound as if they were witnessing something godly.)

MIZUKANE: Tombi, come and behold.

TOMBI: What's up, Mizukane? Hey, what is it, those paintings on the walls?

MIZUKANE: It's the place beyond the sea.

TOMBI: What?

MIZUKANE: Akaoni must have lived beyond the sea.

TOMBI: If what you say is true, then, out of the blue this cave by the sea has come to house the place beyond the sea.

MIZUKANE: We're inside a bottle.

TOMBI: What did you say?

MIZUKANE: There is a place beyond the sea after all.

THE WOMAN: Did you paint these pictures on the walls of this cave, Angus?

*(*AKAONI *speaks in the native language of the actor.)*

AKAONI: This is the place that I come from. These trees that only I know, these golden birds that only I know, the lapis lazuli butterflies, the scarlet fruits, the crystal streams and the coconuts that were imprinted into my memory before I drifted to this shore. And this is a song from my faraway homeland.

*(*AKAONI *sings a song to himself in the actor's native language.)*

MIZUKANE: This landscape is from another world.

TOMBI: These are pictures painted by some evil spirit.

MIZUKANE: He's an evil spirit, he is.

THE WOMAN: He very well may be an evil spirit. But he may also be a god. Gods have always come from beyond the sea.

TOMBI: The words spoken by my little sister put the fear of God into the people of the beach. They had never expected someone who they had called "The Woman," someone they saw in such an eerie light, as capable of invoking the presence of a god. At that, Mizukane said. . . .

MIZUKANE: Right. Nobody knows the place beyond the sea better than me. Don't be fooled, those scarecrows over there have also come from beyond the sea.

TOMBI: And, inveterate liar that he was, he elaborated on his cock-and-bull story.

MIZUKANE: Deceit is a morning sickness that precedes the birth of truth.

TOMBI: That seemed to do the trick.

ELDER: I got it. We will give you the seven days' grace as promised. In return, you, Akaoni, must vanish from here in that time. Go wherever you like, beyond the sea, anywhere.

TOMBI: One miracle had run its course and another was about to befall us. Miracle number two. It happened on the third day. It was a prize beauty.

MIZUKANE: You look down in the dumps. What's up?

THE WOMAN: I just can't get through to him.

MIZUKANE: Get what through?

THE WOMAN: It's like hitting my head against a brick wall.

MIZUKANE: It's because you're hopeless at gesturing. Leave it to me and Tombi, okay?

TOMBI: Yeah.

MIZUKANE: For example, this is "water." Now, this one is "very hot water." So, what do you want to tell him?

THE WOMAN: I want to teach him, "Now is the winter of our discontent." Go on, give it a go.

MIZUKANE: You can't start with something that hard right away.

THE WOMAN: Okay. I got it. How about this one. "The individual who foregoes the pièce de résistance is the politest one."

TOMBI: Even I don't get that one.

THE WOMAN: He and I get along quite well when we talk about easy things.

AKAONI: @@@@@@@@@.

THE WOMAN: Precisely.

AKAONI: @@@@@@@@@@@@.

THE WOMAN: What? Aw, you're pulling my leg.

AKAONI: @@@@.

(THE WOMAN *laughs.*)

TOMBI: Do you really understand him? In just three days?

THE WOMAN: Pretty much.

MIZUKANE: Keep your distance from him when you talk.

AKAONI: @ @ @ @.

THE WOMAN: @ @ @ @ @.

MIZUKANE: Is this what they call being bilingual?

TOMBI: Ask Akaoni if this is the language that everybody speaks in his country.

THE WOMAN: @ @ @ @ @ @ @ @ @ @ @ @ @?

AKAONI: @.

THE WOMAN: Yep.

MIZUKANE: So @ means "yes."

TOMBI: How does he say "no," I wonder.

THE WOMAN: "No" is @ @.

AKAONI: @ @ @ @ @ @ @ @ @ @ @ @ @. (Please stop calling me Akaoni.)

THE WOMAN: @ @ @. (Sorry.)

TOMBI: What'd he say?

THE WOMAN: He wants us to stop referring to him as Akaoni.

MIZUKANE: Well then, what country did he come from?

THE WOMAN: @ @ @ @ @ @ @ @ @ @ @ @.

AKAONI: Red Monde.

THE WOMAN: He comes from Red Monde.

TOMBI: Red Monde? Monde is just demon pronounced backwards.

MIZUKANE: Is this Red Monde beyond the sea? Ask him that. I've wanted to know that for ages. Are the paintings on the walls of the caves pictures of the land beyond the sea?

THE WOMAN: I'm not sure how to say "beyond the sea." Sea? Sea? You understand, sea? *(Gesturing.)* I'm stumped.

AKAONI: @ @.

TOMBI: He understood her gesture for the first time. "Sea" is @ @.

THE WOMAN: "Beyond" is the problem. Here, you understand? Here.

AKAONI: @ @? (Ground?) @ @ @ @? (You mean this beach?)

THE WOMAN: Here. What's "beyond"? Angus. It's not getting through. This sort of thing is the hardest, much harder than winters of our discontent and pieces of resistance.

MIZUKANE: If we can't make him understand "beyond," then we'll never know if there is a place beyond the sea. It's beyond me.

TOMBI: I think Akaoni's beyond help.

THE WOMAN: Nonsense.

TOMBI: Why?

THE WOMAN: All human beings desire something beyond themselves. Why do people go through hell to climb mountains? To see what is beyond the summit.

MIZUKANE: Gee, you're really quite a woman now, you know that?

THE WOMAN: Huh?

MIZUKANE: Before, you couldn't see past your nose. All you did was wash cups and clean windows.

THE WOMAN: Well, from now on I will wash cups, clean windows and polish my Red Mondese. By communicating with Angus I may just ascend the Tower of Babel and, overcoming language, see to beyond the sea.

TOMBI: Mizukane used to make up stories about that place from time to time, but now that I'd heard them from my own little sister, it struck me that they may just be true after all. Everybody desires a place beyond them to see their way to.

THE WOMAN: I have spent my life living off the energy of the dead. There are humans who have sunk to the bottom of the sea, solely clinging onto their grudges. That's the story of our family. So I could talk about how hopeless everything was without losing heart myself. Our mother said the same thing, Tombi, when she sunk to the bottom of the sea. She rowed out onto the mighty deep and died. The white waves, rising in clouds to the heavens, a pedestal for the setting sun. And the crimson eyes peering out from that pedestal, mother's despair. As for me, perhaps I continue to live off the energy of the dead.

TOMBI: Even though we are children of the same mother, I'm such a moron that all I can think of when you say "energy of the dead" is a zombie. Both my mother's despair and my sister's despair are beyond me.

MIZUKANE: Look, gannets.

TOMBI: What's that?

MIZUKANE: I can see gannets offshore. There will be a school of bonito fish below that flock. So many gannets is a sign of a big catch.

TOMBI: But it wasn't a sign of a big catch at all. In fact, the flock of gannets was a warning to us that something untoward was about to occur.

AKAONI: Oh!

TOMBI: Oh!

AKAONI: *(Pointing to the birds.)* Oh, some!

TOMBI: Awesome.

MIZUKANE: Hold on. What'd you just say?

TOMBI: Awesome.

AKAONI: Oh, some!

MIZUKANE: Awesome is awesome even in Akaoni's language.

TOMBI: Awesome, awesome.

AKAONI: Oh, some!

MIZUKANE: Think of it, the same words. Awesome.

AKAONI: Oh, some!

(The four are delighted, repeating the word "awesome.")

MIZUKANE: Hold on. You keep saying awesome. But what's so awesome?

TOMBI: I dunno.

MIZUKANE: I thought so.

TOMBI: I forgot. It was really something awesome, though.

THE WOMAN: Can't be important, then.

TOMBI: If I could've remembered back then, it probably would've turned out to be less awesome than I thought.

MIZUKANE: Sure, awesome. . . .

AKAONI: Oh, some. . . .

THE WOMAN: Mizukane is getting through to Akaoni. Now that's awesome. Just the one word awesome is awesome.

MIZUKANE: *(Deeply touched.)* I talked with Akaoni. Akaoni understands what I say. And, what's more, he's one hell of a nice guy, too!

TOMBI: Before we knew it, the rumor had spread up and down the beach. And in the end, it really turned into something awesome.

Scene 9

(The rumors about AKAONI *have reached everyone by the beach. People are lining up to see him. Four people form a line.)*

MIZUKANE: Stop pushing, for Chrissakes. Wait your turn. Hey, you, no butting in line, eh? Everybody'll get their chance to speak with him, I promise. Don't be in a hurry.

TOURIST 1: *(Played by* TOMBI.*)* Gee, it was really worth coming over the mountains to see it. *(Exits.)*

TOURIST 2: (THE WOMAN) I thoroughly enjoyed that.

TOURIST 3: (MIZUKANE) What a nice demon!

TOURIST 4: (TOURIST 1) Ogle the Ogre, that's what I say.

TOURIST 5: (TOURIST 2) They say that a single word from it prolongs your life no end.

TOURIST 6: (TOURIST 3) It told me three little words. *(Exits.)*

OLD MAN: (MIZUKANE) Here it is, over here, dear.

OLD WOMAN: (TOMBI) Don't go without me.

OLD MAN: We're from two beaches over. I turn 104 this summer. We're twins.

THE WOMAN: You don't look alike at all.

OLD WOMAN: You Ms. Fuku, the one who's letting us speak to Mr. Akaoni?

THE WOMAN: Uh, yes.

OLD MAN: We figured we'd have this as our last memory before going on to greener pastures. Or, if things work out the other way, we figured we could ask about the Prince of Hades while we're at it.

OLD WOMAN: Are you a distant relation of the Prince of Hades? Or might he be your boss?

AKAONI: @@@@@@@@! (Not that one about the Prince of Hades again!)

THE WOMAN: Sorry. They're not shocked by you anymore, but they still can't see you as anything but a red demon.

AKAONI: @@@@@? (What do you expect?)

OLD WOMAN: When I was little, a mermaid landed on our beach, and I ate some of its flesh and that's why I'm still alive and kicking at 103.

OLD MAN: We're here today to eat some of the demon's flesh.

THE WOMAN: You're trying to get my goat, aren't you.

AKAONI: @@@@? (What'd he say?)

OLD MAN: You get my message, Mr. Demon?

THE WOMAN: I don't think he has.

OLD WOMAN: Then you try getting through to him.

THE WOMAN: I can't.

OLD WOMAN: Why?

THE WOMAN: It wouldn't be polite to him.

OLD MAN: What's politeness to a red demon anyway?

OLD WOMAN: You're the one who should learn how to be polite to old folks.

THE WOMAN: Just because you're old it doesn't mean you can act anyway you want.

OLD WOMAN: What's with this bitch anyway, eh? Impudent big-mouth!

OLD MAN: It's no secret that you're riding Akaoni's back so you can be number one big cheese on this beach.

THE WOMAN: Say whatever you like.

OLD MAN: Wash your mouth out with soap. "Say whatever you like."

OLD WOMAN: Just like all these disgusting women who talk about doing whatever they like. And she has a short haircut.

OLD MAN: Have you had a bit of hanky-panky, with it, eh? With Akaoni? One leg up and over, eh? What's gonna pop outta you, a human? A demon?

THE WOMAN: I'd prefer a demon. Humans just get dumber and dumber with the years. You two are living examples of that.

AKAONI: @@@@@@? (What's wrong? What did they say?)

THE WOMAN: Forget it.

AKAONI: @@@@@. (Tell me.)

THE WOMAN: @@@@@@@@@. (They want to eat demon meat.)

OLD WOMAN: What's going on here?

THE WOMAN: I told him you want to eat demon meat so you can live longer.

(AKAONI *walks straight toward them with a fierce look on his face. They cower.* AKAONI *exposes his arm.*)

AKAONI: @@. (Eat and live.)

OLD MAN: What'd it say?

THE WOMAN: "Eat and live."

OLD MAN: Not in the least amusing. Well, that proves that demons have no sense of humor whatsoever.

OLD WOMAN: Well, since he's so kindly . . . *(Pretends to bite his arm.)* . . . Ow! My teeth!

(OLD WOMAN and OLD MAN laugh.)

OLD MAN: Oh, dear me, what a riot.

OLD WOMAN: This definitely will give us a few years extra, I'd say.

(The two leave. MIZUKANE and TOMBI enter immediately.)

MIZUKANE: What disgusting old farts.

TOMBI: There are children waiting outside.

THE WOMAN: Old people are like that. Children treat everyone the same.

TOMBI: They're saying they want to eat devilled eggs with it.

MIZUKANE: And a friend begged me to bring Akaoni trick or treating on Halloween.

TOMBI: And thanks to Akaoni, a lot of people have stopped giving me the cold shoulder. Please thank him for me, will you?

MIZUKANE: Me too. People I never knew say they're grateful to me, and I've even been officially acknowledged. Tell him that.

THE WOMAN: You tell him yourself.

TOMBI: That day my sister was in a terrible mood. The beach people had come to accept him, but only as a demon, not as a human being.

Scene 10

(AKAONI is left alone with THE WOMAN.)

THE WOMAN: I wish someone would accept you as a human being, Angus. I don't think I'm up to this anymore, really. Are you human? Are you? Look, you've been living on this beach for half a year now, right? I'd expect you to be a bit more fluent in human language by now, you know. *(AKAONI cowers.)* I'm at wits' end here. Sometimes I ask myself why I'm going through all this for you. Lately you've been acting like some princess locked up in the tower, longing for home. You're pretty homesick, aren't you. All coconuts are. I guess all you've got to lean on is me. You know, I've been so preoccupied with all the goings-on on this beach I've totally forgotten about the pictures of the land beyond the sea that you painted on the cave walls. There's so much I want to ask you about it. Is it really like the pictures, the land beyond the sea? Do you understand what I'm saying? Beyond. Here. Beyond. No use. Another day down the drain. There's no way I can get him to understand "beyond the sea."

AKAONI: I have a dream.

THE WOMAN: What did you say? Some new word from the back of beyond?

AKAONI: I have a dream.

THE WOMAN: I seem to be able to pick up words better now than before.

AKAONI: I have a dream that one day this world will rise up and live out the true meaning of its creed: We hold these truths to be self-evident, that all men are created equal.

THE WOMAN: Go figure it out. I understood you a lot better when you spoke total gibberish, I mean, growling like a wild beast. But now, the more I can pick out snippets of what you say, the less sense you seem to be making.

AKAONI: I have a dream.

THE WOMAN: I'm basically with you on that. But, Angus, I'm frightened that when I come to put together all the separate words you say I won't have a clue as to what you mean by them.

AKAONI: Let freedom ring.

THE WOMAN: Do you mean that freedom or something should kind of ring a bell or something?

AKAONI: Let freedom ring.

THE WOMAN: I get it. You mean the bell at Notre Dame? The one that Quasimodo rang? This freedom thing should ring the bell, is that it? What for, though? I don't follow you. Who are you, anyway? Where do you come from? Why were you drifting in the sea?

AKAONI: Let freedom ring, I have a dream that one day, let freedom ring from every hill, from every mountainside, every village and every hamlet, from every state and every city.

THE WOMAN: Oh, so that's your dream.

Scene 11

(MIZUKANE *and* TOMBI *appear.*)

MIZUKANE: There are women who say things like, "You got to be kidding. They're a thing, those two? Come off it. You for real? Cross your heart? I'm always the last one to cotton on to those things. I had no idea." Those are the women who are really shrewd, though. They spend half their lives figuring out who's having it on with who. I know 'cause I'm a guy who's just like that type of woman. So I tell you, your sister is having it off with Akaoni. No two ways about it.

TOMBI: They've gone all the way, haven't they.

MIZUKANE: All the way? Have they really gone that far?

TOMBI: Not in that way. I mean, they've gone all the way with each other.

MIZUKANE: In what way do you mean "all the way"?

TOMBI: That way, you know.

MIZUKANE: You're not making any sense. You mean, all the way with each other.

TOMBI: That's right. (*Gesturing a long way.*) Not "all the way." And not "all the way" either. I mean, "all the way."

MIZUKANE: Whatever, one way or another they've gone all the way.

TOMBI: That day Mizukane seemed to have less upstairs than the left side of my brain. Jealousy makes the left side of the brain stupid.

MIZUKANE: Tombi.

TOMBI: Yeah?

MIZUKANE: What I'm about to say to you isn't out of jealousy, okay?

TOMBI: I didn't believe him anymore. But I listened anyway.

MIZUKANE: You said you saw something awesome, didn't you?

TOMBI: Awesome?

MIZUKANE: Yeah, when Akaoni was there, about half a year ago or thereabouts. Don't you remember? It was when there was a flock of gannets flying offshore. No, it's asking too much. You didn't even remember it right after it happened.

TOMBI: Yeah, flew right out of my head. I said awesome 'cause I saw this huge ship, like I'd never seen before in my life, out at sea. And then Akaoni said "awesome" at the same time. But I can't for the life of me recall what it was that was so awesome.

MIZUKANE: You can remember.

TOMBI: Huh? Remember what?

MIZUKANE: You caught sight of a ship offshore, a ship so huge you had never seen one like it in your life.

TOMBI: Uh huh.

MIZUKANE: It's that that was awesome, isn't it?

TOMBI: Is it? Suppose.

MIZUKANE: So a ship has come after all.

TOMBI: A ship?

MIZUKANE: Tombi, it's awesome.

TOMBI: What are you talking about?

MIZUKANE: Since that day an unbelievable number of bottles have drifted onto the beach.

TOMBI: Even without a storm to bring them here?

MIZUKANE: I've been collecting them up in secret.

TOMBI: Probably uncorked empties like always.

MIZUKANE: Not these.

TOMBI: Huh? How many of them had something in them?

MIZUKANE: How many?

TOMBI: One? Two? A whole lot?

MIZUKANE: All of them.

TOMBI: Had something? Something written?

MIZUKANE: In Akaoni's language. Not only that. They were all messages to Akaoni.

TOMBI: How do you know that?

MIZUKANE: Well, I've little by little been jotting down conversations between your sister and Akaoni and, day before yesterday, the meaning of those messages finally began to dawn on me. Just like that day when you noticed the outline of that ship making its way out of the haze.

TOMBI: Yeah. But I didn't get a good look at it, you know.

MIZUKANE: I can't quite see what the messages are getting at either. But it's clear to me that something really awesome is going to happen around here when the beach people realize the truth.

TOMBI: Is what's written awesome?

MIZUKANE: Yes. Awesome.

TOMBI: Awesome.

MIZUKANE: *(Holding his hand over* TOMBI*'s mouth.)* Wait, Tombi.

TOMBI: What?

MIZUKANE: Ever since I was little, everybody said I was like the boy who cried wolf.

TOMBI: I know.

MIZUKANE: That boy . . . when he grows up, he becomes the wolfman.

TOMBI: What?

MIZUKANE: I lie like a rug all the time. I'm the biggest liar on this beach.

TOMBI: If you lie like a rug people will step all over you. There's a saying.

MIZUKANE: You're the only one who believes sayings like that.

TOMBI: You mean people won't step all . . . ?

MIZUKANE: No! But the dough of lies eventually becomes the very bread of truth. Deceit is the morning sickness that precedes the birth of truth. I kept that in mind when I wove my web of lies. But now I, too, am becoming scared. I'm unable to tell whether the messages in the bottles are just run-of-the-mill lies or the kind of deceit that precedes the coming of truth. So, mind what you do, Tombi. If so much as a word of this gets out, your sister's life, not to mention Akaoni's, won't be worth a hoot in hell. I told Tombi to think twice before going around telling people about something awesome. But it wasn't long before the rumor had spread.

*(*TOMBI *becomes* MAN 2; MIZUKANE, MAN 1.*)*

MAN 1: Hey, quick, get that bottle that's just come ashore!

MAN 2: What do you think, I'm another Mizukane or something?

MAN 1: Just check inside it, will ya.

MAN 2: What for, it'll be empty anyway. Hey, what's this?

MAN 1: It's in Akaoni's language. What does it say?

MAN 2: Haven't a clue. But I know one thing: it spells something awesome.

MAN 1: Awesome.

MAN 2: Awesome.

MAN 1: Awesome.

ELDER: Get the red demon and The Woman here immediately!

TOMBI: And then the dawn came, the cock crowed, and the trial on the beach began. There's always someone who lives by a beach who's an expert at fishing out the truth.

Scene 12

(TOMBI *becomes* JUDGE.)

JUDGE: This court will be brief. We wish to hear only that which we need to hear. Woman! According to rumors circulating around this beach, you have formed a point of contact with the red demon. Is that true?

THE WOMAN: What do you mean by "point of contact"?

JUDGE: A point of contact is a point of contact.

THE WOMAN: If I may put our bodies to one side, yes, our hearts and minds may have made contact.

MIZUKANE: Bodies, too.

JUDGE: Mizukane, you are a witness, so be brief and speak up.

MIZUKANE: I'm not gonna say anything that'll get you in hot water, baby. You just got yourself led by the nose by Akaoni, it's that simple.

THE WOMAN: Led by the nose? Fancy that coming from the lips of the biggest liar on the beach! I've heard of a beachcomber before, but a beach-liar, this has got to be a first.

JUDGE: Mizukane, are you still intent on defending her considering what she has just said about you?

THE WOMAN: Defend? Me? You really wanna know? The man is just plain jealous, that's all.

JUDGE: The Woman has made contact with a demon and consequently has turned into a demon herself.

MIZUKANE: Not only with their hearts and minds. With their bodies, too.

JUDGE: Did you say, with their bodies? What exactly do you mean by that? Be brief and speak up.

MIZUKANE: The Woman is banging Akaoni!

(JUDGE *speaks to the audience as if they were beach people.*)

JUDGE: Did you all hear the witness's statement? The Woman is . . . banging the red demon.

THE WOMAN: I most certainly am not.

MIZUKANE: And she won't even bang me.

THE WOMAN: If I had to bang someone, I'd rather bang him than you.

JUDGE: You see, she testifies herself that she has done the banging.

THE WOMAN: I have not!

MIZUKANE: Have too.

THE WOMAN: Who's done whatever-it-is with who . . . is that what this trial is all about?

JUDGE: Please don't think whatever-it-is about this trial, whatever-it-is. It's just that, well, you know, ever since I was a boy I wondered about those stories about cranes and foxes that transformed themselves into men's wives and had it off with them. I'd really like to know. Can you explain it to me?

THE WOMAN: Huh?

JUDGE: I mean, how do you, uh, go about having it off with the red demon.

THE WOMAN: What's that got to do with anything?

JUDGE: But this trial is about, well, having it off or not having it off. Exactly how deep was the contact that you made with the red demon? What sort of contact was it, other than the mind and the body?

THE WOMAN: What are you talking about?

JUDGE: Red demons are coming to invade this beach. Your demon friend is bringing them here.

THE WOMAN: Who's spreading such nonsense?

MIZUKANE: Me. It wasn't no accident, you know, him washing up on this shore.

THE WOMAN: You telling me he washed up on purpose? No accident? Whatever for?

MIZUKANE: To send a signal.

JUDGE: Ah ha! To what or whom?

MIZUKANE: To the awesome ship that Tombi saw.

THE WOMAN: One after another you've extracted a tissue of lies out of your empty bottles, haven't you, Mizukane. Listen, everyone, and don't forget it. This here is the biggest liar on the beach. He hasn't told us how Akaoni is supposed to send his signals. See? Not a peep out of him. It's all a fantasy concocted out of empty bottles by a man racked by jealousy.

MIZUKANE: This is the last bottle that washed up on the beach. I'm not the only one. All the people who live around here have picked them up.

JUDGE: What is inside it, eh? What in the hell's in the thing?

MIZUKANE: I believe it to be a message to Akaoni.

JUDGE: Woman! Instruct it to read it aloud.

THE WOMAN: Angus, read.

AKAONI: I have a dream that one day, let freedom ring from every hill from every mountainside every village and every hamlet from every state and every city.

JUDGE: Well, now, woman, are you familiar with those words?

THE WOMAN: I am.

JUDGE: What does it mean by them?

THE WOMAN: It's his dream.

JUDGE: Explain.

THE WOMAN: I think he's saying, "Ring the bell quickly."

JUDGE: Where?

THE WOMAN: On every shore, in concert, ring all the bells. That's his dream.

JUDGE: And to what purpose?

THE WOMAN: As a signal of his freedom.

JUDGE: A signal of his freedom, you say? Wouldn't it rather be a signal to a ship waiting offshore?

MIZUKANE: The bell will ring on this beach and red demons will make a rush from their ship to this shore. The beach will be crawling with them. That's my opinion. We're being tricked. By it . . . Akaoni.

THE WOMAN: Bear in mind that he's the one who's been tricking everyone on the beach all along. It's all a bunch of lies, isn't it, that your people are preparing to land.

MIZUKANE: Trust it to tell the truth!

AKAONI: @@@.

JUDGE: What did it say?

AKAONI: @@@.

THE WOMAN: . . . That it's not a lie. So you came to this beach for a reason?

AKAONI: @@. (Yes.)

JUDGE: What did it say, yes or no?

MIZUKANE: That was a yes. I know that one.

THE WOMAN: For what purpose?

AKAONI: @@@@@@@@@@@@@@.

JUDGE: What did it say?

MIZUKANE: No lying.

THE WOMAN: He's different from you.

JUDGE: Tell us what it said!

THE WOMAN: Ring the bells . . . to send a signal to his people on board the ship . . . from every shore.

AKAONI: I have a dream.

JUDGE: It's been proven beyond the shadow of a doubt. The demons are going to land and eat the people.

THE WOMAN: They're not demons, they're people. People don't eat people.

MIZUKANE: Then why are they coming here, eh? Answer that one.

THE WOMAN: Listen to what he has to say. Why are they landing on this beach?

JUDGE: To eat people. It's been proven.

THE WOMAN: If, as you say demons eat people, why didn't he eat that baby before? He's human, that's why.

JUDGE: The reason why this particular red demon appears human in your eyes is because you have had "contact" with it. You sold your soul to the demon. The verdict which I am about to deliver shall apply to all red demons. And that includes you.

MIZUKANE: Hold your horses, your honor. Give a little, okay, mate? This

one here is a red demon, we got that. Now, Fuku, just tell the judge
that you'll have nothing more to do with it.

THE WOMAN: He's a human.

MIZUKANE: It makes no difference if it's a human or a demon. Just call
Akaoni a demon and be done with it. That'll make you a human, and
Bob's your uncle.

JUDGE: I ask you once more and once more only. Woman. What do you
see when you set your eyes upon this red demon?

THE WOMAN: A human being.

JUDGE: The sun has set. The trial is over. At the rise of the morning sun,
this red demon and this woman, on this very beach, will be executed
by means of exposure to the rays of said sun. We shall not ring the bell
on this beach. Take them away to the cave. And keep them under strict
guard until dawn.

Scene 13

(THE WOMAN *and* AKAONI *are being held prisoner.*)

THE WOMAN: You know, when all is said and done, I really don't have a
clue as to what you're on about. Maybe I've learned too much of your
language, is that it? What are you here for? Where have you come
from? Where are you going?

AKAONI: @ @ @ @ @—beyond the sea. (This is not the land beyond the
sea.)

THE WOMAN: What did you say just now?

AKAONI: @ @ @ @ @ @ beyond the sea.

THE WOMAN: Is that the way you say "beyond the sea" in your language?

AKAONI: @ @ @ @ @ @ beyond the sea @ @.

THE WOMAN: So these pictures represent beyond the sea for you.

AKAONI: @ @ @ @. (I don't know myself.)

THE WOMAN: You don't know yourself? What are these miraculous
murals that you've painted here?

AKAONI: @ @ @ @ @ @ @ @ @ @.

THE WOMAN: What? Where? When did you manage to carve these letters
into the wall? (*Reading.*) "By the hand of Akaoni, resident of this
cave. This painting represents our homeland. It is located beyond the
sea. Yet, we do not know the land beyond the sea. Ages ago we set
sail. Long before I was born. Ages and ages ago we departed from the
shores of home. The mean temperature there is 38 degrees centigrade.
Our people lived there in perfect bliss. But then, like coconuts drifting
away from shore, we began our days of wandering on the sea. Many
times we were washed up on a beach . . . but they were not the
beaches of home. And we were never taken in and accepted, no matter
where we landed. But when I found myself on this beach, I genuinely

believed that this time I was beyond the sea. My friends are waiting offshore for me to ring a bell. That ringing will tell them all that we have finally come home to the land beyond the sea, free at last. Ages ago we left the land beyond the sea, we who do not know what there is in the land beyond the sea." Then this represents a land beyond the sea that not one of you has ever set eyes on.

AKAONI: @ @ @ @ @ @ @.

THE WOMAN: What? Oh, right. There's something carved over here, too.

AKAONI: @ @ @ @ @ @ @ @ @.

THE WOMAN: "Bottles are arriving on the beach lately without a message. My friends must have tired of waiting forever for the bell that never rang and headed for the next beach over." Leaving you behind?

AKAONI: @ @ @ @ @. (They probably think I'm dead.)

THE WOMAN: They probably think you're dead? They're awful. You're very much alive.

AKAONI: @ @ @ @ @. (They're not awful.)

THE WOMAN: Yeah, guess so. They're not really awful. Whatever, you'll be dead as a doornail tomorrow. But, you know, I haven't lost hope yet. There's still time before sunrise. You saw what my brother's like, but, no matter, he's probably stayed up all night and right this minute is devising some clever way to get us out of this.

Scene 14

TOMBI: For some reason I slept like a log that night. I was awakened by a noise that sounded as if something had stopped dead in my heart. Once awake, I couldn't get back to sleep again. The sound of waves folding over one another reached my ears and then I heard one layer of sand falling, swishing, against another. After that came a weeping noise. At first I was sure that the weeping was coming off the nets of the fishermen. But, thinking back, it might have been Akaoni weeping all along. *(A banging on the door.)* Who is it?

MIZUKANE: It's me, Mizukane.

TOMBI: What's wrong?

MIZUKANE: Can't sleep. I can't come to terms with what's going to happen to your sister. The thought of her dying before I could screw the socks off her really depresses me.

TOMBI: What are you going to do about it, then?

MIZUKANE: I'm going to be the boy who cried wolf again, for the first time in ages.

TOMBI: What, you're going to run all over the beach crying wolf?

MIZUKANE: Perhaps no one'll believe me. They'll brush it off, and that will give them a false sense of security. Meanwhile, I'll steal a boat and you'll steal as much food as you can and bring it to the boat.

TOMBI: You plan to get Akaoni and my sister into the boat and send them away?

MIZUKANE: Are you out of your mind? That'll just throw the two of them into each other's arms. We're going, too.

TOMBI: What? Me too? The hero, the heroine and the heroine's moron brother . . . hmm, got a nice ring to it. Hang on. What's Akaoni's role in this?

MIZUKANE: Navigator.

TOMBI: Huh? You planning to go to the land beyond the sea?

MIZUKANE: I'm more realistic than I look, you know.

TOMBI: I know.

MIZUKANE: The last thing I would do is go on some dangerous journey beyond the sea.

TOMBI: Then how are we . . . ?

MIZUKANE: Akaoni's gonna take us to its buddies who're waiting in the ship offshore.

TOMBI: Aren't you afraid they'll eat us?

MIZUKANE: Come on, he owes us his life, you know.

TOMBI: But what if they eat people they're indebted to?

MIZUKANE: If that happens we'll have you on board.

TOMBI: Oh, I see.

MIZUKANE: Good going. Now, cry wolf real loud.

TOMBI: You mean I'm a wolf boy, too?

MIZUKANE: You should feel honored.

TOMBI: I guess so.

Scene 15

(MIZUKANE *and* TOMBI *go to the cave crying,* "*Wolf! Wolf!*")

MIZUKANE *and* TOMBI: Wolf! There's a wolf here!

AKAONI: @@@.

THE WOMAN: Take it easy. No one in his right mind would come here screaming that sort of thing. Must be my brother and Mizukane.

TOMBI: You okay?

THE WOMAN: Fine, thanks.

TOMBI: Mizukane says that he wants to screw the socks off you.

MIZUKANE: Can't you be a bit more subtle?

TOMBI: But you said there were only two kinds of women, those that you wanna screw and those that you gotta screw. In other words, you and all the rest of womankind.

MIZUKANE: No time for that, Tombi, get into the boat.

TOMBI: Okay.

THE WOMAN: Hang on.

TOMBI: What is it?

THE WOMAN: What do we have here? There's a calendar here with the days marked off.

AKAONI: @@@@.

THE WOMAN: What? We do this, too.

AKAONI: @@@@@.

TOMBI: What'd he say?

THE WOMAN: He's been crossing off the days since he arrived on this beach. He must really have been longing to leave.

TOMBI: And we have been marked by him for our injustices to him.

THE WOMAN: Our mother once went out to sea, overcome with despair. It won't happen to me, though. No matter how alienated I feel here I will not lose heart. On the contrary, I feel a great sense of pride in being able to leave all this behind me. I am going to make my way beyond the sea now, to that land beyond the deep that mother never reached.

MIZUKANE: Just what the doctor ordered. A fog has settled on the sea. We will be enveloped within it, unseen. The beach people will never find us. Untie the rope. Let's leave this shore. We're on our way!

(AKAONI *sings the song of his homeland to himself and the others join in.*)

TOMBI: When the four of us set sail we were overcome by a sense of joy and excitement. We finally understood how the Von Trapp family must have felt when they sang "Edelweiss" fleeing from the Nazis over the Alps. The first of us, though, to slip out of the sense of joy and excitement was Mizukane.

MIZUKANE: What in the hell do you mean?

(*THE WOMAN *and* AKAONI *are in stitches.*)

MIZUKANE: Did you say that the ship carrying its friends beat it out of here a long time ago?

AKAONI: @@@@@.

THE WOMAN: Aha. I thought so, too.

AKAONI: @@@@@@.

TOMBI: Ha ha ha!

MIZUKANE: What are you laughing about, moron? I thought something was fishy. Here we've been out at sea several days already and there's been no sign of a ship. You bastard, you tricked us.

AKAONI: @@@@@.

MIZUKANE: What's it saying now?

THE WOMAN: "I tricked the number one liar on the beach so now I'm number one. From now on you're number two."

AKAONI: Best on the beach, second best on the beach, son-of-a-beach.

(*All except* MIZUKANE *laugh.*)

MIZUKANE: Tombi, we're going back.

THE WOMAN: Back where?

MIZUKANE: The beach!

THE WOMAN: You don't understand a thing, do you? That's 'cause you've never fished before. Take a look at that current. It's whirling around, isn't it? We'll never get back.

MIZUKANE: What are we going to do, then?

THE WOMAN: Just keep going like this until we get beyond the sea.

MIZUKANE: We'll never make it. Hey, Akaoni. Have any idea where beyond the sea is, eh?

THE WOMAN: @ @ @ @ @?

AKAONI: Not a clue.

(THE WOMAN *and* AKAONI *are in stitches.*)

TOMBI: My sister and Akaoni never lost the good mood that they got into after we set sail. I had never seen her like this, like a fish put back into the water. My little sister was a mermaid.

(One-second blackout.)

MIZUKANE: Shit, can't see a single fish for the life of me.

TOMBI: It was like they could smell our presence . . . the only thing that came near us was sharks.

MIZUKANE: If only we could catch a shark we'd have something to eat.

AKAONI: @ @ @ @ @.

THE WOMAN: There's a storm brewing.

AKAONI: @ @ @ @ @.

THE WOMAN: That's why the fish have gone from here.

MIZUKANE: Okay, Tombi, there's nothing else to do but bring out all the food you brought.

TOMBI: Uh huh.

MIZUKANE: What the . . . ? It's all goddamn flowers.

TOMBI: It's food for Akaoni.

MIZUKANE: Where's ours?

TOMBI: Nowhere.

MIZUKANE: What's going on? I told you to get as much food as you could.

TOMBI: I did. Flowers. One, two, a whole lot.

THE WOMAN: Counting's not my brother's forte. He can only get up to two. Three is a whole lot.

MIZUKANE: Well, this is a fine how-do-you-do, a bunch of flowers fit for a demon.

AKAONI: *(Plucking a petal.)* @ @ @? (Want some?)

MIZUKANE: You must be joking.

(MIZUKANE *flings all the flowers into the water.*)

ALL: Ohhh!

(Blackout.)

THE WOMAN: Aren't you a bit hungry?

TOMBI: I'm famished.

AKAONI: I'm famished.

(The three are in stitches again.)

MIZUKANE: Shut the fuck up.

AKAONI: He's angry because he's hungry.

THE WOMAN: When you get a bit hungry, the gas makes you blow your stack. But when you get famished all you do is laugh your head off.

TOMBI: Our laughter just made us even hungrier. And the hungrier we got the more we cracked up. Total joy became our constant state.

(One-second blackout. AKAONI *and* THE WOMAN *are lying down.)*

AKAONI: @@@@.

THE WOMAN: Tombi, Angus wants you to look out there for a second.

TOMBI: What is it?

THE WOMAN: He thinks he caught sight of the land beyond the sea.

TOMBI: Okay, I'll have a look for him.

THE WOMAN: Can you see it?

TOMBI: Sorry. Uh oh, Akaoni's not breathing.

*(*TOMBI *and* THE WOMAN *laugh.)*

TOMBI: It was the storm that took the breath from my laughter. And as it came closer to us, both sea and sky looked increasingly ominous. The only ray of good cheer came from little sister. Its brightness was like the blue sky that shined over her funeral.

Scene 16

(A storm is upon them, as the scene returns to the opening scene with four people adrift. Three are washed up on shore. They bolt up, transformed into three rescuers.)

MAN 1 They're still breathing.

MAN 2: Quick, get them to safety. Make it snappy!

MAN 1: We gotta keep them warm.

WOMAN 1: Are there any more of them?

MAN 1: Only these three.

MAN 2: Look, it's them. They made it back in one piece.

MAN 1: The Woman's here too.

WOMAN 1: That's all I needed! She's not worth saving. Let's just fling her back into the sea.

MAN 2: What do you think you're doing? She's alive. Just leave her where she is, will ya?

*(*WOMAN 1 *is transformed into* THE WOMAN *by being wrapped in a blanket. At the same instant* MAN 1 *becomes* HAG. HAG *brings* THE WOMAN *a bowl of soup.)*

THE WOMAN: Thank you. It tastes good.

HAG: Uh huh, it's shark's fin soup. I don't give this to just everybody, you know. You're getting it 'cause you managed to survive.

THE WOMAN: What was that?

HAG: I said, not everybody gets this.

THE WOMAN: No, I mean the soup. What kind did you say it was?

HAG: Shark's fin. The fin . . . of the shark?

THE WOMAN: This isn't what shark fin tastes like.

HAG: You've had shark fin before?

THE WOMAN: Of course I have, every day out at sea. That's how I know. This isn't it. It just isn't. It's not shark fin. I'm telling you, it isn't! *(THE WOMAN screams and recedes.)*

MIZUKANE: What's got into her?

TOMBI: She's puking back there.

MIZUKANE: Puking?

TOMBI: Her guts out. Even though all that's coming out is a yellowish gastric juice.

MIZUKANE: She's probably throwing up because she ate too quickly after not eating a thing while we were adrift. She wouldn't touch a thing of anything out at sea.
(THE WOMAN comes back with a blank expression on her face. She just stands before them.)

THE WOMAN: Did you say it was shark's fin?

MIZUKANE: Huh?

THE WOMAN: Mizukane, out at sea, you fed me when I was in a daze. You said shark's fin, didn't you.

MIZUKANE: Did I?

THE WOMAN: Yes you did, dammit! What you gave me wasn't shark's fin.

MIZUKANE: Get off my back, will ya? You claim you were in a daze, but you knew, didn't you? You knew full well that that wasn't shark's fin.

THE WOMAN: I didn't know.

MIZUKANE: Ridiculous, you just felt like pretending that you didn't know. Could you really believe a liar like me? Not very convincing.

THE WOMAN: Tombi.

MIZUKANE: You've never believed a word I ever said, so why should you have taken my words at face value then?

THE WOMAN: I want to hear it from my brother, not you.

MIZUKANE: I figured I could keep you alive. I wanted you to live. Because I love you. No, I tell a lie. Because I want to make love to you. If you die, you'll be of no damn use to me.

THE WOMAN: Tombi, please tell me the truth. When I was out there dying, had he . . . had Angus already stopped breathing? Or was he still breathing, faintly?

TOMBI: Huh?

THE WOMAN: Which is it?

TOMBI: I don't follow you, Sis? What are you asking about?

THE WOMAN: No, you do follow. Was Angus dead by the time I ate the shark's fin?

MIZUKANE: Why bother your pretty little head, eh? It's dead. You're alive.

I mean, it's a red demon, not a human being. You would've eaten a shark as soon as anything. Even a red shark, isn't that right. I may not look like it but I really care about you. You were fading fast. We had nothing to eat on the boat. You were so feeble I was afraid you couldn't keep anything down. It was then that I noticed your Akaoni lifeless right under our noses. It was not a human or a demon then, just a thing, a hunk of meat, a chunk of food.

THE WOMAN: So you ate him.

MIZUKANE: I ate it.

THE WOMAN: And you, too, Tombi?

TOMBI: Me too. It was delicious. I was starving.

THE WOMAN: And what about me?

TOMBI: What?

THE WOMAN: Did his flesh go into my mouth?

TOMBI: You had such a blank stare in your eyes, and you were laughing. No matter how hard we tried to force-feed you, you wouldn't open your mouth.

MIZUKANE: So I took it upon myself, lying bastard that I am, to tell you a little fib. "Don't worry, this is shark meat. The fin of the shark. Eat it and live," I said.

THE WOMAN: When I met him for the first time I said to him, "You're a demon. And you're a demon because you eat human flesh." I'm sorry. I was wrong. Demons don't eat humans. Humans eat demons. Humans eat demons to survive. I remember it clearly now. You held out your arm and said, "Eat it and live." So, I ate it. And I lived.

(TOMBI *is now alone.*)

TOMBI: My sister died two days later. She threw herself off the tallest cliff overlooking the beach. From that day on, Mizukane was left without a soul. As for me, I'm pretty much the same as I was before. I guess I survive by not knowing very much about anything. Sometimes I recall Akaoni and my little sister laughing their heads off on the boat. I thought she was laughing, but I reckon that she was without hope then. I too laugh when I picture her like that. By doing that I begin to grasp what it means to live without hope. I won't lose my hope, though. The reason is that even to this day things are being washed up on the beach from beyond the sea. When I inhale, what is beyond the sea comes to this shore. When I exhale, it leaves the shore and goes back out to sea again. I am breathing in concert with the land beyond the sea. And beyond the sea, at the very bottom, lies my little sister's heart.

THE END

CONTRIBUTORS
(in alphabetical order)

MARI BOYD, Professor of Literature and Theater at Sophia University, received her Ph.D. in theater from the University of Hawai'i at Manoa. She has co-authored *Twentieth Century Drama: The World of Japanese Modern Drama*, Volumes 2 and 3 (2002) and has translated plays by Matsuda Masataka, Kōkami Shōji and Ōta Shōgo, including Ōta's *Water Station* (*Asian Theater Journal*, 1990). She has also staged plays by Betsuyaku Minoru and Shimizu Kunio in English translation with the university theatrical troupe, Shakespeare's Dead and We Don't Care.

HASEBE HIROSHI is a theater critic and Associate Professor at the Tokyo National University of Fine Arts and Music. He graduated from the Department of Law at Keiō University. He received the 1998 AICT Theater Criticism Award for his book *Damaged Sexuality: The Artistic Directing of David Leveaux*. He has also authored *Four Seconds of Revolution: The Tokyo Theater Scene—1982-1992* (1993) and *The Stolen Real: Theater of the 1990s* (1998) and has co-authored *Noda Hideki and His Theatrical Company, the Dream Wanderers* (1993). Since 1999 he has served on the selection committee for the Kinokuniya Theater Prize and for the Promotion of Arts and Culture Award's Theater Division, and since 2000 for the Agency of Cultural Affairs Arts Plan 21 Theater Division.

LEON INGULSRUD is a theater actor, director, and teacher. The son of Lutheran missionaries, he was born and raised in Japan. A member of the Suzuki Company of Toga (SCOT) for seven years, he also served as a resident director at the Arts Center in Mito, Japan. After leaving SCOT he earned an MFA in Directing at Columbia University, and helped found the SITI Company in New York with Anne Bogart. With the SITI Company, he directs, acts and teaches throughout the United States and the world.

KAWAI SHŌICHIRŌ, Associate Professor of English at the Graduate School of the University of Tokyo, has received Ph.Ds from Cambridge

University and the University of Tokyo. He has contributed articles in English to the *Hot Questrists after the English Renaissance* (2000), *Japanese Studies in Shakespeare and His Contemporaries* (1998), *"Hamlet" and Japan* (1995), and *Shakespeare Studies* (Tokyo), vols. 25, 30, and 38. His Japanese publications are numerous; his most recent critical work, *Hamlet was Fat* (2001), was awarded the Suntory Literary Prize.

KOBORI JUN, graduate of Aichi University, is a freelance theater journalist and editor with a special interest in modern theater. Until 1982 he was editor-in-chief of the *Nagoya Play Guide Journal* and from 1984 to 1987, of the *Play Guide Journal* in Osaka. In 1988 he served as coordinator of the Seibu Art Museum's "The Art Work of Modern Theater, 1960s-80s." From 1998 to 2001 he was the editor-in-chief of the *Theatrical Universe*, a quarterly that reports extensively on the Osaka Theater Festival. Kobori contributes to the promotion of modern theater, especially of the Kansai area, and is the selection committee coordinator for the Drama Award sponsored by the Ōgi Museum Square.

NISHIDŌ KŌJIN is a theater critic and Associate Professor of Theater at Kinki University, Osaka. From the 1990s, he has held symposia on Heiner Müller and lectures on world theater. Since 1997, he has offered a theater critics training course as part of the Setagaya Public Theater lecture series. His writings include *Adventures in Theatrical Thought* (1987), *The Adventure of Looking* (1991), *Has Little Theater Died?* (1996), *Heiner Müller and World Theater* (1999). He is a member of AICT.

ŌTORI HIDENAGA, theater and art critic, received his MA from the University of Tokyo. He is the programming co-director of the Kyoto Performing Arts Center, Kyoto University of Art and Design, and is adjunct lecturer of Theater at Waseda University. He serves as the Artistic Director of the Laokoon Festival 2002 of Kampnagel, Hamburg, and is a member of the Bush Global Advisory Committee of the Walker Art Center, Minneapolis. He has authored *Reverberation Machines: The Worlds of Richard Foreman* (2000) and *20th Century Polyphonic Theater* (1998). Among his translations are works of Tadeusz Kantor and Andrei Tarkovskij.

MITACHI RIHO is a director and translator. A graduate of Defiance College and Trinity University Graduate School of Drama, she received her professional training and worked as director and actor at the Dallas Theatre Center. After ten years in the United States, she returned to Tokyo and founded Theatre Classics. Besides directing, she teaches acting and conducts creative play-development workshops for professional theater artists. Her directing credits include *Terra Nova* and *Little Victories*. She has translated and published nine plays. She is the recipient of the first Yuasa Yoshiko Award (1994) for the best Japanese translation of foreign plays.

CODY POULTON teaches Japanese literature and theater at the University of Victoria, Canada. He is the author of *Spirits of Another Sort: The Plays of Izumi Kyōka* (2001). His recent translations of Japanese drama include Hirata's Oriza's *Tokyo Notes*, in *Asian Theatre Journal* (Spring 2002) and three kabuki plays for Volumes I and II of *Kabuki Plays on Stage*, edited by J.R. Brandon and Samuel Leiter (2002-2003).

ROGER PULVERS, author, playwright and theater director, has published 22 books in Japan and Australia including novels, essays and his autobiography, *The Unmaking of an American*. His plays and adaptations of the classics have been produced in major theaters in Australia and Japan, including the Sydney Opera House and the Theater Cai in Tokyo; and he has directed plays with such eminent actors as Kishida Kyōko, Hashizume Isao and Emoto Akira. He will publish three books in 2002, including a novel titled *Half*.

CAROL FISHER SORGENFREI is a Professor of Theater at UCLA. She has translated plays and criticism by Terayama Shūji, and is currently completing a book about him. Her articles on contemporary and classic Japanese theater, intercultural directing, and fusion theater have appeared in numerous books, encyclopedias, and journals, including the *Asian Theatre Journal, Modern Drama, Contemporary Theater Review*, and *TDR* (The Drama Review). Her original fusion plays include *Medea: A Nō Cycle Based on the Greek Myth; Blood Wine, Blood Wedding* (a kabuki-flamenco fusion); *The Imposter* (a kyōgen-commedia dell'arte play).

TANIGAWA MICHIKO, Professor of German Modern Culture at Tokyo University of Foreign Studies, is a specialist on German modern theater, particularly Bertolt Brecht, Heiner Müller, and Pina Bausch. She received her M.A. in German literature from the University of Tokyo (1974). She has authored the *Symbiosis of Brecht and his Women* (1988), *Heiner Müller Machine* (2000). Among her translations are *The Collected Drama Texts of Heiner Müller* Vol. 3: 1991-1994 (joint translation with a critical introduction) and Jochen Schmidt's *Pina Bausch—Dance against Fear* (with a critical introduction, 1999).

TONOOKA NAOMI is Associate Professor of English at Aoyama Gakuin

University, Tokyo. She has co-authored several books and published numerous articles in the area of feminism and both Japanese and American theater. Her most recent co-authored book, *Transgressing the Boundaries: An Alternative Reading of American Drama*, was published by Minerva Press in Kyoto (2001). She has also published in *Theatre Research International*, and her most recent article, "The Limits of Speech: Kishida Rio's *Thread Hell*," will appear in *Women & Performance,* vol. 12:1, 2001.